Guests of the State

To Ed, Vera, Jamie and Seán Hassett

Guests of the State

THE STORY OF ALLIED AND AXIS SERVICEMEN INTERNED IN IRELAND DURING WORLD WAR II

T. Ryle Dwyer

BRANDON

First published in 1994 by
Brandon Book Publishers Ltd
Dingle, Co. Kerry, Ireland

British Library Cataloguing in Publication Data is available for this book.

ISBN 0 86322 182 3

Typeset by Brandon
Cover design by P. J. Staunton, Tralee
Printed by the Guernsey Press Ltd, C.I.

Contents

PREFACE

THIS IS THE story of Allied and Axis airmen and sailors interned in Ireland in one of the strangest concentration camps of the war. The prisoners interned at K Lines enjoyed the best sporting facilities in the country and each day were allowed out on parole. Some even brought their wives over from England to join them, while others married local Irish women.

Yet the men were far from content. The Irish Army had to step in to prevent a mutiny among the Germans, following the bomb plot against Hitler and again after his death. The Allied internees, who could mix outside the camp with colleagues on leave from Northern Ireland, were even more frustrated, and continually tried to escape to the North. Being so far from home the German internees had little chance of reaching the continent; the only German who escaped from the camp was caught when the ship on which he had stowed away called at an English port, and he finished the war in a British POW camp.

I only became aware of the existence of the camp while doing research among Canadian diplomatic papers for my first book on Irish neutrality in the 1970s. Thereafter I tried to trace as many of the internees as I could, and their reminiscences, together with the official Irish, British, American and Canadian records, formed the basis of this story. I would like to thank all those people for supplying their wartime reminiscences, particularly Bruce Girdlestone, Chuck Brady, James Masterson, Fred Tisdall, Ralph Keefer, Hugh Verity, Roland "Bud" Wolfe, Kurt Mollenhauer, Kurt Kyck, Arthur Voigt, Georg Fleischmann, Konrad Neymeyr, Willi Krupp and James A. Kelly. I would also like to thank Duncan Fowler's wife, Adelaide; John Holgate's wife, Barbara; Paul Mayhew's brother, Christopher; and Jack

Calder's sisters, Marjorie McNeill and Mary Mason.

Much of my material is taken from reports and contemporary accounts found in the Irish army archives, Department of External Affairs and Department of Defence papers in the departmental and national archives, Dublin; the Dominions Office papers in the Public Record Office, Kew, England; the Canadian Department of External Affairs records in the National Archives of Canada and the United States State Department papers in Washington DC.

I would like to express my thanks to Paddy Cooney as Minister for Justice; Peter Barry as Minister for Foreign Affairs; former Taoiseach Charles J. Haughey; and to the Tánaiste Dick Spring for authorising access to documents which were closed at the time. Finally I would like to thank the late Canadian High Commissioner John D. Kearney, Commandant Peter Young and the staff of the Army Archives, the staff of the National Archives, Dublin, the Public Record Office, Kew, the National Archives, Ottawa, and Kerry County Library.

T. Ryle Dwyer
Tralee, 1994

Irish Neutrality in Perspective

Nobody should have been surprised in September 1939 when the Irish Taoiseach (Prime Minister), Eamon de Valera, announced that his government intended to keep Ireland out of the Second World War. There were a number of reasons for his decision, but the principal one was his belief that a small country like Ireland would only be hurt in the conflict.

On coming to power in 1932 de Valera was seen as a revisionist in the mould of Adolf Hitler or Benito Mussolini, because, like them, he had a reputation as a critic of the Versailles Treaty of 1919, which he campaigned against throughout the United States. He had augmented his revisionist reputation by opposing the Anglo-Irish Treaty of 1921 and actively supporting the Irish Republican Army (IRA) in the civil war of 1922-23; subsequently, he made the revision of the Anglo-Irish Treaty the main plank in his Fianna Fáil party's election platform.

To many people de Valera was the embodiment of the irrational nationalism sweeping Europe, following Hitler's rise to power in Germany, but the Irish leader was a different kind of revisionist. While he had indeed been critical of the more vindictive aspects of the Versailles Treaty, the real emphasis of his criticism was that the framers of the treaty had abandoned some of the loftier ideals of President Woodrow Wilson, the father of the League of Nations. At heart de Valera was an internationalist, and in some respects more Wilsonian than Wilson himself. When Britain and France first embarked on their policy of appeasing the expansionist powers, Germany, Italy and Japan, de Valera, who retained his government's portfolio for External Affairs, was among their most outspoken critics.

During his first appearance before the League of Nations in September 1932, he surprised his critics by calling for international action to stop the Japanese invasion of Manchuria. His government sponsored a resolution calling for the implementation of settlement proposals, but Britain and France vacillated for fear of antagonising Japan and the chance for decisive international action was lost. Later, in 1935, as Italy was making preparations to invade Ethiopia, de Valera again spoke out boldly, emphasising that the League was being given a last chance to prove its effectiveness.

"The final test of the League and all that it stands for has come," he told the Assembly on 16 September 1935. "Our conduct in this crisis will determine whether it is better to let it lapse and disappear and be forgotten."

When the Italians went ahead with their invasion plans a couple of weeks later, the Irish government supported the economic sanctions implemented by the League, and de Valera even intimated his willingness to support military measures. "If military action had been decided on," he later explained, "it would have been our duty to play our part in that action." When the great powers were unwilling to take effective steps to stop Italian aggression, however, de Valera concluded that another major war was inevitable, believing that Italy, Germany or Japan would in the end clash with the major world powers. Ireland, he decided, should try to stay out of the coming conflict.

He knew the major powers would contend that they were fighting for some great moral purpose, but their conduct during the Manchurian and Ethiopian crises had demonstrated that their policies were motivated by self-interest, not moral considerations.

"Peace is dependent upon the will of great states," de Valera told the League's Assembly in July 1936. "All the small states can do, if the statesmen of greater states fail in their duty, is resolutely to determine that they will not become the tools of any great power, and that they will resist with whatever strength they may possess every attempt to force them into a war against their will."

Thus, as early as 1936 de Valera had clearly indicated his intentions. At the beginning of the Second World War, he introduced legislation to provide his government with Emergency

Powers to keep the country out of the conflict.

Within minutes of Britain's declaration of war on 3 September 1939, the Irish were faced with a thorny problem when two Royal Air Force (RAF) seaplanes set down in Irish waters. They had been flying from Pembroke to Stranraer when they became separated. One of them set down in Dún Laoghaire harbour just south of Dublin at about 11.30 a.m. Nobody attempted to disembark. The crew were conserving fuel, waiting for word from the plane which had lost radio contact. Their plane just sat in the water for two-and-a-half hours before taking off again in a northerly direction. At around the same time the missing plane landed off the seaside village of Skerries, north of Dublin. Its pilot, Squadron Leader M.C. Collins, went ashore and made some telephone calls from the Gárda (police) station in the village. While he was there, the first plane flew up from Dún Laoghaire and set down beside the one in Skerries. The two aircraft attracted enormous public attention.

It was a busy day in Dublin with the All-Ireland Hurling Final between Cork and Kilkenny being played in Croke Park. Rumours spread through the city like wildfire that a British invasion force was just off the coast. Numerous people went out to the two aircraft in small boats and they were given guided tours. Squadron Leader Collins waited on shore as the Irish authorities pondered what to do next. As they had taken off before Prime Minister Neville Chamberlain made his radio broadcast announcing that Britain was at war with Germany, it had never occurred to the pilot that he and his crew might be interned.

After consulting de Valera, the Minister for Defence Oscar Traynor ordered that the airmen should be treated as distressed mariners and allowed to leave. Collins was returned to his aircraft and the two planes then took off at about 5 pm. The censor prohibited any mention of the incident in the press, but de Valera complained to Sir John Maffey, a British emissary who visited Dublin on 14 September, that the whole affair had still been the subject of a great deal of public comment. "How could this continue?" he asked.

It was probably more than mere coincidence that de Valera received a telephone call at just that moment. "There you are!" he said, turning to Maffey. "One of your planes is down in Ventry Bay. What am I to do?"

An RAF seaplane with twelve men on board had set down off the Kerry coast, in Ventry harbour, at nine o'clock that morning, and the pilot (Flight Lieutenant Brooks) and a mechanic went ashore with a broken fuel pipe. A passing motorist took them to Dingle, where the mechanic repaired the pipe in a garage.

De Valera said he would have to intern the crew. "It was quite obvious he found this course most unpalatable," Maffey reported. "I said that in view of the Skerries precedent he should warn the British Government before introducing internment in any such cases. The men concerned had probably had no warning of any such possibility."

While they were discussing the matter the telephone rang again and de Valera appeared greatly relieved when he told Maffey that the aircraft had taken off. Since it had been in Ventry for more than five hours, he may well have played up the whole affair deliberately. Whatever the case, Maffey left the meeting convinced that, even though de Valera planned to stay out of the war, he wished "to help us within the limits of that neutrality to the full extent possible".

From Ireland's standpoint the war years can be divided into three quite distinct periods. The first lasted until the German invasion of the Low Countries in May 1940. The second and most crucial period, which was marked by grave Irish fears of either a German or British invasion, ended with the arrival of American troops in Northern Ireland in January 1942. The third and final phase extended to the end of the conflict. Looking back in May 1945, Joseph P. Walshe, the Permanent Secretary of the Irish Department of External Affairs, listed twelve different crises, ten of which occurred during the second phase, with only one in each of the other two phases.

During the initial phase the Irish government was able to concentrate on internal security matters. Although there was little doubt that Ireland ultimately had a constitutional right to remain neutral, the legal position was not without its complexities because the country was still attached to the British Commonwealth. It was therefore arguable, from a purely legal viewpoint, that Britain's declaration of war committed all members of the Commonwealth, and if the Irish had wished to remain neutral, they should have withdrawn from the Commonwealth beforehand. They were therefore really at war, according to Winston Churchill, the new First Lord of the Admiralty.

"Legally," he wrote, "I believe they are 'At war but skulking'."

Of course, not all of the dominions accepted this narrow interpretation. Before declaring war on Germany, for instance, the Canadians waited for a week in a symbolic gesture demonstrating their right to remain neutral. For his part, de Valera had foreseen the possibility of legal complications and had taken the precaution of altering Ireland's relationship with the British Crown during the abdication crisis of 1936, when he had legislation enacted formally stipulating that the country's link with the Crown was essentially only symbolic.

The British authorities accepted that Dublin's actions were compatible with the Statute of Westminster of 1931, but they balked when de Valera tried to get them to appoint a British minister to Ireland rather than a high commissioner – the title normally given to a diplomat from one British dominion accredited to another. As de Valera was unwilling to accept a high commissioner, the British had no diplomatic representation in Ireland when the war began. It being no time to argue about semantics, the two governments soon agreed on a compromise in which Sir John Maffey returned to Dublin with the title of British Representative to Ireland.

Maffey was in his late sixties. A tall, thin man, standing six-foot-four, with a crop of long grey hair and a strong nose, he spoke rapidly in a clear, deep voice and had sparkling eyes under full eyebrows. He had had a distinguished career in colonial service in India and British North Africa. In 1933 he was recalled to London, where he was appointed Permanent Undersecretary of State at the Colonial Office. Shortly before the war he retired but was persuaded to come out of retirement to take up the new post in Dublin. Even though his long imperial career did not dispose him to a favourable view of Irish neutrality, he was a superb diplomat who knew how to keep his feelings under control. He proved himself an excellent choice. Discreet and capable, he soon won de Valera's confidence.

Professor Desmond Williams, the noted Irish historian who worked for British intelligence during the war, concluded that Maffey and the German minister to Ireland, Edouard Hempel, "acted as a brake on the more tempestuous alarmists or optimists who were pressing for a more active policy vis-à-vis Ireland. Their job was hard, uninterrupted and none the less impressive because the details sometimes involved unimportant, unattractive and squalid personalities. The activities of conspirators, agents, provocateurs, idiots and journalists were a frequent cause of much distress in all official quarters."

The Irish were also lucky to have someone like Hempel in charge of the German legation. He was a diplomat of the old school, trained in the foreign service before Hitler's rise to power. A tall, polite, slightly balding man with dark eyebrows and a penchant for flashy bow-ties, Hempel was in his early fifties. Prior to his Dublin posting in 1937, he had been primarily concerned with the administration of German foreign ministry property. This involved a lot of foreign travel without implicating him in the Nazi intrigue of the German foreign service. His membership of the Nazi party was nominal and reluctant, and his Irish appointment was attributed to the fact that a real Nazi would not get on with de Valera. Before leaving Berlin Hempel had been personally briefed by Hitler, who impressed him with his knowledge of Ireland. The *Führer* seemed to be well-informed about Anglo-Irish difficulties but realised that de Valera had an aversion to the Nazi regime on religious grounds. Hempel therefore kept a low profile in Dublin and, clearly not anti-semitic, was in fact liked by the city's Jewish community.

At the very end, following the death of Hitler, de Valera's attitude towards Hempel may have influenced his policy, but throughout the war there was never any real doubt about his sympathy for Britain. From his first meeting with Maffey on 14 September 1939, de Valera went out of his way to emphasise this sympathy. "England has a moral position today," he said. "Hitler might have his early successes, but the moral position [will] tell."

De Valera knew that the British would not stand for German

submarines or aircraft sheltering in Ireland, but if he were to deny the Germans access and at the same time allow British military planes or warships to use Irish facilities, he would risk retaliation from Germany. Hence his government decided that Ireland should be closed to all belligerent planes and ships. He promised, however, that when the Irish coastwatching service observed any of these, the information would be broadcast at once.

"Not to you especially," de Valera said. "Your Admiralty must pick it up. We shall wireless it to the world. I will tell the German minister of our intention to do this."

Reporting all sightings to both sides may have seemed impartial, but it worked against the *Luftwaffe* on two counts. Germany was too far away to make use of reports of Allied flights, whereas British forces could react quickly to sightings of German aircraft and submarines. And the messages, which were broadcast on a radio frequency agreed with the British, informed Allied planes of their positions if they were lost over Ireland.

The first test of the country's neutrality occurred when the British asked for permission for the Royal Navy to use Irish ports. It was politically impossible for the Dublin government to comply with the request, even if it had wished to do so.

"There is no gainsaying Mr de Valera's view that any tampering with the neutrality of the ports would raise a storm here, the consequences of which are beyond computation, and which would certainly bring him down," Maffey reported. "It is remarkable how even the 'pro-British' group, men who have fought for the Crown and are anxious to be called up again, men whose sons are at the front today, loyalists in the old sense of the word, agree generally in supporting the neutrality of Éire. They see no possible practical alternative."

The Irish were afraid, however, that the British government would ignore their refusal. These fears were not without justification: Churchill in particular was reluctant to accept the situation. In October 1939 he advocated that Britain "should coerce" Dublin for bases, but the cabinet rejected the idea, at least until the need for such facilities became a question of life or death.

In order to placate the British and ensure that Irish neutrality would not hurt them, de Valera agreed to the routing of all Irish cable communications through London, and raised no objection to a system which compelled all Irish ships to call at British ports for a navicert, a kind of naval passport, before proceeding to or returning from the continent. The British were also given permission to take over seven new Irish-registered oil tankers and, in order to keep chartering rates down by minimising competition, the Irish agreed not to charter any neutral ships. In return, Britain promised to provide Ireland with a certain amount of shipping space.

De Valera remained his own Minister for External Affairs throughout the war, but he relied on career diplomats and civil servants to take care of day-to-day diplomacy. Joseph P. Walshe, the Permanent Secretary of the department, was thus cast in the role of a virtual foreign minister.

Walshe was a linguist with proficient French, Italian, German and Dutch. He had spent some years training for the priesthood as a Jesuit and taught languages in Clongowes Wood College for a number of years before securing a law degree, but he never practiced. As a staunch nationalist, he served in Paris under the Irish rebel emissary Seán T. O'Kelly during the War of Independence. With the establishment of the Irish Free State in 1922, Walshe was appointed to take charge of the Department of External Affairs. He served de Valera's opponents loyally, but dutifully afforded full allegiance to the Fianna Fáil government when it came to power in 1932. He was credited with recruiting some of the best brains in the country for his department.

Secretive and mistrustful, Walshe ruled the department in an autocratic fashion and had a reputation for deviousness. Ministers abroad often complained that their requests for advice were left unanswered. He had the highest regard for his own intellectual capacity and was not averse to moving on his own initiative even when it came to policy matters that should strictly have been the preserve of his political masters. Intensely religious and with inflated views on the power and influence of the Roman Catholic Church, he was always particularly interested in trying to enlist the support of the Catholic hierarchy for the various governments under which he served.

While recuperating from an illness in Nazi Germany in 1933, he wrote to de Valera about "the most interesting political situation" that had arisen as a result of Hitler's rise to power. He was impressed with "the general atmosphere of the great experiments which are being carried out here – and the essentials of which we may well have to imitate in Ireland". He advised de Valera, for instance, "to give Parliament a holiday for an indefinite period," because the situation in the 26 Counties was "at least as parlous as that of any other states in which the ordinary constitutional forms have been set aside for a time by the majority as is absolutely within their right".

Foreign diplomats stationed in Dublin found him a charming, cultured and warm-hearted individual, and his diplomatic skill was such that he convinced Hempel that he was sympathetic to Germany. In the early months of the war, when the Nazis looked almost invincible, he undoubtedly tried to ingratiate himself with Hempel in subtle ways, such as expressing hope that the Germans would not allow Ireland to be sacrificed to the wrath of Britain after they had won the war. He implied that Irish neutrality was so favourable to Germany that he was afraid that the British would seek revenge after the conflict, unless Germany were prepared to protect Ireland. The Allied representatives realised that he was not sanguine about their prospects of victory, and they suspected his loyalties, but de Valera felt he could rely on him. In fact, he used Walshe as his principal liaison to establish some extraordinary secret co-operation, first with the British, and later with the Americans, who found Walshe so helpful that they approached him to go on an espionage mission to the continent before the end of the war.

There was never any doubt in the minds of either the Allied or the Axis representatives in Dublin that de Valera personally favoured the Allies. The British probably posed the greater danger to Ireland; they behaved as if they had a right to Irish bases, and the London government repeatedly ignored de Valera's requests for an assurance that Britain would respect Irish neutrality. Yet de Valera was always available to Allied representatives, but kept his contacts with Hempel to a minimum, at least until after Hitler's death.

De Valera relied on Walshe's protegé and deputy, Frederick H. Boland, the Assistant Secretary of the department, to liaise with Hempel. A dapper medium-sized man with a ruddy complexion, in his mid-thirties, he had done post-graduate research in the United States, at Harvard University among other institutions. He represented a younger generation who came to External Affairs without any political or ideological baggage. Diplomatic, urbane, witty and a good speaker, Boland had all the qualities necessary to get to the very top of his field. He served as First Secretary of the Irish legation in Paris in the early 1930s before being recalled to head the League of Nations section at the Department of External Affairs in Dublin. Throughout the war he advocated that Ireland should be as accommodating as possible to the British, because he firmly believed that the fate of western Europe lay in the closest possible Anglo-American alliance. He was always more positive than Walshe about Britain's chances in the war.

During the so-called phoney war de Valera concentrated on the threat posed by the outlawed IRA, with which he had broken during the 1930s. In January 1939 the IRA declared war on Britain and begun staging a series of bombing outrages in various British cities, the most notorious of which was a bomb that killed five civilians in the streets of Coventry in August 1939. Blinded by their own Anglophobic prejudices, many in the IRA were ready to support the Nazi war machine. "England's Difficulty – Ireland's Opportunity has ever been the watchword of the Gael," the IRA proclaimed in October 1939. "British cities and ports are now beleaguered by Germany's aeroplanes and submarines. Now is the time for Ireland to take up arms and strike a blow for our Ulster people."

As the IRA sought to exploit Britain's difficulties, de Valera gradually tightened the screw on his former comrades. Following the outbreak of war, some 70 members of the IRA were rounded up and interned without trial. A number of men went on hunger-strike for their immediate release, and tension mounted as de Valera emphasised his determination not to accede to their demands.

"If we let these men out we are going immediately afterwards to have every single man we have tried to detain and restrain going on hunger-strike," he declared. But his government was dealt an embarrassing blow in early December when the president of the High Court ruled that it had acted unconstitutionally in interning the men under legislation which had been implemented prior to the outbreak of hostilities on the continent. Rather than appeal to the Supreme Court, the government released the internees, only to be quickly faced with a further setback.

On 24 December the IRA raided the Irish army's magazine fort in the Phoenix Park, Dublin, and made off with arms and over a million rounds of ammunition. The government retaliated with a nationwide search and introduced legislation to close the loophole exploited in the High Court. When other members of the IRA, jailed following the magazine fort incident, demanded to be treated as prisoners-of-war and went on hunger-strike in support of their demands in February 1940, de Valera again talked tough, and this time he meant it.

As the prospect of world war intensified following the invasion of Norway in early April 1940, the hunger-strikes were reaching a critical point. Two of the hunger-strikers had particularly high profiles: Jack Plunkett was a brother of one of the leaders of the Easter Rebellion of 1916 and Seán MacCurtain was a son of the Lord Mayor of Cork who had been murdered by British agents in 1920. But De Valera resolutely refused to compromise even though the political pressure became intense.

"Prisoners [will] not be allowed to dictate the conditions under which they [will] be kept in detention," de Valera insisted. The issue became a test of wills. This time the IRA backed down after the first hunger-striker, Tony Darcy, died. Another man, Jack McNeela, also died, but both Plunkett and MacCurtain survived. These events left de Valera and his colleagues in an unenviable position on the home front. On one side they had alienated their former Civil War allies, while their Civil War opponents had still not forgiven them for a war which had been fought less than 20 years earlier.

On the international front, the war on the continent entered a new phase on 10 May 1940 after the German invasion of the

Low Countries, which was quickly followed by the election of Churchill as British Prime Minister. He was known to be deeply irritated by the denial of Irish bases, with the result that Dublin had to reckon with the possibility of Britain using any pretext to justify their seizure.

The Irish authorities found themselves in a delicate situation on 22 May following a raid on the Dublin home of Stephen Held, a member of the IRA. Evidence was found that he had been harbouring an *Abwehr* spy. Although the spy, Hermann Goertz, escaped and remained at large for a further 18 months, his transmitter and papers were seized in the raid. Among his papers the police found a crude IRA plan for German forces to land in Donegal and announce that they had come to liberate Northern Ireland, while at the same time the IRA would call on the Irish people to assist the Germans. Held had personally presented this plan to the Germans during a visit to Berlin some weeks earlier. His passport indicated that he had crossed into Germany from Holland and that he had returned home via Britain.

The Irish authorities thought it ominous that he had not been picked up in Britain when he had a German stamp on his passport and feared that the British, aware of Held's activities, intended to use them as a justification for a pre-emptive invasion of Ireland. De Valera had perhaps more reason than most to be suspicious and apprehensive. In 1918, following the arrest of an Irishman who had been dropped on the Irish coast by a German U-boat, he and some other Sinn Féin men had been arrested for supposedly being involved in a "German Plot". Neither de Valera nor any of his colleagues had been involved, but they were transported to England nonetheless and deposited in jail until after the end of the First World War.

As Europe slid towards war in May 1940, de Valera's played the belligerents off one another, convincing each side that it had more to lose than gain by violating Irish neutrality. In the event of a German invasion, he made it clear that Ireland would open her bases to the British, and if Britain invaded, that his government would help the Germans, and would call on Irish-Americans to use their influence to block American aid to

Britain. There was no doubt, however, about the Taoiseach's sympathy for the Allies and his aversion to the Nazi regime. On 23 May Hempel predicted that because of geographic and economic considerations, "as well as his democratic principles", de Valera would "maintain the line of friendly understanding" with Britain, "even in the face of the threatening danger of Ireland becoming involved in the war". That same day, as Hempel telegraphed his report to Berlin, the Taoiseach sent Joe Walshe and Colonel Liam Archer, the head of G2 (Irish military intelligence), to London to assure the British that Dublin would have no truck with Hitler and "would fight if attacked by Germany and would call in the assistance of the United Kingdom the moment it became necessary". The Irish delegates were instructed to suggest secret talks between the British and Irish military to prepare a joint defence strategy.

As the British Expeditionary Force in Belgium was literally being driven into the English Channel, British officers visited Ireland and were shown the disposition of Irish defence forces. Contingency plans were drawn up to deal with a possible German invasion, and de Valera moved decisively to check the IRA's quisling activities. Over 500 suspected members were rounded up and interned without trial for the duration of the war at the Curragh in Hare Park – or Tintown – a prison camp which had been used in the 1920s by the British during the Irish War of Independence and by the Irish Free State authorities during the subsequent Civil War.

In spite of the secret Anglo-Irish co-operation, Irish fears intensified in June 1940 when Britain showed a renewed interest in Irish bases and asked the various dominion governments to use their influence to persuade de Valera. South Africa's premier Jan Christiaan Smuts, who had played a major role in organising the talks that led to the Anglo-Irish settlement of 1921, saw little point in persuasion. "The Irish Atlantic ports should be seized at once, even in the face of Irish opinion, to prevent them suffering the same fate as the Norwegian ports," Smuts insisted.

"Although as a last resort we should not hesitate to secure the ports by force," Churchill told his cabinet on 16 June, "it would be unwise at this moment to take any action that might compromise our position with the United States of America, in view of the present delicate developments."

In the following days the British made frantic efforts to move de Valera, going so far as secretly offering to end partition in return for the use of Irish bases. Neville Chamberlain was put in charge of negotiations for the British side and Malcolm MacDonald was sent to Dublin as an emissary with an offer to declare a united Ireland immediately in return for Dublin's support in the war. A constitutional committee would be set up to work out the practical details of the new united Ireland. However, as there was no guarantee that the Northern unionists would not scupper the constitutional talks, de Valera and his cabinet reacted cautiously.

"Will you come into the war if we create a united Ireland straight away?" MacDonald asked.

"If we have a united Ireland," de Valera replied, "it will be neutral for at least twenty-four hours. We will then call a meeting of our assembly and it will decide if we – as an independent nation – will come into the war."

During the talks he candidly told MacDonald that nationalist sentiment was so strongly against involvement that a united Irish parliament would still probably defeat a declaration of war, even if he supported it himself. This assessment was endorsed by James Dillon, the deputy leader of the Fine Gael opposition and the only member of the Dáil to advocate openly the abandonment of neutrality.

"If de Valera were to try to carry the country for abandoning neutrality on the strength of the present British promises," Dillon said, "he would be beaten."

The British softened their position, and argued that if certain Irish bases were given to Britain, Ireland would not have to declare war at all. It could try to stay out of the conflict by reaffirming its determination to remain neutral. However, it was generally felt that handing over the bases would in itself be tantamount to a declaration of war. De Valera told Maffey that he was turning down the offer brought by MacDonald. "It has gone hard with him to turn down any scheme which would bring about a united Ireland, the dream of his life," Maffey reported.

"But in the present circumstances acceptance was impossible. It would have meant civil war."

"The real basic fact is that it is not partition which stands in the way at this moment, but the fear of Dev and his friends that we shall be beaten," Chamberlain believed. "They don't want to be on the losing side and if that is unheroic[,] one can only say that it is very much the attitude of the world from the USA to Roumania and from Japan to Ireland."

Churchill was now desperate for Irish bases, and the Germans deliberately aggravated the situation. On 28 June Hitler ordered "all available information media" to indicate that a German invasion of Ireland was imminent. "Sooner or later," one German newspaper warned, "Germany may have to act in consequence as in the case of other small European neutrals."

On 14 July the British notified Dublin that they had information that German would invade Ireland the following day and that they had been about to invade ten days earlier; these incorrect warnings were probably the result of the deception ordered by Hitler. Irish suspicions of British intentions had been raised on 12 July when a British spy was arrested. Major Edward Byass, who was serving with the British army in Northern Ireland, had been travelling about Ireland in civilian clothes with his wife, collecting military information to be used by British forces in Ireland. The Irish had already shown their facilities to the British, so they were at a loss to explain his spying.

Maffey apologised and assured de Valera that London had nothing to do with the Byass mission. The major had been sent by his superiors in Northern Ireland to gather information in case British forces were invited to assist the Irish army, he explained. There was nothing sinister about the mission, and London had ordered that "nothing of the kind is to occur again without prior consultation with the Éire authorities".

De Valera was satisfied with this assurance and, although all German spies caught in Ireland were imprisoned for the duration of the war, Byass was quickly freed. It was but another of the growing examples of neutral Ireland's secret benevolence towards Britain.

The First Internees

THE BATTLE OF Britain was raging across the Irish Sea, but there was little for the men to do in the look-out post at Brandon Point, Co. Kerry, on Tuesday, 20 August 1940. The whole area was shrouded in a thick fog and visibility was only a matter of yards. Through the fog they could hear an aeroplane approaching. Although it was flying low and passed near by, they could not see it.

The crew of the four-engined Focke Wulf Condor had left their base in Abbeville, France, early that morning, primarily on a weather reconnaissance mission, but they also planned to attack any Allied shipping they might come across. As they moved up the west coast of Ireland a warm front approached from the Atlantic and very soon there was little they could do but gather weather information. The plane penetrated the front at different heights while Dr Eric Kruger, their meteorologist, took repeated readings.

After three hours of this the commander, *Oberleutnant* Kurt Mollenhauer, had enough. He asked the navigator, *Feldwebel* (Sergeant Major) Ludwig Wochner, for a course home.

"*Herr Leutnant*," Wochner said, after giving the reading, "any height you like until I tell you to climb; we will be well to the south of the mountains of south-west Ireland – but just in case."

He called for the plane to climb to 5,000 feet and hold that course for 30 minutes. Then they descended to 1,000 feet in the hope of spotting some shipping. They thought they were out over the ocean when the clouds suddenly broke and they saw the Magharees peninsula, forming the western boundary of Tralee Bay, off their port wing. They could only guess their location because they were too far away to get a bearing on their own radio beacons. They tried to find Radio Éireann, the Irish broadcasting service, but it was off the air for the afternoon. In the circumstances Mollenhauer took what seemed like the safest option in ordering the pilot to head west back into the mist and away from the Irish coast. They had no idea they were over Brandon Bay and were turning towards Mount Brandon, Ireland's second highest mountain, then shrouded in thick cloud.

It was only at the last moment that the pilot, *Stabsfeldwebel* Robert Beumer, saw the mountain. He instinctively raised the nose of the plane, but as he did, a large rock tore off the under turret. Had Beumer planned it, he could hardly have done any better. The rock slowed the plane's momentum and by sheer luck the aircraft with its nose up was flying virtually parallel to the mountain slope and proceeded to make a belly-landing on the treacherous slope.

Only two of the six-man crew were injured. Mollenhauer fractured his right ankle, and Beumer suffered a painful back injury. His colleagues used a rubber dinghy to drag him away from the scene, and Mollenhauer ordered the crew to burn what they could of the remainder of the plane.

It was three-quarters of an hour before an official search party reached the crash site. By then there were already some 50 local people at the scene. The airmen were sharing chocolates with the people and passing three bottles of brandy around among themselves. They were helped to Faha, a tiny, remote Irish-speaking townland in a staunchly republican area whose people were sympathetic towards the Germans and quite hostile to the official search party. One local man, who offered the hospitality of his home to the security forces, was stuffed into a closet by local republicans.

Mollenhauer and Beumer were taken to St Catherine's Hospital in Tralee, while the other four were held overnight in the local army barracks, where they aroused considerable curiosity. They were treated as celebrities, with curious callers requesting their autographs.

"They appeared to be men of fine moral and physical fibre and were picturesque figures in their brown knee-top boots, leather jackets and curiously tilted soft caps which they wore in place of flying helmets," the *Kerry Champion* reported.

Kruger and *Unteroffizier* (Sergeant) Hans Bell from Dusseldorf spoke some English, and they chatted affably in a somewhat fractured manner. Wochner, the oldest member of the crew at 30, explained that he was married with children back home in St Polten, Austria.

"War is not good for wives and little children," he said. "We would like to spare them. When this is over I will go back to them and then we will all be happy when peace comes."

Because of the presence of the meteorologist, the Irish authorities rightly concluded the plane had been primarily on weather reconnaissance, but the crew refused to speak about the mission, though they were willing to speak about general matters of a non-military nature. "The topics ranged from the weather to the all-Ireland football semi-final," according to the *Kerry Champion*.

A couple of days earlier the Kerry football team had defeated Cavan to qualify for the all-Ireland Gaelic Football Final, so football interest – usually high throughout Kerry – was at fever pitch just then. Indeed it was almost as if the local reporter thought the airmen might have dropped in for news of the match. "The Germans," he noted, "were particularly interested in newspaper photographs and accounts of the game."

Next day the four men fit enough to travel were transferred to Collins Barracks, Cork, where they were detained for ten days. From there they wrote their first letters home. Three of them commented on the friendliness of the Irish people.

"You need have no anxiety about me, since we are here removed from the vicissitude of the war," the 25-year-old Kruger assured his mother. "I have here a lazy life, and perhaps the abundance of sleep and good food will have a good affect even on me."

His sentiments were shared by both the oldest and youngest members of the crew. Wochner wrote to his father that "all the people we have to do with here are very nice to us and they do everything to make our life as bearable as at all possible." Twenty-year-old *Gefreiter* (Corporal) Kurt Kyck from Allenstein also noted that "the people are very friendly and put everything at our disposal that we need, the food even first-rate, only we are interned and must put up with it. When the war is over I shall probably come home again. I hope it won't be long now."

On 31 August 1940 Mollenhauer and Beumer were transferred from Tralee to the Curragh military hospital, and the four others were moved from Cork to "K Lines", or the No. 2 Internment Camp, as it was officially called. It was a newly constructed barbed-wire compound at the Curragh, about a mile from Tintown, the No. 1 Internment Camp, in which members of the IRA were being held.

The Curragh itself was a twelve-square-mile plain about 30 miles south-west of Dublin. In ancient times it had been used for chariot racing, and now it was the site of the country's most important racetrack. All of the horse-racing classics – the Irish Derby, Oaks, St Leger, 1,000 and 2,000 Guineas – were run there annually.

At the start of the Crimean War in 1854, a small instruction camp was built on the plain to serve the military in the nearby garrison towns of Kildare and Newbridge, each of which was about three miles away. The new camp expanded rapidly and the Curragh became one of the first examples anywhere of a complete military town. It was here that the British army's infamous mutiny took place in 1914. After Irish independence in 1922, the Irish army took over the Curragh and its seven red-brick barracks, which were re-named after the leaders of the Easter Rebellion. These barracks housed 227 officers and 5,340 men, with married quarters for 86 families. By Irish standards the Curragh camp was a fairly large town, with the various conveniences normally associated with urban centres. Being a military camp it had the added advantage of having some of the country's most advanced sporting facilities.

At the outset there was a certain amount of tension between the internees and their guards, who were not as easy-going or as friendly as the soldiers had been in Cork. The guards at the Curragh initially did interchangeable duty between the K Lines and Tintown camps. This was unfortunate because relations between the guards and the IRA internees were very strained, and it was inevitable that the tension in Tintown would affect the attitude of the guards towards the internees in K Lines. In each case, after all, the duty of the guards was the same: to prevent the internees escaping.

When the German minister visited K Lines on 2 September he found the German airmen uneasy about the tight security. They complained of being treated like prisoners-of-war. In the strict sense they were not prisoners, but guests of the Irish state, which was merely obliged to ensure that they took no further part in the war. However, Colonel Thomas McNally, the officer-in-charge of the Curragh command, certainly thought of them as prisoners and he ordered the most stringent security.

"These prisoners in my opinion are the type who consider it a duty to effect escape at the first available opportunity," he wrote. "As a race they are very tough and methodical and I feel will avail themselves of any laxity in the regulations which govern their internment."

Commandant James Guiney was responsible for both internment camps, but, preoccupied with Tintown, he left the day-to-day running of K Lines to Lieutenant James A. Kelly, who was selected because he had attended a Jesuit secondary school in Germany and was able to speak the language fluently. Of course, he had no experience of running an internment camp and was thrown in at the deep end to feel his own way, which he did rather cautiously.

In Cork the men had been permitted to drink alcohol, read Irish newspapers, and even listen to the radio. Now these facilities were denied. The Germans were not even allowed to have garden implements with which they might have relieved their boredom. Hempel found the camp authorities in a quandary when he brought Mollenhauer six bottles of wine. They were anxious to inspect anything he brought and they also wished to supervise his meetings with the internees, but they accorded him and his staff unhindered access in deference to their diplomatic status. With other than the diplomats, however, it was initially decided that each of the men would have only one visitor a week and that the meeting would be supervised in a special visiting room.

While in the Curragh military hospital, where he and Beumer remained for twelve days, Mollenhauer complained of not being able to get even enough fresh air. Large nails had been driven into the window frames to prevent the windows being opened more than a few inches for fear they might try to escape, although there was already an iron grill on the window, Mollenhauer had his leg in plaster and his colleague was still recovering from a painful back injury. Given the stifling atmosphere of the military hospital, the pair initially welcomed their transfer to the barbed-wire compound in K Lines, where they were able to get all the fresh air they wanted, but now they had the nuisance of being woken at regular intervals throughout the night by noisy guards checking their rooms and shining torches in their faces.

The six internees were housed in two separate wooden bungalows – the officers in one and the NCOs in the other. However, all ate together in the same mess, at their own request. Mollenhauer and Beumer were still recuperating, so they made regular visits to the military hospital, and they were allowed to exercise outside their compound under guard. Mollenhauer asked Hempel to secure the same exercise privileges for the other men.

After thanking the Department of External Affairs for the way that the men were treated in Cork and Tralee, Hempel went on to ask for a relaxation of the prison-like procedures at K Lines, but the wheels of the bureaucracy moved slowly until his request was given a new urgency with the internment of the first British airman on 29 September 1940. This added a whole new dimension to the internment question, especially as Flying Officer Paul Mayhew was the son of a prominent British businessman.

As a separate compound was being prepared for Mayhew in K Lines, Frederick Boland, Assistant Secretary at the Department of External Affairs, warned G2 that the internment of the British airman was going to "give rise to questions in some ways more difficult than we have to face with the present six men". The guards would be obliged not to show any favouritism, so he thought it advisable to anticipate and make concessions to the Germans immediately rather than be compelled to make them later under British pressure.

"What we must be sure of," Boland wrote, "is that we do not

withhold reasonable and usual amenities which it might later be deemed to be expedient to grant to military internees of another nationality to obviate, for example, attacks in the British press." He was undoubtedly reflecting the views of de Valera himself, but the latter had to move delicately when it came to relations with the army. Less than 20 years earlier de Valera had supported the IRA in the Irish Civil War, while the top brass in the army had fought on the other side. Before coming to power in 1932 he had promised not to victimise his Civil War opponents, and he had faithfully upheld his promise. In the process he won the respect of many of those opponents, but the old bitterness and distrust still ran deep. He had to tread warily when it came to relations with the army, which, in turn, adopted a professional approach towards him.

As a result of Boland's intervention the army was more receptive when Hempel next intervened on behalf of the German internees. Mollenhauer had been complaining about various matters and was anxious that his men should be allowed to buy civilian clothes. As a result a conference between representatives of the Department of Defence, the army, and the Department of External Affairs was convened on 2 October 1940. The attendance included Colonel Archer of G2, Boland from External Affairs and his counterpart at the Department of Defence, General Peter MacMahon, as well as Colonel Thomas McNally, the officer commanding the Curragh.

Boland argued that the internees should be as content as possible with their lot in order "to minimise their anxiety and quite natural desire to escape from our custody". Believing the German requests were reasonable, he saw no grounds for denying the men a radio, newspapers or magazines. "None of the points are very serious," he explained. Hempel, whom he described as "a difficult character", had put forward the suggestions "in a reasonable conciliatory way".

The Irish felt that Hempel was in a difficult position because of Henning Thomsen, the counsellor at the legation. Hempel played the role of the diplomat but Thomsen acted like a strutting Nazi. An *SS* officer in his mid-thirties, he was considered the Gestapo's man, sent to keep an eye on Hempel. He had joined the *Reiter SS*, the mounted *SS* at the Brandenburg Gate Riding School, because he was told that he had little chance of being appointed a diplomatic attaché without some form of party affiliation. He later claimed that he had no contact with the *SS* and was employed mainly as an escort at state functions. In Dublin he acted as the legation's intelligence officer and consorted with a variety of pro-German Irish people whom Hempel avoided out of a sense of diplomatic decorum. Thomsen held loud boisterous parties and his wife – who was an architect with an Irish firm – moved freely in Irish social circles.

The Irish were acutely conscious that Hempel might be compelled to be awkward when it came to the treatment of the men. Boland summarised the views of the Department of External Affairs in this way:

> We are under international obligation to keep these men in this country and to ensure that they do not escape and return to Germany. Any failure on our part to carry out this obligation would land us in a diplomatic incident. Within the limits of this general obligation to ensure the safe custody of the men, however, our view is that once their safe custody is assured the men should be granted every facility and amenity calculated to soften their captivity and relieve their monotony. There is no point whatever in our view in refusing them any amenity that does not detract from the measures taken for their safe custody. On the contrary, the task of everybody and particularly the officer immediately responsible would be lightened by a policy directed towards making the men as satisfied as the circumstances of their internment allow. I am satisfied that this is not only the only course dictated by the general practice of neutrals in the treatment of military internees, but the best in our particular circumstances. It is the wisest policy to pursue.

As a result of Boland's prompting, it was decided to provide the men with civilian clothing and to suspend the use of flashlights at night. It was also decided to approach the German government about getting permission for the men to sign parole.

Under Article II of the Hague Convention the Irish government could "decide whether officers can be left at liberty on giving their parole not to leave the neutral territory without permission". As far as de Valera was concerned, the internees could be permitted to move about relatively freely, if they would promise on their honour not to try to escape or take part in any activities relating to the war effort. As things stood, however, the men were under an obligation to try to rejoin their units, and Hempel was unwilling to authorise parole without permission from Berlin.

While this approval was being awaited, it was decided the men should be allowed to attend church services under guard. This was to facilitate Wochner, the only Roman Catholic among the internees. The others were free to attend services in the churches of their choice, but they were not greatly concerned about doing so.

Gradually the army relaxed its restrictions. When Henning Thomsen presented the internees with a radio, the army erected an aerial for it. The nightly inspections were discontinued and the officers were given an allowance of £3 per week and the others £2 per week, as well as £5 each to purchase civilian clothes. This money, along with the cost of their food and medical expenses, was to be recouped from the German government. The internees were also given gardening tools, and they quickly set about cultivating a vegetable garden. Although their food was identical with that served to Irish soldiers, the Germans found difficulty in adjusting to the diet. They complained of getting too much meat and not enough vegetables.

When Berlin authorised the internees to sign a limited parole, a system was introduced allowing them out of the camp each day; in return they gave their word of honour that they would return to the camp by a specified time. In the strict sense only the officers were eligible for parole, because in the class-ridden structure of the military only officers were regarded as having any honour, but the Irish accorded the parole privileges to all ranks, on receiving an assurance from Berlin that the enlisted men would abide by the same conditions. Initially the freedoms granted were quite modest and only expanded slowly.

A Lone Englishman

Flying Officer Paul Mayhew, the first British pilot to be interned in Ireland, made an emergency landing in his Hurricane fighter near Kilmuckridge, Co. Wexford, on the afternoon of 29 September 1940. Earlier that afternoon his plane had been one of eight Hurricane fighters which scrambled from their base in Bristol to intercept a flight of German Heinkel 111 bombers approaching from the south. In the ensuing engagement one of the RAF fighters was shot down. Mayhew managed to bring down one of the bombers, but he spent too much time following the others and lost his bearings in the process. It took him so long to find land again that he was running dangerously low on fuel. Thinking he was over southern Wales, he landed in a field with barely enough fuel for a further five minutes flying. He was taken into custody by members of the Local Defence Force (LDF). Ironically the major in charge of the unit was a former member of the RAF. Mayhew's plane was undamaged, but his arrival attracted so much attention that the Irish authorities felt they had to intern him.

Unlike the previous British airmen who had landed in Ireland, Mayhew had just shot down a German bomber and the bodies of its crew were soon washed up on the south coast. Having interned six Germans only the previous month, it would have been stretching Irish neutrality too far to let Mayhew go, especially with the war at such a delicate stage. The Battle of Britain was still in progress and the Irish people were understandably anxious not to antagonise the Germans, especially when few people held out much hope of a British victory.

The previous month the first casualties of the war on Irish soil had occurred in Campile, when an apparently disorientated crew of a German plane bombed a creamery, killing three women workers. People were acutely conscious of the danger of being dragged into the war.

The British did not protest against Mayhew's internment because they believed that "unconditional internment" would operate in their favour. Unless a stringent rule of internment was adopted by the Irish government and accepted by London, the British feared that German combatant planes would be able to exploit the international law applicable to combatant ships needing repairs. The planes would "alight on Irish soil under the pretence of needing repairs, there obtain fuel, and then continue on their combatant patrols, having had the benefit of southern Ireland as a fuelling station," Maffey told the American minister. Moreover, the British were so heavily dependent on American aid that they were in no position to retaliate against the internment of their pilot. Violating Irish sovereignty in the matter would undoubtedly inflame Irish-Americans and have repercussions on American public opinion, especially in an election year in which President Franklin D. Roosevelt, a staunch Anglophile, was running for an unprecedented third term.

Mayhew was initially held at the Curragh under armed guard in Ceannt Barracks, while a new barbed-wire compound was built as an extension to K Lines. He was allowed a certain amount of freedom, such as the use of the billiard room, and had access to all reading material in the officers' mess. His food, which was served to him in his room, was the same as that being served to Irish officers. He was permitted to have visitors and take whatever walking exercise he desired. At all times, however, even when going to the toilet, he was accompanied by an armed guard, who was in fact under secret instructions not to use his gun. He was to let the pilot go rather than shoot him in the event of an escape attempt.

On 17 October 1940 Mayhew was transferred to K Lines, where he was to remain the lone British internee for almost two months. Physically, the camp was not unlike many other concentration camps scattered throughout Europe. There was a rectangular perimeter fence made of barbed wire stretched between large wooden poles, with a large double gates made of barbed wire on strong wooden frames at the outer entrance. There was another barbed-wire fence inside. Between the two fences there was a grass corridor connecting four gun-posts, one at each corner. Camp guards patrolled within the corridor, and there was a residence hut inside the main gate so that extra guards were on call in the event of trouble. The rectangular area within the inner barbed-wire fence was divided into two separate compounds by a corrugated-iron fence topped with barbed wire. There were separate entrances, consisting of two smaller barbed-wire gates. Just inside the gates a parole hut stood on the dividing line between the two camps, with a door and a window in each compound. The Germans were interned in what was known as G Camp, and Mayhew in B Camp. The name B Camp (for British Camp) stuck even after other Allied nationals were interned.

Mayhew was paid directly by Maffey's office. The Irish wanted his salary restricted to £3 a week, because they feared he would be able to bribe the guards, most of whom were paid less than £1 a week, but the British refused to comply. He was given his full salary and was provided with an army cook free of charge, though he had to pay for his food.

The 21-year-old Mayhew found life boring. One letter to his fiancée, for instance, was largely taken up with accounts of chasing a mouse and trying to find a flea. "Did I ever tell you of my mouse hunt a week ago?" he wrote. "It was a graphic affair – very lone battle of wits. But it ended sadly as I leapt full length on the floor with a very disarranged sitting room, clutching the coal shovel to my middle while the mouse disappeared triumphantly down a hole behind the coal scuttle."

Mayhew was more successful in his hunt for a flea which had bothered him for a couple of days. He took a hot bath, went through his clothes carefully and then searched his bed, where he found the offending insect beneath his pillow. "After the war," he joked, "I shall demand compensation from the Irish Army for introducing vermin to British officers."

The camp censor, lacking in humour, took offence at the remark and demanded it be cut out of the letter.

"I should like to make it plain that it was intended solely as a personal joke and that it is in no way reflective of my treatment here which has always been excellent in every way," Mayhew wrote to the officer in charge. "Since my letter will lead to a misunderstanding of my conditions of internment in this country, I should be obliged if you would destroy it."

Instead, the letter was kept on file – a testament to the touchiness of the guards and the sterile rigidity of their censorship. The affair was only one of the silly, annoying facets of censorship that was to irritate all the internees during their stay at the Curragh. Mayhew wrote to his fiancée:

"Though I would like to see how many times I could write 'I love you' on one sheet of paper, I'm afraid it wouldn't tell you anything fresh and the authorities would assume that I had gone mad," he wrote. "But I can say that even at this distance of three hundred miles you are as great a distraction as ever. I can't do any work without thinking of you... In internment one must get as much joy out of one's memories as in old age and though we really didn't have a hell of a long time together before this catastrophe occurred we made it pretty eventful, didn't we, darling?"

Mayhew's letters to his older brother Christopher, who later became defence secretary in Harold Wilson's first government in the 1960s, dwelt on various matters, including Anglo-Irish relations in which he took a keen interest, especially during November after an outburst by Churchill in parliament sparked a propaganda campaign in the British and American press.

On 5 November 1940, the day of the American presidential election, Churchill gave vent to his frustration at the Dublin government's refusal to allow Britain to use Irish bases. "The fact that we cannot use the south and west coasts of Ireland to refuel our flotillas and aircraft and thus protect the trade by which Ireland as well as Great Britain lives is a most heavy grievous burden and one which should never have been placed on our shoulders, broad though they be," he told the House of Commons.

The outburst, which was highlighted by the press on both sides of the Atlantic, was apparently provoked by a distress call from mid-ocean. The convoy, HX84, which had set out from Halifax, Nova Scotia, with some 40 ships under the protection of only a lightly armed merchant cruiser, reported that it was being attacked by a German battleship in mid-Atlantic. This message was followed by radio silence. Since the merchant cruiser, the *Jervis Bay*, was no match for a battleship, there were fears for the safety of the whole convoy, and those fears were intensified that night when German radio announced the convoy had been "wiped out". All further Atlantic convoys were suspended for twelve days.

"Emotions are all very 'het up' here about these damned naval bases," Mayhew wrote. "God knows we've given the Irish cause for suspicion, but all this seems faintly ridiculous. Can one really see the British fleet bombarding Cobh? I can't and you can't, but apparently the Irish can, and the talk is all of fighting to the last man, etc., etc.

"I quite honestly think the most colossal mountain is being made out of a worm-cast," he continued. He thought Churchill had only made a statement of fact, and the issue was then blown out of proportion by "a few irresponsible members of parliament, supported by the *Daily Mail* and the *Daily Express*," which exaggerated the whole thing "a lot too tactlessly.

"As a study in psychology, it's perfect to see a crisis being created out of nothing. If you talk enough about crisis, of course there'll be a crisis," Mayhew wrote. "If it wasn't so tragic, rousing up all the latent 1916 feelings, it would be excessively funny."

The story of convoy HX 84 took an ironic twist the week after Churchill's speech when ships began straggling into port, and continued to arrive for the next twelve days. The *Jervis Bay* with its captain, Commander Fogarty Fegen from Ballinunty, Co. Tipperary, had managed to engage the battleship long enough for most of the convoy to escape. It was indeed ironic that, while Churchill was denouncing Ireland for not helping to protect the trade of the British Isles, an Irishman was playing the leading role in averting what could have been a maritime disaster. Fegen, who went down with his ship, was posthumously awarded the Victoria Cross, Britain's highest award for gallantry. He became the third of eight Irishmen born in the 26 Counties to be so honoured.

It was some months before the anxiety generated by

Churchill's remarks subsided in Ireland. In the interim Maffey used his influence to get permission for Mayhew to enroll for correspondence courses at Trinity College, Dublin. He was given facilities to borrow books by mail from the college's world-famous library, and these helped to relieve the monotony of his internment.

"I have at least ample time for the 'highest activity of the human soul,' philosophic speculation," he wrote to Christopher. "Life might be very considerably worse. I'm very comfortable. I'm doing lots of work, and listen to hours of good music on the wireless. In the last hours I've heard Beethoven's 4th Piano Concerto, which I love, and a good programme of Bach chorals, very well sung, from Germany. I'm very much afraid that my work will never be any good to me, but I enjoy it."

He had plenty of time to think about the war and his own part in it. Traditionally, grounded pilots were pretty discontented individuals, and he was no exception. He missed the excitement of flying.

"I found for myself personally a hideous enjoyment in my few weeks of active war," he wrote. "I loved, and always shall love, the exhilaration of flying; and though I realised the moral iniquity of shooting down wretched Germans, and didn't like it at all when I thought of it, I refused to think of it more than I had to. In the air it is impossible to worry about it, as the inhibitions of civilisation slipped away and one went back to 'it's him or me' of the cave-man. Apart from this, there is the thrill of being in real danger for the first time in my life, and the knowledge that your continued existence depended on your personal wits in a way strange in modern warfare. Now I shall never again have the excitement and real satisfaction of seeing tracer bullets slipping past me, or the pride of finding bullet holes later on the ground."

He also had time to think about his regrets. "The worst thing I ever shot down," he confessed, "was a wretched seaplane in mid channel that I strongly suspect was picking up survivors. But it had no Red Cross marking, so we had no choice." In his combat report of the incident he wrote that he opened fire "reluctantly".

Mayhew's commanding officer was "one of the very old

school" who seemed to think that a dutiful soldier or airman should have no compunction about killing any of the enemy. He complained to the assembled pilots afterwards that he was "ashamed to hear that any pilot of his squadron was reluctant to shoot a body, whether he's in a bomber or swimming in the water". Mayhew stood his ground and a heated argument ensued. Although colleagues thought it imprudent of him to argue with a superior officer, they told Mayhew privately that they agreed with his point of view. "So there is some dreg of humanitarianism left!" he concluded.

Although Mayhew initially had to use his own imagination to provide diversion from the boredom of his solitary confinement, the system of parole was gradually relaxed. At first the various internees were only allowed out to exercise in the afternoons, but the camp had the advantage of having the country's most modern recreational facilities: a gymnasium, indoor swimming pool, squash, handball and tennis courts, as well as a golfcourse and playing fields for various outdoor sports. The internees were offered the run of these. They were allowed out of their barbed-wire compound provided they signed a promise to return to K Lines by a specified time which they wrote on a sheet of paper:

> I hereby promise to be back in the compound at o'clock and, during my absence, not to take part in any activity connected with the war or prejudicial to the interests of the Irish State.

Mayhew availed of parole most afternoons to play golf. He usually played with retired officers from the British army, or with serving Irish officers. "I expect to be British Amateur golf champion in 1944," he remarked facetiously in a letter to his father.

Sir Basil Mayhew was not amused. Worried that the British censor might think his son a shirker, he chided Paul for playing too much golf and not spending enough time trying to escape. In fact, however, young Mayhew had actually been trying to lull his guards into a false sense of security by appearing content with things. He assured his father he was only joking about becoming amateur golf champion. "I recognise my first and foremost duty to escape. But you can't expect me to write letters about that," he explained. "It is only honest to say that the opportunity to give parole is an extremely welcome concession, which I am certain I have never abused in any way. I think the Éire authorities will bear me out that never have I acted as a 'holiday maker'."

Being allowed out on the Curragh plain for three hours each afternoon in the dead of the Irish winter was hardly a dream vacation. Whatever novelty it may have had quickly wore off, and army authorities gradually extended the privileges to include parole two nights a week to attend movies at one of the Curragh's three cinemas, and this was soon expanded to include cinemas in the neighbouring towns of Newbridge, Kilcullen and Kildare. While going to those towns, Mayhew and the five German internees had to dress in civilian clothes. They were not supposed to enter any hotels or bars, with the exception of the bar at the Curragh golf club. They were not to talk to civilians in the street, or visit any private homes without the prior permission of the camp commandant. And they were shadowed by Irish soldiers.

While Mayhew accepted this without objection, Mollenhauer resented being tailed and felt it was a slur on his honour. The escort, however, was also for their protection. The authorities were genuinely afraid that Mayhew might be attacked by some of the republican elements, or that the German internees could get into trouble with some of the many pro-British people living in the area. De Valera had agreed that the guards should keep an eye on the internees while on parole, and Lieutenant Kelly was promised a car for this purpose. Instead he was issued with a military truck, so that at first the internees were shadowed by a truck driven at walking pace and trying to be inconspicuous. It was some time before the practice was discontinued.

THE RESTLESS ONES

THE PRESS CAMPAIGN sparked off by Churchill's remarks on 5 November continued for several weeks. Although Maffey warned that this campaign was having an unhealthy effect on relations with the Irish, Churchill refused to intervene. "I think it would be better to leave de Valera stew in his own juice for a while," he wrote, adding that Maffey "should not be encouraged to think that his only task is to mollify de Valera and make everything, including our ruin, pass off pleasantly. Apart from this, the less we say to de Valera at this juncture the better, and certainly nothing must be said to reassure him."

The attitude of the American minister to Ireland, David Gray, only made matters worse. He was a most unusual diplomat. Already in his seventieth year when he was appointed to the Irish post in the spring of 1940, he had no diplomatic experience and owed his appointment to his relationship with the Roosevelt family. He was married to an aunt of Eleanor Roosevelt, the president's wife.

From the time of his arrival in Ireland, he tried to impress on de Valera and everyone else he met that the United States was anxious for Ireland to give Britain as much assistance as possible. Maffey found him very helpful. Just how helpful is probably best understood from a letter he wrote to the Dominions Office on 25 February 1943:

> It would be ungracious on our part not to recognise how great a debt we owe to Mr David Gray, the American minister in Dublin. He came to Dublin in April, 1940, and was there during the dark weeks when France fell, when we stood alone and when Dublin opinion formed a very low estimate of our chances of survival. Although America was still

> neutral (and it was Mr de Valera's declared belief that this neutrality was unshakeable) Mr David Gray was outspoken in his condemnation of the Axis aggressors, in his support of Britain's determined stand for liberty and in his criticism of the unhelpful attitude of the de Valera Government towards our cause... He recognised the need of extreme patience on our side of the table and continued to say exactly what he thought in the ideal setting of the American Legation where, with Mrs Gray, he extended to a wide circle a generous hospitality and friendliness. It would be difficult to estimate the importance of the help which the Legation gave to the British cause here during those difficult days. His association with me was overt and significant. It had a profound effect on Irish opinion at a critical stage of the war. Though it may escape the notice of the historian, Mr David Gray's arrival in Dublin was a milestone in Irish history, and Irish history means a great deal more than the history of Ireland. An American minister had the temerity to make it plain to Irish Nationalists that they were no longer the darling Playboy of the Western World, and to point out that the audience were bored. This rang down a curtain and raised a new one. We have been able to co-ordinate our policies with Mr Gray in every way.

Maffey had only to drop a hint and Gray would enthusiastically adopt the suggestion as if it were his own. While Churchill agonised over the wording of an appeal to the Americans to use their influence with de Valera, for example, Gray took the initiative and tried to persuade the Irish to allow Britain to use the ports off his own bat. Then, when Washington instructed him to approach de Valera, he went back and adopted a distinctly threatening tone on 22 November 1940.

If the Irish government did not at least explore the possibility of further co-operation with Britain in the matter, he warned, there could be a deterioration in relations between Dublin and Washington. "Americans [can] be cruel if their interests [are] affected and Ireland should expect little or no sympathy if the British [take] the ports," Gray explained to de Valera. He went on to say that the United States would soon be in the war and would require Irish bases, so Ireland might just as well anticipate the moment by allowing Britain to use the ports immediately.

There appeared to be no limit to the American minister's determination to help Britain. He thought, for instance, that President Roosevelt's avowed policy of giving Britain all out aid short of war was ridiculous, if that assistance was not going to be sufficient to defeat Hitler. "We either ought to cut our losses and declare out now or put up what is needed to push Hitler over," Gray wrote to the president. "I am sure that you feel this way about it."

Roosevelt never contradicted him. Indeed, in many ways he would confirm Gray's judgement in the coming months. Gray was perhaps doing a service in explaining American policy so candidly, but de Valera was far from impressed, and regarded the American minister as no more than an enthusiastic amateur. He expressed his views with such reckless imprudence, especially in the circles in which he socialised, that the Taoiseach feared that Gray was giving the impression "that America wants the British to seize our ports".

The propaganda campaign waged by the British press and echoed on the other side of the Atlantic involved a series of distortions. Ireland was depicted as infested with Axis agents, and it was rumoured that the German legation in Dublin was heavily over-staffed. The German legation actually had only six Germans, not more than 100, as reported. In addition, Ireland was reputed to be affording refuelling facilities to German U-boats. In late November the *Washington Evening Star* published an article asserting that Galway was being used as a U-boat base. Even if the Irish had wished to do so, they could not have refuelled U-boats, which used a heavy oil not available in Ireland. The British, who supplied all of the country's oil, had no doubt that the rumours of U-boat bases were absurd, and Lord Snell, the Deputy Leader of the House of Lords, had actually dismissed this rumour on behalf of the British government some weeks earlier. But although all such rumours were authoritatively denied, they resurfaced time and again during the war.

The second group of German airmen to arrive in Ireland came

unnoticed and remained undetected for a number of days. Shortly after three o'clock in the afternoon of 25 November 1940 they set their Bolhm & Voss flying boat down beside Innishvicillaun, one of the Blasket Islands off the coast of Kerry. The plane had been on a reconnaissance mission, searching for Allied shipping in the Atlantic, when it developed engine trouble. *Leutnant* Konrad Neymeyr, the pilot, decided to put down at the first opportunity, and he chose the sound between Innishvicillaun and the Great Blasket as it provided some shelter.

Weather conditions were so bad at the time that nobody on the mainland, or the nearby Great Blasket Island, noticed the plane or heard the shots fired by the crew as they used a machine-gun to destroy the aircraft. For three days the five-man crew remained on the uninhabited island. They lit a fire to keep themselves warm and to attract attention from the other islands, but without success. They shot a sheep and cooked some rabbits for food, and found some condensed milk and flour in an empty house that was sometimes used by shepherds.

On 28 November they set out for the Great Blasket in two rubber dinghies. A very heavy sea was running and the dinghies became separated. *Unteroffiziers* Hans Biegel and Wilhelm Krupp were swept away, but they made it to the island and climbed the steep cliffs to safety. Neymeyr, *Feldwebels* Erwin Sack and Ernst Kalkowski, reached the island shortly afterwards. All five men were brought to the mainland by fishing boat. They were suffering from exposure and were held overnight in hospital in Valentia before being transferred to Collins Barracks, Cork. There they were interrogated by Captain Joseph Healy of G2.

The 23-year-old Neymeyr had good English and seemed to have a greater knowledge of Irish matters than any of the previous Germans. At least he knew that the country was neutral and predominantly Roman Catholic. He also knew something of the difficulties between England and Ireland over the centuries, but he assumed that Anglo-Irish relations were still strained, and he hoped that the Irish authorities would secretly connive at allowing him and his crew to escape to Germany. Nevertheless he was secretive about his mission.

"You will appreciate my position," he told Healy rather apologetically. "I trust you completely, but we are warned to give no information whatever lest it might perhaps fall into the hand of our enemies."

Unlike Mollenhauer, whom Healy had earlier found aloof, Neymeyr was chatty and friendly. He talked freely about conditions in Germany and joked about rumoured food shortages by observing that he and some of his crew were overweight. Despite Neymeyr's affable nature, Healy was uneasy about the way that he talked about Germany's "Jewish problem" and asked whether Ireland had any such problems. In an effort to learn about the crew's mission, Healy plied Neymeyr with alcohol, but, he lamented, "the consumption of seven glasses of Irish whiskey seemed to have no noticeable effect other than diuretic upon him."

The crew spent two nights in Cork. At one point Sack sent a note about their treatment to the Irish officer in charge. "Without beer it is good," the note read. "With beer it is better." Some beer was then provided. The airmen were transferred to the Curragh on 1 December 1940.

Georg Fasenfeld, a native of Hamburg who had set up a meat factory in Roscrea before the war, invited all the German internees to his home for Christmas Day, but Mollenhauer's request for permission to travel to Roscrea was turned down, though not before it had gone all the way to de Valera. With wild rumours circulating abroad about Ireland crawling with Axis agents, Fasenfeld's invitation could hardly have come at a worse time, especially as there was also a threat of a serious confrontation with the Germans in the offing.

On 19 December Hempel informed Joe Walshe that a Lufthansa airplane would fly into Rhinanna airport, Co. Clare, in two days time, with additional diplomatic staff for the German legation in Dublin. There were nearly three times as many people in the British mission, all of whom had been sent to Ireland since the start of the war, so the Germans had good grounds for increasing their six-man staff. Hempel was taken aback when he was told that the Irish government feared British retaliation for any such move. De Valera ordered the army to be put on alert and the runways in Rhinanna blocked. He made it clear that the Germans would be arrested if they landed. He insisted that they would have to arrive "by the ordinary ways of travel", which was a commercial flight from the United States to Portugal, and from there to Britain and then on to Ireland. This, of course, was impossible, as the British would undoubtedly arrest them.

On the day that the Germans had planned to arrive, 21 December 1940, five further British airmen were interned, following two separate crashes. Two of the men were pilot officers from a Miles Master training aircraft which landed in a field near Dundalk. William A. Proctor, a Scot from Blairgowie, Perthshire, and Aubrey R. Covington from Kingston-on-Thames, had taken off from England in clear weather to return to the Isle of Man, where they were stationed. Confident that they would have no difficulty finding the island, they did not prepare a flight plan and got lost when they ran into heavy weather. They landed in Co. Louth, thinking they were in Northern Ireland.

On learning from a farm labourer that they were just south of the border, they tried to take off again but the surface was too bumpy and their propeller struck the ground, causing the plane to flip over. The two men were very lucky. Proctor was trapped in the cockpit and had to be helped out, but he was little the worse for the incident. Covington, on the other hand, was thrown clear and received superficial injuries, but he became very agitated when he was told by Irish officials that the two of them were being interned.

The other three airmen interned around the same time were Englishmen who baled out of a Blenheim bomber over Co. Donegal while returning from patrol duty over the North Atlantic. The plane, which was running out of fuel, crashed three miles north of Buncrana. The whole neighbourhood was roused by the crash and the explosion of the bombs on board. The men were only a few miles from Northern Ireland, but two of them, Sergeant Douglas V. Newport and Sergeant Sydney J. Hobbs, were quickly picked up by the LDF. The pilot, Sergeant Herbert W. Ricketts, was the last to jump from the aircraft. He was fortunate to land on an island in Lough Swilly, where he remained overnight. Next morning he swam ashore and was promptly taken into custody, none the worse for his narrow escape.

There was a particular air of expectation in Ireland next day, Christmas Eve. A German plane was reputed to have been seen in the Rhinanna area, but it made no attempt to land. Elsewhere Hempel sent the internees a Christmas hamper and Fasenfeld arrived at K Lines, bringing with him a phonograph and some records, as well as a lavish assortment of meats and several bottles of wine for the men. This was his way of contributing to the German war effort.

Christmas must have been a lonely time for the internees, miles from home and family, with little to do. In the circumstances it was inevitable that they would think of home, and in the case of the Allied airmen this prompted thoughts of escaping and making it across the Northern Ireland border, less than 70 miles away.

Mayhew had been working on an escape plan for some time with the help of his brother, Christopher, who was in the Special Operations Executive (SOE). Efforts to interest the SOE in arranging Paul's escape were rejected because the operation would take up too much time for just one pilot, but Christopher was given permission to go ahead on his own. He compiled a list of Irish people who would be willing to help and he made a rough map of the internment camp with the help of his father, who visited Paul in early December. The initial plan was for Paul to hide in the roof of his hut while the BBC announced that he had escaped to Northern Ireland. Since he was the only internee in the compound, it was felt that the Irish guards would then be withdrawn and Mayhew would be able to slip out under cover of darkness. Before the plan could be implemented, however, the five other British airmen were interned.

Aubrey Covington had not been in the camp even a week by Christmas, but it was already too long. Only 19 years old and already a veteran with more than two years flying experience, he had seen action in both the Battle of France and the Battle of Britain. He had survived being shot down twice and bore the scars of having been wounded on one occasion. As a result he looked much older than his years. Standing six feet tall and weighing just over eleven stone, he had a dissipated look, with stooped posture and a pale complexion, exaggerated by his dark hair and moustache. Blinking repeatedly, especially when excited, his nerves betrayed the hectic action he had seen. A less determined individual might well have welcomed his internment under the circumstances, but Covington had no intention of submitting meekly. In the following weeks, months and years he became a thorn in the side of his Irish guards as he made numerous escape attempts, some in the most blatant circumstances.

Shortly after nine o'clock on Christmas night he walked out to the main gate and began climbing it. He was straddling the top of the gate when the startled sentry called on him to halt and threatened to shoot him. Covington, gambling that the guards were under instructions not to shoot any British internees, just jumped off and walked away. The guards had not actually been ordered, but they had been advised not to shoot at internees attempting to escape. The sentry found himself in an unenviable position. Unwilling to shoot and not daring to leave his post, he was reduced to blowing his whistle in impotent frustration.

Hearing the whistle Sergeant Denis Diver of the camp guard stopped Covington, who tried to brazen his way out by saying he was just going over to the officers' mess. He invited Diver to join him for a drink.

"He said it was Christmas time – apparently treating the incident as a fake," Diver noted. "He told me to say nothing about it. I brought him back to the camp and reported the incident."

Questioned later by Kelly, Covington admitted he had been trying to escape. And he was making no apologies.

"I have a duty to my country and I am aware that you have a duty to yours," he explained defiantly. "My country is at war and I wanted to be in the racket. I attempted to escape; it is my duty, and I shall keep on trying while I am here."

Following the incident, the Irish authorities reconsidered the issue of having the guards use their guns. Commandant James Guiney issued clarifying instructions to the sentries at K Lines. Each was to carry a rifle and 50 rounds of ammunition. They were to have a clip with five rounds in their gun, but the breach was to be empty. They were authorised to open fire in five different circumstances: to stop someone trying to break into the camp, to prevent themselves being disarmed, to protect the post they were defending, to protect their own lives or the life of a comrade. These were the only occasions, so henceforth it was clear that they were not supposed to fire at an internee simply trying to escape, as in Covington's case.

On 20 January 1941 there was a mass break-out from the camp. This time it was more than an impromptu effort: the break was carefully planned and five of the six Allied airmen managed to escape for a time. They had waited for a particularly dark night. Around nine o'clock a metal poker, attached to a rope taken from a parachute which Hobbs had been allowed to retain, was thrown over the electric wires and then dragged back up so it made a connection between two wires, fusing the lighting system.

Four of the internees had already escaped before a sentry noticed somebody running from the barbed wire in the darkness. He gave chase and caught Hobbs. When the lights were restored half an hour later, the guards discovered that Mayhew, Proctor, Covington and Newport were missing. The only trace was a scarf and a coat caught in the barbed wire. The Gardaí in the nearby towns were notified and army search parties scoured the area. Newport was captured near Naas on the road from Kilcullen shortly before three o'clock the following morning, while Covington and Proctor were arrested on a bus at Rathcoole some six hours later. Mayhew was caught in the same place on another bus that evening.

The three arrested in Rathcoole were taken to Portabello Barracks, Dublin, where they were questioned and, much to their indignation, accused of violating parole by "a typically English trick". Just what the "trick" was was not spelled out, but the same accusation was also made when they were brought back to the camp. This, of course, merely added insult to the injury of having been caught, and the three officers made a formal complaint to Colonel McNally.

"We are still accused by certain officers here of having abused our privilege, although we are not told in what way we have," they wrote. "We consider these accusations most unjust as there is no truth in them whatsoever, and there can be no foundation for making them. It is our duty as members of the Royal Air Force to escape, if possible. And there should be no ill-feeling when we legitimately attempt to do so. We consider it essential that steps be taken to publicly deny these rumours as they are an insult not only to us but to the force we represent."

The complaint was not taken as seriously as the internees would have wished. It was a full week before they received a reply, and this was only from McNally's adjutant, who wrote that there was no ill-feeling and all Irish officers realised the internees had a duty to try to escape.

There was no doubt the internees had a legitimate grievance, and in the circumstances it was hardly surprising that they decided that if they were going to be accused of violating parole, they might just as well exploit the situation. Henceforth the cardinal rule would be simply not to get caught.

Kelly, the officer in charge of K Lines, was painfully aware of his own ignorance of matters relating to internment and escapes, and asked that somebody with experience should be assigned to the camp staff. Captain Frank Fitzpatrick, a middle-aged veteran from Monaghan, was duly appointment. He had been interned in Frongoch, Wales, in the aftermath of the Easter Rebellion of 1916. There he was a colleague of one of history's greatest escape organisers, Michael Collins, who had masterminded de Valera's famous escape from Lincoln Gaol in 1919, as well as the escapes of many others from a whole range of British and Irish prisons. Fitzpatrick was quick to notice the tell-tale signs of escape schemes, and he would frustrate many Allied efforts in the coming months.

He came up with a ploy to keep the internees away from the barbed wire for a while and disabuse them of the idea that the guards would not fire on them. Noticing a dead sheep on the plain one day, he had the guards drag the animal's remains to the perimeter fence that night and used some red ink to create the impression of a bullet wound. Then he told one of the guards to fire at the dead sheep. This, of course, roused the whole camp, and at this Fitzpatrick put on an act, pretending to upbraid the soldier for shooting the unfortunate animal.

A Busy Six Months

In the first three days of 1941 a number of Irish localities were bombed. There were were no fatalities, but the bomb fragments were identified as German and a strong protest was lodged in Berlin by the Irish chargé d'affaires.

Many Irish people suspected, however, that the British might have dropped German bombs in an attempt to inflame the Irish population against the Germans. David Gray, the American minister, reported that the IRA seemed "certain" that the British were responsible, and he added that "a general majority" of the Irish people "appear to think it probable".

There was deep suspicion in Irish government circles that the British were deliberately exerting economic pressure by cutting back drastically on the shipping space promised to Ireland at the start of the war in return for the transfer of seven oil tankers and Irish agreement not to compete with Britain in the hiring of neutral shipping. Although the British claimed that they needed the space for themselves, British cabinet records indicate that Britain's prime motive was to put pressure on Ireland.

The Irish had naturally been anxious to avoid antagonising the British needlessly. There were so many British overflights that the government ordered that "EIRE" be spelled out at prominent sites throughout the country. Written in six-foot block letters painted a bright white, 83 signs were posted, mostly on coastal headlands. Nevertheless in the first six months of the year, 20 belligerent planes crashed or made forced landings in Ireland.

There were no survivors in four of the crashes, while a British seaplane with a nine-man crew was treated as a ship in distress and allowed to leave, following the example set in Skerries and Ventry at the start of the war. Thirty-three survivors – 18

German and 15 Allied – were interned.

The first two of those interned in 1941 baled out of a Whitley bomber which crashed near Letterkenny, Co. Donegal, on the night of 24 January 1941. They were returning from a routine sea patrol. Unable to find their base in Limavady, they crossed and re-crossed the Scottish coast and went up and down the west coast of Ireland before the pilot, Flying Officer Leslie J. Ward from Vancouver, Canada, gave the order to bale out as they were running out of fuel. Unfortunately, the first three to jump landed in the ocean and were drowned, while Ward and the radio operator, Sergeant George Victor Jefferson from Belfast, were lucky to land on firm ground. The plane itself crashed about three miles from Quigley Point.

The army and LDF were immediately alerted and the 20-year-old radio operator was captured within ten minutes of the crash. Ward, who injured his leg in the fall, sought refuge in a private home, where he was arrested in the early hours of the following morning as he awaited promised help to bring him across the Northern Ireland border.

Later the same day an RAF Hudson bomber made a pancake landing on the beach near Skreen, Co. Sligo, with four men on board. They were running out of fuel and the pilot thought they were landing in Scotland. The crew consisted of three English pilot officers, John W. Shaw from Gildea Park, Essex; Denys Welpy from London, and Roderick Cowper from Richmond, Surrey, together with a Scottish NCO, Sergeant Norman V. Todd from Dunfirmline.

The *Luftwaffe* crew of a Focke Wulf 200 bomber were not so lucky when they crashed in thick fog into Cashelfeane Hill, about four miles from Schull, Co. Cork, in the early hours of 5 February. Five members of the six-man crew perished in the crash while a sixth, *Feldwebel* Max Hohaus of Breslau, survived with horrific burns. He was taken to St Brichin's military hospital, Dublin, where he remained for the next two-and-a-half years.

The next belligerent plane to arrive made deliberately for Ireland on 3 March 1941. Viennese *Leutnant* Alfred Heinzl's Heinkel 111 bomber had been hit during an attack on an Allied convoy in the Atlantic. One engine had been knocked out, the other damaged and the 23-year-old rear gunner, *Gefreiter* Gerd Rister, shot dead. They had been able to put out a fire in the rear of the aircraft but had no hope of returning to their base in France. When the navigator, *Feldwebel* Arthur Voigt, explained they would have to choose between landing in Britain or Ireland, the choice was straightforward.

"All we knew was that Ireland was supposed to be neutral so we opted for there," Voigt recalled. "I picked out a spot in Co. Wexford and we limped in our battered aircraft towards it." It was three o'clock in the afternoon when the plane landed with its wheels up on the beach at Rostoonstown.

The four surviving crew members immediately alighted, dismantled a machine-gun from the turret and removed Rister's body. They walked about a hundred yards into the sand dunes and began firing on the plane. As some local people approached, the crew warned them to take cover because the plane was about to blow up. Suddenly there was a loud explosion and bits of the plane went hurtling into the air. Heinzl, Voigt and their two comrades, *Gefreiter* Maximillian Galler and *Feldwebel* Rudolf Hengst, were taken into custody and interned in the Curragh with the minimum of delay.

An equal number of Allied airmen were interned later in the month. These four included the first of those from outside the British Commonwealth. The first two, from a Whitley bomber which got into trouble over Galway Bay and crashed into the sea on 13 March, managed to bale out before the crash; three other members of the crew went down with the plane. Pilot Officer David Midgely landed in the water between Ardfree Point and Renville pier and managed to swim ashore. He walked some miles to a farmhouse, where he was arrested by the LDF. Sergeant Robert G. Harkell was fortunate enough to land on the golf links at Salthill, but he was picked up when he asked a Garda how far it was to the border.

Sergeant David Southerland was also interned the same day after his Blenheim fighter made a forced landing at Termonfeckin, Co. Louth. Although not far from the border, his chances of escape were destroyed when he broke an ankle in the crash.

Next night saw the internment of a pilot with a Russian background. Thirty-nine-year-old Sergeant Stanislau Kerniewski had been stationed at Kemble in England as part of a Free Polish unit. He got lost on a training flight when, seeing the lighted city, he realised he was over Dublin, so he put down safely in the water off Clontarf and swam ashore. He refused to give much information about himself except that he considered himself Polish. He was born in Minsk when it was part of the Russian Empire and he grew up in Moscow, but fled the Soviet Union in the 1930s. While he had very little English, he claimed to speak fluent Russian and Polish, neither of which were of much use to him in Ireland. He absolutely refused to give any details about his family, other than that his wife was in Poland.

April and May 1941 were probably the most tense months of the whole war for Ireland. The Dublin government expected that the postponed German invasion of Britain was likely to occur any day during the spring, and there was a real danger that the Germans would launch at least a diversionary attack on Ireland, which was virtually defenceless. Despite Maffey's support, de Valera had been unable to purchase arms from the British. He sent Frank Aiken, the Minister for Co-ordination of Defensive Measures, to the United States to try to buy arms there, but this mission turned very sour. Aiken got into a heated argument with President Roosevelt in the White House and then proceeded to associate himself publicly with some of the president's most vocal opponents. Gray was instructed to protest and he, in turn, got into a bitter exchange with de Valera, who let it be known that he would demand Gray's recall if it were not for his close relationship with the Roosevelts.

All of this unfolded as Ireland was being dragged closer towards war. On the evening of 1 April, a Heinkel 111 bomber made a forced landing on a beach four miles from Dunbratten Head, Co. Waterford. The plane had been shot up during an attack on some ships in the Bristol Channel. An engine had been knocked out and there was no question of their being able to return to their base in Tours, France, so they decided to make for Ireland, even if it meant internment. Since their rubber dinghies had been damaged and one of the crew, *Leutnant* Heinz Grau of

Vienna, had a seriously wounded arm, the crew decided against baling out. After landing successfully they set a time switch to blow up the plane. When it failed to go off, they fired into the craft with a machine-gun in order to destroy its instruments.

They walked to a local farmhouse, where they were given tea and Grau's arm was bandaged by a doctor, Pat O'Callaghan, a famous athlete who had won gold medals in the hammer throwing event at both the 1928 Amsterdam and 1932 Los Angeles Olympic Games. If it had not been for a split in Irish athletics, he would have defended his title at the Berlin Olympics, at which one of the men he was now treating – *Leutnant* Georg Fleischmann from Graz, Austria – had been an official cameraman. O'Callaghan and some colleagues got the crew's blessing to siphon fuel from the aircraft, as petrol was extremely scare in Ireland at the time. Fleischmann warned them that they would not be able to use the high octane fuel in a motor car, but O'Callaghan explained that they would dilute it with paraffin oil. The German airmen were taken to Waterford, where a doctor at the local hospital advocated amputating Grau's arm.

James Kelly of the Curragh internment staff, who was sent to pick up the men, was given the unenviable task of explaining the situation to Grau, who insisted that he would take his chances with his arm, as he had been an architect in civilian life and felt that he could not do without an arm in his profession. He was adamant that he would rather risk death than lose the arm. He was transferred instead to St. Brichin's Hospital, where his arm was saved. Kelly brought Fleischmann and the others – *Oberfeldwebel* Ernst Lorra and *Unteroffiziers* Otto Jaeger and Ernst Gensen – to the Curragh.

Shortly after midnight on 8 April six German Heinkel 111 bombers, which had detached themselves from a raid on Glasgow, bombed Belfast, killing 13 people. It was probably just an exploratory raid to test the defences of the city.

A couple of days later there was a curious incident when an RAF Lerwyck seaplane with nine men aboard set down in Bundoran Bay. It was decided to treat the crew as distressed mariners. Under international law, they had 24 hours to effect repairs and leave. In this case they were simply short of fuel, which was brought by road from Northern Ireland only 20 miles away. Within four hours the plane was able to leave again.

The following Monday, Dublin celebrated the 25th anniversary of the Easter Rebellion, and the people would soon find that they had good reason to be thankful for Irish independence. Next night, more than 200 German bombers attacked Belfast in what was one of the deadliest bombing raids of the whole war. Large areas of the city were devastated and 745 people were killed, which was far worse than the infamous bombing of Coventry in which 554 people lost their lives. The extent of the carnage in Belfast was played down at the time, because it dramatised the fact that Britain had left Northern Ireland relatively defenceless. Of course, this justified Dublin's decision to keep the even more poorly defended part of the island out of the conflict.

Nevertheless de Valera did get involved in the aftermath of the raid when he was asked to send southern fire brigades to help fight the fires raging in Belfast. Thirteen brigades were dispatched from Dundalk, Drogheda and Dublin. The Taoiseach was apparently worried that the Germans might consider his actions a violation of neutrality, but Hempel was understanding.

"I think we could have protested, but it would have been cruel," he told an Irish journalist afterwards. "I know that the Irish Government felt a bit uneasy that the German Government might protest, but it was a deed of sympathy for your people, your Irish people, and we fully understood what you felt. Nobody from Germany protested and I had no intention of doing so. Your own people were in danger."

A couple of days later five more Germans were interned after their bomber ditched in the sea between Calf Island and Goat Island off Schull, Co. Cork. The crew were *Leutnant* Ernst Muller, *Feldwebel* Karl Macht, *Feldwebel* Georg Sigl, *Obergefreiter* Alfred Jackel, and *Gefreiter* Willi Salbenblatt. Sigl, who was injured in the crash, was taken to Mallow Hospital, while the others were rushed to the Curragh wrapped in blankets.

A second Pole was interned on the Allied side exactly one week later. A professional pilot, Lithuanian-born Captain

Kazimiers Baranowski had had an aristocratic upbringing before the Russian revolution, when he fled to Poland. In September 1939 he fled his home in Warsaw to join the Free Polish forces in Britain. On 24 April, running low on fuel, he spent about half an hour hovering over the area between Waterford and Dunmore East looking for a suitable landing spot before setting his Fairly fighter down on the main Tramore-Waterford road at Corbally in the late afternoon. At 41 years of age, he was the oldest of the Allied internees.

On 30 April a Whitely bomber crashed near Askill on the border road from Ballyshannon, Co. Donegal, to Garrison, Co. Fermanagh. Four of the crew baled out over Northern Ireland, but the pilot, the last to leave, landed on the Donegal side of the border. He tried to buy a bicycle from a man he met on the road, but even though that proved unsuccessful he had little difficulty in crossing the border on an "unapproved" road which had no custom's post.

The month of May was even more difficult for the Dublin government. It was marked by a grave political crisis surrounding the possible introduction of conscription in Northern Ireland and it finished off with the most serious bombing incident of the war as far of the people of the 26 Counties were concerned.

In the early minutes of 5 May the Germans launched another massive bombing raid on Belfast. Some 95,000 incendiary bombs were dropped by 204 German bombers and de Valera again sent the fire brigades north.

Next day a German bomber was shot down by a British fighter some three-and-a-half miles off the Irish coast. Two of the four-man crew went down with the aircraft, while the other two, *Oberleutnant* Walther Hollborn and *Unteroffizier* Josef Emmerich, managed to scramble into a dinghy and make it to shore at Blackwater, Co. Wexford, where they were arrested. They had been shot down over international waters, so they should have been considered as distressed mariners under international law, but the niceties of neutrality were overlooked in favour of the Allies.

But Churchill was still so annoyed over the denial of bases that he was unwilling to give Dublin credit for anything; instead he sparked off a major political crisis on 19 May 1941 by suggesting the possibility of introducing conscription to Northern Ireland. This was something de Valera had long feared, believing that the nationalist population in the North would resist conscription violently, and the rest of the island would inevitably be dragged into a conflict with the British by the IRA. Indeed, there were reasons for believing that it was not the Easter Rebellion of 1916 so much as the British attempt to introduce conscription in Ireland in 1918 which had driven the Irish people into the arms of the radical nationalists in the lead-up to the Irish War of Independence. Now the Taoiseach was afraid that another conscription crisis would drive the people into the arms of the IRA.

As this drama was being played out, the most senior of the Allied airmen to be interned, Flight Lieutenant Hugh Verity, was arrested on 22 May 1941 after his Beaufighter made a forced landing in a field adjoining Leopardstown racecourse in south Co. Dublin. The plane, which was on a flight from Gibraltar to England, sustained considerable damage, but none of the crew was seriously injured. A crowd quickly gathered at the scene and watched as Flying Officer John Holgate smashed instruments in the cockpit with a hammer. The other member of the crew was a Scot, Sergeant William Barnett from Crossgales in Fifeshire.

Local police and members of the LDF arrived and took the men into custody. A doctor, Hugh Wilson, a veteran of the First World War, treated the men at the scene. Wilson was one of a number of veterans who were in the process of setting up an "escape club" to help British airmen get out of Ireland. Some bystanders invited the crew for a drink, but the police refused to permit this.

James Dillon, the deputy leader of Fine Gael, warned Maffey and Gray that de Valera would rouse anti-British feelings, and would use the conscription crisis to escape from economic and political realities by enlisting the support of the Roman Catholic cardinals for "a Holy War" against the British and the Unionists. Joseph Cardinal MacRory – who had approached Hempel on the eve of Churchill's statement about conscription with a request that the Germans should not bomb the cathedral town of Armagh – issued a strong statement denouncing the conscription proposal. There were public demonstrations throughout Northern Ireland, with major gatherings in Derry, Armagh, Newry, Omagh, Dungannon, Enniskillen and Belfast.

"If Mr Churchill is determined, as he seems to be, to go ahead with the proposal, the prospect is indeed as dark as it can be," de Valera privately told the American minister. "Almost inevitably this will lead to a new conflict between Ireland and Britain in which we shall all be involved. We are truly in a world gone mad."

Even *The Irish Times*, one of the last bastions of unionism in the 26 Counties, was opposed to the move. There was also widespread press hostility to the conscription proposal in Britain, with doubts about its propriety being expressed in newspapers like *The Times*, the *News Chronicle*, the *Daily Express*, and the *Daily Telegraph*. According to the Belfast correspondent of the *New York Times*, "The opposition to conscription has brought about almost complete unanimity between the various factions in Southern Ireland, as well as nationalists and those with nationalist tendencies in Northern Ireland." Despite these criticisms, and the reservations expressed by President Roosevelt and Prime Ministers W.L. Mackenzie King of Canada and Robert Menzies of Australia, Churchill was unwilling to back down. He feared further loss of face following the German victory in the Atlantic when the *Bismarck* sank the pride of the Royal Navy, HMS *Hood*. Nonetheless he was overruled on the issue by his cabinet on 26 May.

Next day, giving full play to his sense of the dramatic, Churchill exploited some good news on the war front. He told the House of Commons that British planes had located the *Bismarck* and damaged its steering mechanism. As he was speaking, he said, the Royal Navy was moving in for the kill. "He then went on to speak about conscription in Northern Ireland and left the House with a sense of *coitus interruptus*," a colleague noted. As a Unionist MP began to object to the dropping of the conscription proposal, an aide arrived with a message for the Prime Minister. "I crave your indulgence, Mr Speaker," Churchill interrupted. "I have just received news that the *Bismarck* has been sunk." The chamber erupted in loud cheering and, amid all the euphoria, the conscription crisis passed quietly into history.

The danger to Ireland, however, had not yet passed. In the early hours of Sunday, 30 May, a German plane bombed the North Strand area of Dublin, killing 34 people and wounding 90, and destroying some 300 homes. It was by far the worst incident of the war to occur in the 26 Counties.

"Nazi planes dropped their loads of death over a wide area of Dublin, killing and wounding more than a hundred people," *Pathé News* reported. "The Éire Government has protested to Berlin against the wanton attack on their professed neutrality – but unfortunately protests will not bring back the dead or heal the wounds of the injured! Maybe this is the price that Éire has to pay for sitting on the fence."

The bombing did not provoke the kind of public backlash against Germany that the *Pathé* organisation evidently desired. Although there was no doubt that the damage was done by German bombs, there was still so much distrust of the British – just 20 years after the rampages of the Black and Tans during the War of Independence – that people did not rule out the possibility that German bombs might have been dropped by British planes.

On 10 June 1941 the country got another small taste of war when a Heinkel 111, trying to land shortly before ten o'clock in the morning near Churchtown, Co. Wexford, struck a small stone wall and burst into flames, killing the five members of the crew. The plane had been shot down by a Free French pilot, Pilot Officer Maurice Motte (alias Remy), who had made a forced landing himself not too far away at Kilmacthomas, Co. Waterford, about an hour earlier.

Following the German invasion of the Soviet Union on 26 June, the focus of the German air war turned to the east and there was a distinct slackening in *Luftwaffe* activity around Ireland thereafter. Indeed, from then until the end of the war, only eight more German planes came down in Ireland, and one of those was in the last hours of the conflict. Ireland was largely by-passed as Germany concentrated on submarine warfare in the Atlantic.

LIFE IN G CAMP

ON 26 JANUARY 1941, when there were eleven German and twelve Allied airmen in K Lines, Hempel suggested that the Irish government should repatriate a similar number of each to their home countries. Maffey seemed to like the idea, but when he went over to London for consultations, the authorities there would not hear of it. They were afraid that the German airmen would be able to provide valuable information about Ireland to their people in Germany, who were poorly informed about the country. The idea was scrapped, though the German minister was to bring it up again several times during the war.

Most of the German airmen were model prisoners as far as the Irish guards were concerned, though Mollenhauer did give the authorities headaches by protesting on behalf of his men with a militant zeal. They generally observed the letter and the spirit of parole, but in return they expected to be trusted as men of honour and not be subjected to any petty restrictions while on parole. Mollenhauer could not understand, for instance, why he was refused permission to go to Cork for the funeral of colleagues from his squadron who were killed near Durrus, Co. Cork, on 5 February.

Five members of the six-man crew had perished in the crash, but the Irish authorities refused to permit any of the internees to attend their funerals. When Mollenhauer and Wochner, together with Henning Thomsen of the German legation, went to visit the injured *Obersfeldwebel*, Max Hohaus, at St Brichin's military hospital on 14 March, the staff told them they were under orders not to permit any internees to see him. The three men lodged a strong protest and left vowing to return that afternoon, by which time they hoped the senseless restriction would be lifted. The matter was brought to the attention of Army Headquarters, who saw no reason for the ban. The Adjutant General was about to order that the men be admitted when he learned that the barring order had been issued by Oscar Traynor, the Minister for Defence. Hence the internees were again refused admission later in the day.

"This is not the first time for us to experience mean and annoying measures without any reason whatsoever and even against international law," Mollenhauer exploded upon his return to the camp. It was the last straw. He gave vent to all his pent-up frustrations over the petty restrictions – his delayed mail, McNally's occasional refusals to see him, the denial of facilities to telephone the German legation when he wanted to complain about something. On top of that he and his colleagues had been denied parole for a time following the *British* escape attempt of 20 January 1941.

"I cannot but have the impression," he wrote to McNally, "that all these unintelligible measures are deliberately taken by some source – sources – in order to make our life here still more difficult." He formally requested permission to see Hohaus on his next visit to Dublin. When he had still not received a reply a week later, he repeated the request, only to be told that a visit was out of the question for "medical reasons". Mollenhauer, however, persisted. He was trying to establish the principle that once there were no medical objections he and his colleagues would be allowed to visit the injured airman, and he demanded a "final decision soon".

Officials at the Department of Defence resented his tone. They decided to tell him that he and the other internees were allowed to come to Dublin each month "for the purpose of visiting the Legation only and that it is not proposed to widen the privilege in any other way", but the Department of External Affairs intervened before the reply could be sent. De Valera felt the Germans had a valid point. Traynor was persuaded to reverse his earlier decision and the internees were informed that they could call on Hohaus as soon as he was well enough to receive visitors.

Frustrated and homesick, Mollenhauer tended to be quite critical of conditions at the Curragh. When he complained about these in a letter to his father on 3 May 1941, however, the censor insisted the critical passage be excised or the letter destroyed. This, of course, only made matters worse, because there was no military or security justification for the censor's demand.

"The extract in question concerns as far as I know a complete and truthful description of our treatment here," he wrote to McNally. "It was described truthfully and certainly is not dangerous to the State. It is not clear to me why the censor thinks that he should suppress the truth. If he is of the opinion that it would create a bad impression in Germany then the matter would be better amended by altering our treatment here."

The camp authorities disliked what they regarded as Mollenhauer's sense of German superiority. They felt that he was contemptuous of the Irish army because it was small. Although as an *oberleutnant* Mollenhauer was outranked by Captain Frank Fitzpatrick of the camp guard and even more so by Commandant James Guiney, he still insisted in taking his complaints directly to Colonel McNally, the senior officer in charge of the whole Curragh Command. He seemed to feel that as the senior German officer he should deal directly with the most senior Irish officer, which of course offended the sensitivities of the Irish officers with whom he was in regular contact.

Among the things which annoyed Mollenhauer intensely was the retention of personal belongings taken from him and his colleagues when they were first arrested. Article 6 of the Geneva Convention on prisoners-of-war stipulated that all personal affects and articles for personal use, except arms or military equipment, should remain in the prisoner's possession. Mollenhauer demanded that his cap, leather gloves, briefcase, lighted pencil and a portrait attachment for his camera – all of which had been seized at the police station in Cloghane – should be returned to him. Other colleagues had had similar items taken. When the *Irish Press* – a newspaper largely owned and controlled by de Valera – published an article on the rights of prisoners-of-war stating that only arms or military items could be legitimately seized, Mollenhauer renewed his demands.

"We want our property in our own custody, because we cannot believe it is safe now," he wrote. "Should things be lost or damaged, we shall claim damages. Should they not be returned I shall be obliged to take other steps, for instance, by my government or the International Red Cross."

De Valera asked that Mollenhauer's demands should be treated "as being of great urgency". By then, of course, it was impossible to trace many of the items, which had been taken as mementoes by arresting personnel.

This did not end the pilfering. On 17 April Ernst Muller and three members of his crew were rushed to the Curragh after they were rescued in the water off Schull. They were taken in an open truck wrapped only in blankets because their uniforms were wet. Muller objected to being transported in such a fashion, but he was told the army had orders to bring them to the Curragh immediately. When they got their uniforms back two days later, they were in a shocking state. They had been bundled together with no effort made to dry them and were damaged by souvenir hunters ripping off all rank and flight insignia.

Hempel protested to the Department of External Affairs on 15 May 1941. He listed Mollenhauer's various complaints, especially the unnecessary restrictions. Freddy Boland contended, in reply, that those restrictions were necessary because the Germans would only give a qualified parole. They were only willing to sign for the period that they were out of the camp, rather than give a blanket commitment not to take any further part in the war for the duration of hostilities. If they would give such a commitment, he said, the restrictions could be dropped and even the barbed wire removed.

Mollenhauer was really getting up the nose of the Irish army with his constant complaints and his repeated insistence on going directly to McNally over the heads of Kelly, Fitzpatrick and Guiney. Boland told Hempel that McNally was very busy and could not meet Mollenhauer every time the German officer asked to see him, but Guiney, as the officer-in-charge of internment, would be "available for all reasonable discussions".

Not all the German internees saw things as negatively as Mollenhauer. Arthur Voigt, who was interned on 3 March 1941, had been a prisoner-of-war of the British for some days after his aircraft was shot down over Belgium in May 1940, but he was left behind when they evacuated Dunkirk. As a result he had a broader view of the conditions under which he was being held.

"At first we were depressed about being taken to the Curragh," he recalled. "We hoped we would be set free." But he quickly found his life-style was much different from that of a prisoner-of-war. "Our way of life was unbelievable," he wrote. "We were all treated extremely well by the Irish authorities."

Within the camp each of the officers initially had his own room, although later as the camp became more crowded they had to double up. The NCOs doubled up from the beginning. The men were housed in 20 x 120 foot huts divided into six rooms, each with electric light, wardrobe, chest of drawers, mirror, bed, table, chair, curtains and a mat. There was also a small, coal-fed iron stove to provide heat, which was often much needed during the winter months. Two of the resident huts had large washrooms attached. In each of these there were two toilets, three handbasins, and two showers, with hot water available from eight o'clock in the morning until nine-thirty at night.

A normal day began with a breakfast of bacon and egg with tea, bread, butter and jam. From ten until noon on two mornings a week the *Luftwaffe* internees had the exclusive use of the Irish army's swimming pool. Later this was extended to three mornings weekly and eventually to one hour daily. The main daily meal was served at one o'clock in the afternoon. It usually consisted of roast beef, potatoes and turnips, with rice pudding for dessert, followed by tea. The kitchen was staffed by Irish army personnel and the food was similar to that served in the Irish barracks near by. Although the meals were wholesome, they were monotonous; the daily menu seldom varied, except for fish on Fridays. Mollenhauer complained so much about the food that the German legation authorised Willi Krupp, a gourmet cook in civilian life, to buy and prepare some different meals.

"Suddenly we were eating tinned pineapples and peaches, asparagus tips and steaks," Voigt recalled. A hefty bill for this was run up and sent to the German legation. Hempel paid the bill, but this "ended our fancy dishes", Voigt lamented.

The internees were free to go out on parole between two and five o'clock each afternoon. They could use the swimming pool, though they had to share it with Irish soldiers and Allied internees in the afternoon. They also had the full use of the other sporting facilities, or they could visit the three nearby towns to do some shopping.

"The first thing I did was to go into nearby Newbridge and order a new suit," Voigt explained. "It was the first time in my life I had a handmade suit."

Back at the camp at five o'clock the Germans had daily lessons in English, conducted by two local primary teachers. This was followed by the evening meal, consisting of tea, bread, butter and jam. At seven-thirty they were again free to go out on parole, usually to attend movies, or they could relax in their own bar in the compound, in which beer and spirits were served by an Irish army bartender at duty-free prices. A glass of beer or spirits cost only 5d (2.4 pence) per glass.

Unlike the Allied internees, who had segregated dining areas and separate anterooms for the officers and NCOs, the German officers and men ate in the same dining-room and had a community recreation room in which they mixed freely without any apparent class distinction. The enlisted German airmen never showed anything like the resentment towards their officers that was apparent among their Allied counterparts. The level of discipline, too, always seemed to be higher amongst the Germans. Each time they entered their recreation rooms they would face a picture of Hitler and give a Nazi salute, though they did not give formal salutes to each other, except on ceremonial occasions.

Within the camp they dressed in well-tailored uniforms and looked very smart, and their morale was such that they maintained that smart appearance while on parole in civilian clothes. As a result they had a particular appeal for young women. One foreign dignitary, who brought his wife on a visit to the camp, kicked up a bit of a rumpus when she went missing. It was the cause of some amusement among the guards, who were aware that she was in bed with one of the *Luftwaffe* officers. "Exclusive types of glamorous females, not normal to the confines of the Curragh, were attracted by the German airmen," one envious Irish soldiers recalled. "If they were not winners in war, they certainly succeeded on many other fronts."

LIFE IN B CAMP

AS FAR AS the Allied internees were concerned anything was permissible, if they could get away with it. But the authorities had a very good intelligence network when it came to such matters, especially as the parole area was invariably crawling with off-duty soldiers from the Curragh. There were several reports, for instance, that British internees were seen violating regulations by going into the bar of the Central Hotel in Newbridge. One Irish officer reported that, on 30 January, he had seen Covington and Proctor outside the parole area in Naas, where they met a local man and his daughter.

"They had obviously been expecting each other," according to the officer, who added that they had then entered Lawlor's Hotel and gone into a private room. On the night of the recent escape, Covington and Proctor had passed by the local man's house. G2 wondered if the man and his daughter might be preparing to assist in a further escape bid. The situation was discussed at a conference between representatives of the army, and the Departments of Defence and External Affairs, which had been requested by McNally to draw up formal parole regulations.

At the meeting the Assistant Secretary at External Affairs, Freddy Boland, again emphasised that they "should be granted all possible concessions consistent with the necessary precautions against their escape". The German internees resented being followed by guards while they were on parole, even at a discrete distance, but McNally argued that the tail was necessary to protect them. It was decided to persist with the surveillance, but to permit the men to avail of parole for an extra four hours each night and to allow them to visit designated hotels in Newbridge, Kilcullen and Kildare, as well as visit their respective diplomatic representatives in Dublin once a month instead of every three months. At Boland's insistence the senior British and German officers were to be permitted to telephone their diplomatic representative at any time. McNally was uneasy about this concession. He grumbled that Mollenhauer was "somewhat neurotic" and would be making interminable complaints. Hempel recognised this, according to Boland, but was anxious that the senior officer should have the facility all the same.

Next day instructions were issued to the camp guards. The internees could have parole for three hours each day for exercise and for four hours each evening for recreation. If necessary, the evening period could be extended for a further half-hour to facilitate them in the event of an extra long movie.

William Proctor, the fair-haired Scot from Blairgowie, Perthshire, was at first the only Allied internee who was married and had already asked for extended parole, if his wife visited him. De Valera's department, wishing to have parole as liberal as circumstances permitted, suggested that Proctor should be allowed parole from noon till about nine o'clock, or even ten o'clock, but certainly not beyond ten-thirty. The camp authorities eventually granted a twelve hour parole until ten-thirty. By the time this was settled Proctor had been joined by another married man and they made arrangements to bring their wives to Ireland. The same privileges were also available in theory to the married Germans, but they were never able to benefit from them.

Parole conditions were further liberalised in April 1941 after Dublin had time to enquire about parole conditions in other countries. They learned that Norway and Belgium had both allowed internees out on parole while they were neutral. Sweden gave officers unsupervised parole and allowed enlisted men out under supervision, while in Spain internees stayed in local hotels and merely had to report to the military daily.

In B Camp the separate recreation rooms "were the scenes of many wild evenings, darts parties, and nights of crap shooting," according to one of the internees. There was, however, only one bar in the Allied compound for both the officers and men. It was a particularly popular gathering place.

"Our bar was run on RAF lines," one of the men recalled. "That is to say that it was always well stocked and well attended."

While the Germans cultivated vegetable gardens and grew flowers, the Allied compound was a shambles. The grass was overgrown and little effort was made to raise anything. They were afraid that if they planted a garden it might give the impression they were content with their lot, whereas they wanted everyone to know they could not get out of the place fast enough. The Allied internees were a highly disgruntled group of individuals whose discipline and morale often appeared to be particularly poor. The enlisted men seemed to resent the special privileges given to their officers, who had, for example, Irish orderlies assigned to them. In comparison with the Germans, some of the Allied internees dressed in ill-fitting, dirty uniforms, and their perpetual sloppiness did not endear them to their military guards.

The Allied airmen from overseas had all volunteered for service, and, like Mayhew, they were frustrated by their grounding for the remainder of the war. Shaw had given up a job in Argentina and returned home to fight, not to sit out the war in Ireland; likewise Ward, who had come all the way from Vancouver, Canada. Baranowski, who spoke little English and did not seem to have much motivation to learn any, was particularly depressed. He had left his wife and family in Warsaw and had no word of them since the German invasion of Poland. "His internment," one colleague recalled, "was an existence full of brandy drinking and spasmodic outbursts of broken English."

Military intelligence, which was in charge of censoring internees' mail, noted with satisfaction that the men were frustrated by the efficiency of the camp staff: Captain Fitzpatrick and Lieutenant Kelly, Sergeant Denis Diver, two corporals and 25 acting corporals. Fitzpatrick seemed to know most of the tricks that the internees might use.

The guards were ordered to keep a particular eye on the activities of Proctor and Covington, in view of their recent visit to Naas in blatant disregard of their parole conditions. This paid off within a fortnight when a guard investigating a suspicious noise entered Norman Todd's room and found Covington standing on a bed trying out a homemade rope ladder that was dangling from the ceiling. It had been made of rope from a parachute tied around pieces of timber.

"I have just about had enough lately and I am getting a bit brassed off," Todd wrote to his mother in Dunfirmline. "There is too much spying and 5th Column work going on, for every time we make any plans at all we are always caught. It's inexplicable."

A message hidden in a cake which a local woman sent to the British internees, was found by G2. "If you get another chance to escape call here and we will do our best to help," she wrote, adding details of her house and its location. She ended with a request that they burn her note.

Although Covington had been caught with the rope ladder, it did nothing to dampen his ardour to escape. He made another dramatic bid on 20 March 1941. He was cycling around the compound as one of his colleagues was preparing to go out on parole. Cowper had just signed out and, as the guard opened the gate for him, Covington raced through on the bicycle and peddled off furiously in the direction of Newbridge.

The corporal at the gate explained that he did not try to stop the internee for fear of injuring him. "I was afraid to knock him off as he would be injured in the barbed wire," he said. "But I called him back and he took no heed of me."

The alarm was raised immediately and a corporal took off after Covington on a bicycle. Other guards soon followed and the Gardaí in Newbridge were alerted. Covington managed to lose his pursuer and stayed at large for an hour. Camp guards checked all buses leaving Newbridge. After checking one bus bound for Dublin a guard noticed Covington running up a side street and getting on the bus. The guard requested the police to stop the bus at a checkpoint over the Liffey bridge.

Covington immediately came forward.

"You are Mr Covington?" the guard asked.

"Yes, and why, what's all this about?" he replied. "I'm on parole. I signed the parole form coming out as I always do."

"I know you always do, but you didn't do it today and that is why we are here."

"Why are you on that bus?" another of the soldiers asked.

Covington said he was going to the Central Hotel, but the bus had already passed the hotel. He tried to make a run for it but was quickly overpowered.

Commandant Guiney took a very poor view of the episode. He thought the sentry's reason for not trying to stop Covington at the gate was "a very lame excuse" and the unfortunate soldier was fined for dereliction of duty. At the same time the commandant was bitterly critical of Covington for causing a "considerable amount of commotion" in Newbridge when he tried to bolt after having lied about signing parole. In Guiney's view an officer should not lie under any circumstances, even to further an escape attempt. Moreover, he felt it had not been honourable to rush the gate when it was being opened for a colleague on parole.

An Irish army waiter in the Allied compound overheard Covington being admonished by the senior Allied officer, Leslie Ward. "The RAF will never countenance this," Ward said, "because it was nothing short of abusing parole."

"Would you not do the same thing yourself, if there was a gate open to you?" Covington asked. "And, besides, my name was not on the parole list."

"No," Ward replied. "It certainly wouldn't be my way of doing things." At that point they saw the waiter and changed the subject.

Welpy and Cowper also expressed misgivings about their colleague's tactics. "Whether Covington's action was honourable is a debatable point," Welpy told one of the Irish officers, "but I personally do not consider it honourable." Cowper, who was particularly sensitive to the possible accusation that he might have violated parole in helping Covington to escape – seeing that the break was made as he was going through the gate – agreed with Welpy that the attempt was not honourable, and he added, "It could be put down as abusing parole."

However, Covington had not violated the letter of the parole system, and McNally acknowledged this in a report to Army Headquarters in Dublin. He was nevertheless very critical of the young airman.

"Pilot Officer Covington is the greatest source of trouble we have," McNally wrote. "He is constantly endeavouring to annoy us by making these spectacular efforts at escaping." The view that Covington's escape attempts were only carried out to annoy senior officers was rather naive. Describing the 19-year-old airman as "irresponsible" and "not endowed with a lot of honour," Guiney wrote that he was "a very difficult internee to deal with".

But the guards themselves took a much more realistic view of the situation. They knew that Covington was simply determined to escape and made no bones about his willingness to use just about any means to do so. Even if he was not always of the happiest disposition, they could understand that too.

"What is wrong with you?" one of the guards asked him one day when he looked particularly glum.

"I'm sex starved," he replied.

The guard was amused. When he reported the conversation, McNally came to an outrageous conclusion. He wrote to Army Headquarters that Covington suffered from a sexual disease, which was totally untrue. Even though McNally admitted that Covington had not violated parole in cycling through the gate, the young airman's parole privileges were suspended for three weeks. He was clearly getting under the skin of some of the camp authorities.

In time even those internees who had apparently been critical of Covington's methods would exploit a comparatively similar situation at the gate in a mass escape attempt. Their criticism may well have been contrived in order to persuade the camp authorities that it was not necessary to tighten up procedures. Although the Irish had intercepted various escape-related notes, they had not noticed that one of the Allied internees knew a letter code used by MI9, the British services escape organisation. The January break-out had failed because the men had been unable to get out of the Kildare area. Now arrangements were made for another break, and MI9 was to provide transport to the border.

FIVE EVENTFUL WEEKS

ON 22 MAY 1941 Flight Lieutenant Hugh Verity was delivered to the camp and promptly took over from Ward as the senior Allied officer. His initial reactions were rather mixed. Conditions in the camp did not seem too uncomfortable, though he found "life inside the huts was not that easy.

"As Commanding Officer I had a room to myself, but the place was always too noisy, with junior officers and NCOs rarely keeping quiet," he explained. "Discipline was pretty relaxed. Our greatest form of relaxation was playing cards all night."

It was indeed an unusual kind of concentration camp. Next morning Paul Mayhew left for Dublin, having been granted extended parole in order to sit the first-year examinations at Trinity College. He was given permission to spent the next four nights at the home of one of Maffey's staff in the city.

Verity was immediately struck by the presence of the Germans on the other side of the fence, but he had very little contact with them. "We were always polite to each other but never friendly," he noted. "A simple nod or a curt thank you was as far as the conversation went.

"We had a good reporting service through the Irish officers on what was going on next door in the German camp." Most of the time the Allied internees could not have cared less, but Verity's first few days were somewhat different, because of the political crisis generated by the possible introduction of conscription in Northern Ireland, as well as the dramatic news from the war front. When they heard that the German battleship *Bismarck* had sunk HMS *Hood*, the Allied internees were sickened, and their dejection was aggravated when the German internees held a noisy celebration. A car from the German legation in Dublin brought a group of girls down to the camp and they pasted brown paper over the windows of the huts and held "an enormous party/orgy", according to Verity. "We could hear the merriment going on all night behind the corrugated iron fence."

Four days later came the announcement of the sinking of the *Bismarck*. It was the first really good war news that any of the Allied internees had heard since being interned. Just to be different, they held a low key celebration. "We had a quiet drink," Verity recalled years later. These events brightened the early days of his internment, which was short and eventful.

Sydney Hobbs's fiancée came over from London, and he was given extended parole from nine o'clock each the morning until midnight over the holiday weekend. This was the weekend on which Dublin was bombed, but Hobbs did not allow events there to spoil his break: he and his girlfriend decided to get married the following Sunday at Ballysac's church. He was the first of the Allied internees to get married at the Curragh. Five of his colleagues would follow suit, four to Irish girls whom they met during their internment in K Lines.

Three days after the Hobbs wedding the Allied internees had as their latest addition their one and only Frenchman, Maurice Motte, or Maurice Remy as he called himself. He had shot down a German bomber, killing everybody aboard, so his addition to the camp was hardly likely to enhance relations between the Allied and Axis internees. But he turned out to be a quiet, solitary man, or "a rather strange individual", according to a fellow internee. Standing a little under five-foot-six, he walked with a distinct military carriage, but he was delicate looking, despite his sallow complexion. The 28-year-old Remy was non-smoking, an ardent teetotaler, with a mistrustful disposition which rendered him something of a recluse. He seems never to have disclosed his real name to his colleagues. Much of his time was spent studying the *Oxford Dictionary*, but he was an enthusiastic participant in the various organised escape attempts, and his colleagues liked him for that.

The Irish authorities proceeded with their gradual relaxation of regulations. Mollenhauer and his two senior colleagues, Neymeyr and Muller, had already been invited to attend a conference on internment at the Department of Defence in Dublin.

They were joined by representatives of the German legation, the Irish army, and the Departments of External Affairs and Defence. At this meeting it was decided to extend the parole area to Naas and to permit the men to engage in horse riding. In addition, Colonel McNally was given authority to determine the hours of parole.

The three internees had a number of complaints. They wanted more coal for their sitting-room fires and they objected to the guards waking them up in the middle of the night to check that they had not escaped. They were promised more coal and it was agreed the last check would be at midnight. The Irish authorities were apparently feeling particularly amenable on this occasion, because they gave the three internees special permission to travel outside the parole area to attend the funerals of the men shot down by Remy.

The following week representatives from Maffey's office and three of the Allied internees, Verity, Ward and Mayhew, attended a similar conference in Dublin at which they extracted further concessions – all of which applied to both sets of internees. The Irish army assigned orderlies to the internee officers – one orderly for every four officers. It was also agreed to permit the internees to attend local dances within the parole area and to visit private homes. When the men complained about the censorship of their letters, it was decided that the censoring would henceforth be done by someone not in personal contact with the men.

The conference took place in a friendly atmosphere. The British were less than a week away from an elaborately planned escape attempt, so they went out of their way to lull the authorities into a false sense of security. According to the official report, the internees and the two representatives from Maffey's office – Norman Archer and G.D. Craig – "expressed appreciation" for having been given the opportunity to raise the various matters and they thanked the Irish authorities for "the kindness and consideration shown at all time to the internees".

After the internees left the meeting, Colonel McNally explained to the diplomats that he was trying to improve the morale within the camp by promoting friendly exchanges between the internees and the Irish army with organised get-togethers in the various Irish messes. He also made arrangements with the committee of the Curragh racecourse to get free passes for the German and British officers to attend the Irish Derby, which was to be run the following week. Eight of the German officers and a similar number of their Allied counterparts availed of the free passes. Ward, Midgely and Proctor were also invited to bring along their wives.

In the circumstances it was easy for the men to pretend they were happy with their lot. While Mollenhauer never seemed to tire of complaining, Verity went out of his way to give a different impression when the Red Cross contacted him as a result of the German complaints. There was no truth that their letters were delayed, or that they were short of clothes, Verity wrote to Captain Frank Fitzpatrick at the camp on 20 June. They were not tramps or orphans and while they were "glad of presents, there is no need". He genuinely enjoyed the plentiful supply of food available in Ireland, and he managed to send a food parcel containing butter, bacon and marmalade to his parents in England. However, Verity had no intention of staying at the Curragh a minute longer than necessary. After learning that escape plans had already been made with MI9, he took charge of the operation. He had already met Dr Hugh Wilson, the doctor from Foxrock who had treated them at the crash site in Leopardstown, who was one of the leaders of the Escape Club set up by MI9.

Verity pretended to be settling in for a protracted stay at the Curragh. He opened a bank account in Newbridge and arranged to enroll for correspondence courses at Trinity College, Dublin. For the benefit of the camp censor, he wrote a series of letters to his wife about coming over to set up house in Ireland: he gave an Irish friend a secret message for her, telling her to stay put for the time being. "If my break succeeds, hope to see you soon, darling," he wrote. "Please suspend plans to come here now." Irish military intelligence got hold of the message. Camp authorities were duly notified and told to be on their guard.

The break was planned for the night of the Irish Derby. The many visitors in the area would enhance the escapees' chances of getting away, and MI9 had made arrangements to provide cars.

At different times during the evening the Allied airmen gave out a tremendous roar from their huts. Lieutenant Kelly investigated a couple of times: once he found one of the officers making a speech, and on the other occasion they were holding a birthday party. Things seemed quite normal at eleven o'clock when he made his last check before going off duty. Ward and Shaw were each playing solitaire, while the rest of the men were reading or listening to the radio, which was playing dance music at full blast.

When Captain Frank Fitzpatrick made what was intended to be the final check at midnight, two of the officers were in bed, two more were in their bedrooms and two were making tea. One was in the toilet, and five were still in the officer's anteroom. Six of the sergeants were in their anteroom and another was in bed. Harkell and Barnett were out on special parole for their monthly visit to Dublin and were not due back for another 30 minutes.

They arrived at the front gate with about ten minutes to spare, apparently quite drunk. Barnett – a stoutly built, balding 24-year-old Scot – was admitted first, but he stopped just inside the gate, blocking the entrance. He bent over clutching his stomach and groaning as if he were about to vomit. Harkell waited outside, singing in a drunken fashion. The guard, Corporal Reilly, asked Barnett to move out of the way. Suddenly he was distracted by John Holgate at an inner gate, which had been locked since midnight. He was impatient to be allowed through as he wished to send a telegram. The men had been sending numerous telegrams in recent days. What with the new internees, the Hobbs wedding and the recent birth of Verity's first child, the telegrams seemed incessant.

Corporal Reilly was in a dither, with Barnett blocking the gate, Harkell acting the fool and Holgate demanding attention.

"What about the wire?" Holgate snapped.

"Hold on, please," Reilly replied, calling a second guard to look after him. As the second guard went to allow Holgate out, he was rushed from inside the compound by Welpy, Verity and Shaw. Holgate and Welpy jumped him and pinned him against a light pole. Verity raced forward and tied the handle of the door of the patrol hut in order to delay the guards inside from coming to the aid of their colleagues. Shaw rushed to help overpower Reilly, then preoccupied by the drunken antics of Harkell, pretending to be so drunk that he did not know what he was doing. In exasperation Reilly pushed him aside and forced the gate shut. After slamming the bolt home, the corporal had just put the bar of the padlock through the eye of the staple when Harkell pushed him aside; Shaw grabbed him, pinning his arms to his side and holding onto the strap of his pistol and holster. Barnett and Harkell then bustled the guard away from the gate.

"Help, help!" Reilly shouted, but his cries were drowned out by a sudden burst of cheering from the huts.

The plan agreed with MI9 was for six pilots to be picked up by two cars at a crossroads a few miles away. Anyone else who escaped was to make his own way without MI9 help. At first everything fell into place. The six men found the gates open and, as the struggle with the guards continued, three others also managed to slip through.

In the melée Reilly, Shaw, Barnett and Harkell collapsed onto the wire in a heap. Barnett and Harkell got up and rushed towards their huts, showing no signs of drunkenness now, while Shaw hung on to the guard, who tried to get his whistle from his breast-pocket. In an effort to stop him, Shaw let go of the holster, and Reilly managed to grab his gun and fire off three shots. The alarm bells sounded immediately.

Shaw tried to run through the open gate but Reilly ordered him back to the compound. With the gun pointed menacingly, the Englishman did not tempt fate. He turned sheepishly and walked back towards his hut, while Reilly picked up the lock and key from the ground and finally locked the gate.

Amid the confusion the guards initially thought that only two internees had escaped. Fitzpatrick raced from his quarters and ordered that the searchlight be turned on and the stand-to party called out. He also notified Colonel McNally to set up cordons and road-blocks in the area of the Curragh. Contingency plans for this had already been drawn up and a number of vehicles raced off with men to set up the different road-blocks.

Kelly inspected the camp and reported that nine internees

were missing: Verity, Mayhew, Ward, Covington, Welpy, Holgate, Proctor, Cowper and Hobbs. On hearing this, Fitzpatrick rounded up a posse, and they set off towards Athgarvan on bicycles.

"What arrangements were planned after the pick-up, I do not know," Verity later explained. "I guessed we would just be driven through the short June night to the border and across at some secluded spot. However, by the time we got to the rendezvous it was already guarded by Irish soldiers, as were all the other crossroads around the Curragh, and there was no sign of the cars."

Fitzpatrick and his bicycle party arrived at Athgarvan Cross to learn that two cars with Northern Ireland registrations had passed through, but none of the three occupants were internees. The captain raced off to the nearest telephone to ask the police in Naas stop the two cars: FZ1101 and FZ9671. When they were apprehended, they had four occupants, all with Belfast addresses. They said they had come down for the Irish Derby and had stayed at the Marine Hotel in Dún Laoghaire the previous night. Following the races they had dinner at Osberstown House and said they drove to Kilcullen afterwards to visit Lord Glentoran's secretary, a Major Wickens, who confirmed their story. The Garda chief superintendent who questioned them noted that "all were normal and quite sober". But although their story checked out, he was convinced that it just a cover for their real mission – to help the internees escape.

Covington was the first to be recaptured after little more than ten minutes of freedom. Midgely and Ward managed to stay out all night but they were caught next morning while having breakfast in a bar. The others managed to go into hiding: while on parole they had made friends in the area, so they knew where they could turn to for help. One family actually put up four escapees – Verity, Mayhew, Holgate and Hobbs – while an MI9 officer from Dublin organised some safe houses in the capital. After two days in hiding in the Curragh area, the four were smuggled out. "We were driven to a safe house in the Dublin area where we were looked after by the family," Verity explained. "During the ten days or so that we were there we had various far-fetched proposals for evacuation by sea or air but eventually went to Belfast by train, heavily disguised and with false identities." The disguises and false papers had been provided by MI9. Verity wore a false paunch filled with silk stockings, which were still available in Ireland, though not in Britain.

Given the availability of such luxury items and the plentiful supply of steak dinners, many British soldiers visited Dublin from Northern Ireland on leave, and Verity was able to mix with them on the train. The trip was uneventful, though at one point he had the satisfaction of hearing two returning soldiers talking about the escape.

"I see from the paper that they have not yet caught all those RAF fellows," the soldier said. "I wonder where they are now?"

It was hardly surprising that nobody recognised Verity on the trip. "The disguise was so good that my own father did not recognise me when I went to his home in London," he recalled with satisfaction.

After reaching Belfast, Mayhew sent a telegram to the camp announcing their safe arrival. And when he got home to England he wrote to Proctor:

> Well, we made it and have now dispersed to our various homes for some leave of indefinite duration. I would not write you the details of the escape and anyway it would most properly be censored if I did but let it rest at the fact that it entailed a vast amount of violent walking. There is hardly a field in Éire that we have not visited so far as I remember, and by the time we got out we were all suffering from flat fleet, fallen arches, and every ailment know to chiropodists. Morale, however, was perfectly good; we got terribly depressed at intervals, but being together naturally cheered us up, and our hopes grew with every step. Incidentally, I haven't even mentioned yet that "we" is Hugh, Johnny, Jack and Self, but I gathered you learned that from the telegram I sent from Belfast, if the Irish allowed it through. We had a hell of a binge to celebrate in Belfast before coming over. We heard by rumour that nine got out, but that we were the only survivors. If you were one of the unlucky five, as I imagine you were, I sympathise very much with you and the other

four. It's rotten luck but I trust that soon you will be treading a more successful path. Finally, and most sincerely, will you thank the gents who helped us in the break? It really went like a piece of cake and the memory of those gloriously open gates will live with me for ever. I don't want to over do the sentiment but it required a quantity of unselfishness and co-operation that you can all be very proud of. We really are incredibly grateful to you all. I promise you all a Fortnum's parcel, but alas I had no time when in town. I'll send it off as soon as I can get back to town, and it will be good.

Yours till all's blue,

Paul Mayhew

While Mayhew's letter was ostensibly written to Proctor, it was really for the camp guards. He knew that G2 would examine it carefully, so the reference to the long walk was included as a ruse to throw the Irish off the scent of the Escape Club. Whether he knew at that point that Cowper and Proctor had also escaped to Northern Ireland by a different route is not clear.

Verity was not trying to be facetious or sarcastic, when he wrote to thank McNally on 7 July:

I hope you will not mind me writing a line to thank you for looking after us so fairly.

As senior officer I always found the Irish Army extremely courteous and considerate and also extremely impartial. I will be delighted to tell my friends over here how well we were fed and housed.

The patience of Capt. Fitzpatrick seemed inexhaustible. I was always worrying him about everything from sour milk to mess furniture, and he was always most helpful.

Please give my regards to your brother officers who were so very courteous to us.

Yours sincerely,

Hugh Verity

Verity had only been in the Curragh for five weeks in early summer, and he regarded the camp more favourably than those who were compelled to spend the dreary winter months in Kildare. Roderick Cowper had been there for five months but he, too, wrote to thank McNally "for all the kindness.

"After that good treatment I may appear rather ungrateful but I am sure that you will understand my feelings," Cowper wrote. "I nevertheless regret all the trouble I may have caused by my escape."

Both men meant what they wrote and McNally was wrong to think that they were merely trying to salve their guilty consciences. All the escapees returned to active service after a short leave, during which Mayhew married his fiancée. While at K Lines Hobbs had written to his future wife: "I am no shirker Old Girl, so if the least chance presents itself, or if Éire should enter the war on our side, I should be back on the job like a shot." He meant what he wrote. He was quickly back in action, only to be killed even before his belongings could be forwarded from the Curragh.

More Allied than Axis

Eighteen Allied airmen were interned in the second half of 1941, by far the largest number interned in any six-month period of the war. Seven others were quietly allowed to leave.

The first of those secretly released were the three-man crew of a Hudson bomber that landed at Roskeeragh beach, Co. Sligo, on 21 July. As the unarmed plane was merely being delivered from Newfoundland, de Valera decided that it should be treated as a civilian aircraft and the crew were allowed to leave after a quick meal. They only had fuel for 30 minutes flying, but once the three Canadians were informed of their exact location they were able to fly to the British air-base at Limavady.

The first member of the Royal Canadian Air Force (RCAF) to be interned in Ireland was Sergeant Ros Tees from Thorold, Ontario. He got lost while on a flight from Halvington, near Bristol, to Clyde on 21 August 1941. At the time he had only been in Britain for ten weeks. He had taken off with three Hurricane fighters but he got hopelessly lost after his radio went on the blink. Running low on fuel, he made a forced landing near Athboy, Co. Meath, thinking he was somewhere over Scotland. A member of the LDF was first on the scene, followed by a local Garda, who took Tees into custody.

Five days later, a *Luftwaffe* JU 88 bomber left Brest early in the day on a bombing raid. When their plane developed engine trouble and the crew realised they had no hope of making it back to France, they decided to land in Ireland. They crash-landed at Balgooly, a few miles from Kinsale. None of the four crew members were injured. On the ground they proceeded to destroy the aircraft. The crew, *Leutnant* Rudolf Laurer, *Leutnant* Ludwig Stockbauer, *Gefreiter* Herbert Schulze and *Gefreiter* Gerhard

Dreschel were quickly arrested and taken to the Curragh.

A Fairy Fulmar landed on Trynure strand near Rosbeg, Co. Donegal, next day. Not knowing where they were, the two-man crew raced into the sandhills and began burning documents. When John Cochrane – a 17-year-old student home on vacation from Eton College, England – came on the scene, they asked him where they were, and he showed them on their map. Although they were low on fuel, they had enough to get them the 50 miles to Northern Ireland. The student helped them to turn the aircraft and they took off again.

There were international complications, however, after a Lockheed Hudson landed at the Irish Air Corps aerodrome at Baldonnel, near Dublin, on the morning of 27 September 1941. Captain L.R. Dubue from Montreal and Sergeant F.G. Goodwin were both members of the RCAF, while the third member of the crew, S.R. Kenny, was a civilian radio operator. They were delivering the plane to Northern Ireland and landed in the hope of obtaining fuel. They were given a meal and the Department of External Affairs instructed that the plane should be treated as a civilian aircraft because it was not armed and there was a civilian on board. After being refuelled, it took off for Belfast that afternoon, but crashed in the mountains near Jenkinstown, Co. Louth, killing all on board.

The Toronto *Globe & Mail* reported that they lost their lives because they were trying to avoid being interned in Ireland. "Although short of gasoline, they tried to make for Northern Ireland rather than be imprisoned in a neutral country until the end of the war," according to the report. "As a result there was a crash and all were killed."

The Irish protested and Canada's high commissioner in Dublin reported that the crew in question had been "treated with every kindness" at Baldonnel. There was therefore no justification whatever for the *Globe & Mail* report. Thereafter Canadian authorities became quite sensitive about allowing the internment question to receive publicity in Canada. It also began to take some interest in the welfare of its men in Ireland.

The week after the Jenkinstown crash Sergeant Fred W. Tisdall from Moncton, New Brunswick, Canada, was interned. He was the navigator on a Hampden bomber which got lost after its radio was knocked out by anti-aircraft fire while returning from a bombing raid over Germany. They were running out of fuel and the Welsh pilot, Sergeant H.J. Newby from Cardiff, gave the order to bale out. They thought they were over Scotland at the time. The other two members of the crew were Sergeant James Wakelin from Newcastle, and a Scot, Sergeant David Reid. All landed safely and their plane crashed into the Glenadown mountains.

Although Tisdall was actually the third Canadian to be interned, he was the first that the Canadian authorities knew about. And they only learned of his internment when a letter that he had written to his parents was published in the Toronto *Globe & Mail* on 7 November 1941. By then four more Canadians were interned. Two of them – Sergeant Paul O. Webster of Vancouver and Sergeant Charles Brady of Toronto – had been on board a Blenheim bomber which came down in the sea off Long Island, near Schull, Co. Cork, on 23 October 1941. Also on board was Sergeant Douglas Woodman of St Catherine, Ontario.

"We hit the sea very hard and poor Doug Woodman was flung through the nose of our aircraft," Brady recalled. "I was able to get our dinghy out and inflated but, because we did not have a knife to cut the line from the dinghy to the aircraft we had to saw it off with a rough bit of metal from the aircraft. We got Doug into the dinghy, but he was in very bad shape. In fact his chest was crushed and the bones were sticking out of his left knee. After what seemed to be about five hours, we were picked up by a fishing boat and towed into the harbour." Woodman was immediately transferred to Mallow Hospital.

"An Irish priest visited Webster and I, and seeing how cold and exhausted we were got us a bottle of brandy," Brady continued. "Paul and I drank the whole bottle."

They were taken to a military barracks in Bantry and placed under guard, which was the first indication they had that they were not going to be allowed to return to their squadron. Next day, Woodman died and the other two were taken to the Curragh, where they vowed to escape. "Paul and I made the same remark that all newcomers to the camp were to make: 'They won't keep us here very long'," Brady recalled.

The following night, 25 October, two more Canadians found themselves in trouble after they had inadvertently overflown Britain while returning in their Wellington bomber from a mission over Germany. They were running out of fuel and unable to find a landing place in the darkness. They fired off distress flares, but there was no response from the ground.

"I always wanted to make a parachute jump anyway," joked the pilot, Pilot Officer Ralph Keefer from Montreal.

"But not under these circumstances," replied his Ontario-born navigator, Pilot Officer Jack Calder. "It's a long walk home."

They had been rooming together in England for the past four months and had thrived on the excitement of bombing raids from Brest to Bremen. With only five minutes fuel left, Keefer ordered the crew to bale out. The four English sergeants went first – Alex Virtue from Newcastle, Maurice Browne from Middlesboro, Leslie Diaper of London, and Albert Dalton of Dinnington, near Sheffield. Then came Calder's turn.

"Jumping was easy," he wrote. "As my feet went, the slipstream caught them and I was speeded through by the rush of air. I pulled the rip cord, in a moment my head was jerked back and I felt as if I were being sawn through. The sensation ended quickly and the first thing I noticed was the desperate quite after eight hours of listening to the buzz of the engines and the crackling of the telephone."

He and the pilot had planned to link up on the ground to try to escape together. "I shouted for Keefer and got no reply," Calder continued. The pilot had planned to head the plane out to sea but, as he prepared to jump, he noticed that it had come back round and was going inland, so he returned to the controls, pointed the craft for the Atlantic and jumped.

"For a long time I seemed not to be falling at all, just swaying a little in the breeze," Calder recalled. "I turned around to make sure that I wouldn't be carried out to sea and I inflated my 'Mae West' just in case. Suddenly I realised the ground was near and I relaxed for the impact." He landed in a bog and found that no matter where he tried to walk, he was walking into water, so he waited until dawn. In the daylight he was able to extricate himself by picking his steps carefully. Then to his delight he came upon a gate with a sign: "Keep Gate Shut."

"Well, we speak the same language," he thought. He felt he walked several miles before he was arrested by a Garda. The police and army were out looking for them, because the plane had not gone into the Atlantic, but crashed near Quilty, Co. Clare. Soon Calder found himself reunited in the Garda station with his five colleagues, while curious local people gathered outside to get a glimpse of the latest visitors.

During the autumn of 1941 it became apparent that the Americans were building a naval base on Lough Foyle in Northern Ireland. Officially those involved were said to be American civilians working for the British, but in fact they were military. To many people it seemed only a matter of time before the United States would be openly at war with the Axis powers. Immediately after Tokyo joined the Rome-Berlin Axis in September 1940, David Gray had actually predicted in a letter to President Roosevelt that the United States would probably become involved in the war as a result of a surprise Japanese attack in the Pacific. In the following year he seemed to become even more convinced.

"Before you get this," Gray wrote to Roosevelt on 21 October 1941, "Japan may have touched things off. You have handled that situation as miraculously as every other as far as I can see." He seemed to be congratulating the President for provoking Japan to attack the United States. This was still six weeks before Pearl Harbour.

Even though Gray had a good grasp of the American political scene, he tended to believe the worst of the Irish authorities, and the worst was particularly distorted, because he had some extraordinary sources. He was a strong believer in spiritualism and actually forwarded seance transcripts to the White House. On 8 November the ghost of the late British Prime Minister Arthur J. Balfour supposedly warned him that Joe Walshe of the Department of External Affairs "was hand in glove with the German minister". In the transcript Walshe was described as "a leading quisling" who had helped to organise a fifth column which would set up a puppet government if the Germans went ahead with a plan for an invasion of Ireland the following spring.

"I believe de Valera will go down on his knees and thank God if the USA takes forcible possession of this country," Balfour supposedly continued in the transcript which Gray sent to the White House. "There will be no resistance only welcome, and it will be a sound strategic stroke in the war. Are the Allies always going to be late in moving? That is what you have got to ask Washington."

Ireland had enough problems without having Gray listening to the advice of ghosts in the American legation. What was probably even more disturbing was that President Franklin D. Roosevelt was quite happy with the job Gray was doing.

The first and only American to be interned at the Curragh arrived exactly one week before the Japanese attacked Pearl Harbour. People coming from Sunday Mass at Moneydarragh, Co. Donegal, on 30 November 1941, heard a plane overhead but could see no sign of the RAF Spitfire in the foggy conditions at the time. Suddenly they saw a man descending by parachute and heard his plane crashing in the distance. The pilot, PO Roland "Bud" Wolfe, an American serving in the famed Eagle Squadron of the RAF, was taken into custody and transferred to the Curragh, where he was to remain for the best part of two years. His unique distinction of being the only American to be interned in Ireland during World War II was all the greater when one realises that at least 260 other American airmen came down in Ireland during the next three-and-a-half years, but all of them were quietly let go. He was not only held, but suffered the humiliation of probably being the only American in any war who was ordered to return to a concentration camp because his superiors did not approve of the way he had escaped.

Of course, the Irish could not have known that the United States would be in the war so soon after Wolfe's internment. Even Gray had been given grounds to question his own astute assessment of the situation in the Pacific. On 2 December he had another seance at which the ghost of the late President Theodore

Roosevelt supposedly belittled the danger of a Japanese attack and suggested that there would be "no immediate" attack and possibly no attack at all.

"Four days after this communication," Gray wrote to the White House, "the Japs attacked Pearl Harbour." It may be wrong to read too much into Gray's dabbling in spiritualism, but he did betray a distinct tendency to believe what he wanted to believe. Even though he had been given such bad advice, he never doubted that he had been in touch with Teddy Roosevelt's ghost; instead he concluded that the Japanese had simply fooled the late president. "They had T.R. fooled," he wrote. "I suspect that if these communications come through pretty much as given our friends on the other side don't know very much more than they did on this side."

De Valera considered Gray naive to the point of being extremely dangerous. This may well have influenced the whole internment policy in relation to the Allies after the United States entered the war, or, to be more specific, after the Americans stationed troops in Northern Ireland in January 1942.

Before that, in December 1941, there were three further Allied crashes, as a result of which airmen from as far away as Canada and New Zealand were interned. Two of those occurred on 16 December. In the early afternoon a Spitfire piloted by Sergeant G. Duncan Fowler, whose home was in Victoria, British Columbia, Canada, made a pancake landing on the strand near Clogher, Co. Donegal. He was promptly arrested by a member of the LDF. Later that evening a Sunderland flying boat tried to land in Galway Bay in stormy conditions. The pilot, Flight Lieutenant Grant Fleming of Calgary, Alberta, Canada, recounted what had happened:

> We had been out on patrol from 4 a.m. on the morning of 15/12/41 from Lough Erne, Northern Ireland. That evening owing to running short of petrol, I decided to try to come down in the sea off the coast. I succeeded in doing this but the float on the port wing snapped off and I found it necessary to take off again. I was then undecided what course to adopt but finally came down in the sea again. This I accomplished but unfortunately the outer engine of the port wing

> broke off. This caused the boat to list and it began to sink. I ordered the other members of the crew to abandon the plane, which they did. I left the boat last but was carried under the water and had to dive deeper to extricate myself. I came to the surface and managed to climb on to one of the rubber boats which I found floating. I was almost immediately washed off this and had to keep myself afloat the best way I could. After what must have been a couple of hours I felt sand under my feet and was washed ashore by the breakers and taken to a house nearby.

In fact, he was in such an exhausted state, he apparently did not realise that he was helped ashore by three people. Seven members of his crew perished in the freezing water. Only Sergeant Jimmy Masterson from Great Yarmouth managed to get ashore unaided; he made his way to a nearby house and collapsed on the doorstep.

On 21 December 1941 Sub Lieutenant Bruce Girdlestone from Wellington, New Zealand, took off from the aircraft carrier *Illustrious* in a Grumman Wildcat, on a flight to the fleet aerodrome on the Mull of Kintyre. He had no radio and no maps and soon lost his way.

"Evidently I passed between the Mull and Fair Head without seeing either and made landfall near Stranraer," he recalled afterwards. "Realising that I was too far South I turned out to sea again hoping to pick up the Mull but on again making landfall which evidently was the coast of Northern Ireland, I attempted to cross it due West thinking it was the East coast of Kintyre. Finally I became weather-bound amongst the mountains, found a valley running North, and carried out a precautionary landing in a field just as it was getting dark. The field's surface which looked sound enough from the air, failed to take the plane's weight on landing and with a violent tearing of metal I came to rest upside down in a most undignified fashion."

Girdlestone was pinned under the aircraft and had to be dug out by two local policemen. "I crawled out into a semicircle of perhaps fifty gaping onlookers. The two perspiring policemen who had wielded the spades told me that their station was about two hundred yards up the road. A car was taken from one of the interested onlookers and off we went after leaving two fairly intelligent looking bystanders to guard the wreck."

Still shaken, Girdlestone did not realise he was not in Scotland. "The first indication that things were not as they should be occurred as I entered the police sergeant's office," he wrote later. "The door was locked behind me, two policemen stood in front of it, and the sergeant with a sweet smile that broke up the map of Ireland on his face told me that I would have to be detained!"

Even when he was told he had landed in Ireland, Girdlestone was sure it must be Northern Ireland. He had actually landed on the most northerly peninsula on the island, so he was surprised to learn at the police station that he was actually in "Southern Ireland".

"Sure, if this were Scotland you would be right," the Garda sergeant told him, "and if it were Northern Ireland you would be right also, but this happens to be Northern Éire."

"But Éire is south of Northern Ireland," the New Zealander argued.

"So it is, but this is Northern Éire and it's north of Northern Ireland, and it's neutral like southern Éire which is south of Northern Ireland."

At that point the dialogue, which Girdlestone thought sounded like a comedy sketch from an Abbot and Costello movie, was interrupted by the arrival of a Roman Catholic priest.

"Ah me poor boy, God has indeed been kind to you," he said.

"How's that?" Girdlestone asked.

"You have landed in Northern Éire!"

"I left it at that and welcomed the next visitor who was a doctor," Girdlestone explained. The doctor stitched a cut on his forehead and he was then handed over to the Irish army.

"I was escorted out of the station and handed over to a waiting military guard, neat in their green uniforms and rifles at the ready," Girdlestone wrote. "It looked frightfully dramatic. Even the huge crowd of onlookers were awed. A woman rushed up and gave me a packet of cigarettes." He was kept overnight in a barracks some miles away before being driven south to the Curragh next day.

At this point in the war the internment policy was working

against the Allies. With the Germans heavily committed on the Russian front, it meant that there was a distinct fall off in the number of Axis flights around Ireland, but, with the increase of American aid to Britain, there was a lot more Allied activity. In the second half of 1941 18 Allied airmen had been interned in comparison with just four Germans. And with the United States now in the war, there was bound to be an increase in Allied air traffic.

No further Allied pilots were interned for the next ten months. On the same day as Girdlestone was taken into custody, de Valera ordered that Pilot Officer Leslie Lee Garlow should be released after his plane was refuelled at Gormanston military camp, where he had landed while delivering the aircraft from the factory to Aldergrove, near Belfast. This action signalled a change in de Valera's policy in regard to Allied aircraft.

"He will make his neutrality as friendly as possible," Maffey explained, "but he has to tread warily where overt actions are concerned." Henceforth all aircraft being delivered were promptly released, usually after being refueled. In return the British furnished an incentive bonus by replacing Irish stocks of scarce aviation fuel with twice the amount used in refuelling any Allied aircraft.

On the day after Christmas there was a German landing some six miles from Waterville, Co. Kerry. The crew, who realised they were over Ireland, had decided to land because of engine trouble, and none of the four men aboard the JU 88 were injured. One crew member, *Inspektor* Arthur Klanke of Verblem, had previously been interned in neutral Sweden. He had a good command of English but, like all other German airmen, was unwilling to give details of their mission. Also on board were *Unteroffiziers* Werner Kipp, Bruno Hullmann and Rudolf Beckmann. There was a certain amount of international press speculation about this landing, following reports that Field Marshal Heinrich von Brauchitsch, who had resigned as Commander-in-Chief of the *Wehrmacht* a few days earlier, was on the plane. The Dublin government killed the speculation by announcing that there was no one on board with a military rank higher than sergeant.

Settling In

As far as McNally was concerned, the Allied internees had played fast and loose with their parole privileges by planning the Derby night escape to coincide with the return of the two internees. "They have admitted that their position is very thin but took up the attitude that it is better to have the point argued from the outside rather than from the inside," McNally told a court of inquiry. "They cannot defend the action of the incoming internees in assaulting the policeman before the gate was actually locked."

Ward, who again took over as the senior Allied internee following Verity's escape, told McNally that it was never intended that Harkell or Barnett would actually assist in overpowering Corporal Reilly at the gate. They "were merely to be used as decoys to ensure the gate was kept open long enough for those attempting to escape to overpower the guard," he explained.

The military court set up to investigate the circumstances of the escape questioned why an air-lock system had not been set up so that the internees would always have to pass through two guarded gates. Captain Fitzpatrick was asked if he had ever considered constructing "a cage" with a separate entrance and exit around the parole hut.

"I thought about it," he told the court, "but as I had already received numerous protests from the internees about the erection of so much barbed wire, I considered that the erection of a cage would lead to further protests by the internees." He had applied for three extra guards instead, but these had not been granted, so the court exonerated him and the other guards.

The report was particularly critical of the actions of Barnett and Harkell. They had helped those trying to escape even though the conditions of their parole specifically precluded them from giving "any assistance whatever" to fellow internees seeking to escape until they returned to their quarters in K Lines. "The court is satisfied that Sergeants Barnett and Harkell broke parole by their actions on the night," the court concluded. "Even from a purely legal point of view they had not returned to their quarters but when dealing with parole there can be no hairsplitting over phrases. Parole is a gentlemen's agreement. It must not and should not be used to affect the escape of even other internees. The court are of the opinion that the escaped internees, particularly the officers, were not entitled to use the dishonourable action of Sergeants Barnett and Harkell to facilitate their escape."

The army asked the Dublin government to demand the return of the six airmen, but the Allied internees contended that once they got inside the gate, Barnett and Harkell were entitled to assist those attempting to escape. Maffey made it clear that the men would not be returned and he warned that such a request was likely to lead to diplomatic complications. Consequently, de Valera did not pursue the matter.

For three days after the June escape, parole was suspended for the Allied internees while security at the gate was strengthened with the erection of an air-lock system in the form of a barbed-wire cage around the side of the parole hut in B Camp. Henceforth the Allied internees had to pass through a guarded gate to get to the parole hut and another guarded gate to get out of B Camp proper. No attempt was made to erect a similar cage on the German side of the fence, because Mollenhauer had been doing so much complaining that the army were afraid of offending him. He took umbrage at anything which even hinted at questioning the honour of German airmen in the matter of parole.

The censoring of their local mail, of course, was a different matter. The Germans – like their Allied counterparts – frequently ignored camp regulations and deposited letters in public mail boxes while out on parole. A number of these letters were intercepted. Most were to Irish girlfriends, and some proved rather embarrassing to internees in each of the compounds.

During the summer of 1941, for instance, military intelligence intercepted a love letter from one of the Allied officers to the wife of an Irish officer. Another intercepted a letter from a German officer to a married woman who was using the house of a friend in Dublin for her extra-marital activities. He wrote to her at the Dublin address to arrange a date there for the following Saturday, even though he was not entitled to travel to the city on that day. When he learned that his letter had been intercepted, he had to cancel the trip.

Although the internees were supposed to submit all letters to the camp censor, this was just a camp regulation. Their conditions of parole merely obliged them to stay within the parole area and not to do anything to further escape attempts, with the result that mailing letters outside the camp was not a parole violation. Mollenhauer thought this regulation was particularly unfair to the Germans, because they frequently suffered delays that never had to be endured by the British. In August 1941, for instance, the man censoring the German mail went on holidays and there was no one unconnected with the internment staff with enough German to act as censor. As a result all their letters, including ones written in English, were delayed. Mollenhauer wrote to a woman in Kildare thanking her for an invitation, but his letter took more than a week to get to her.

"It arrived only today, which is particularly intolerable for me because it lets me appear impolite," he complained to Fitzpatrick. To make matters worse, local letters mailed to him had also been delayed. This, he contended, was further "proof of the inefficiency of the Military Censor. If I do not get a reasonable explanation and compensation, I shall hand the matter over to my Legation."

The camp authorities were again annoyed at Mollenhauer's tone. They felt he was looking down on them, and they were right to a degree. With his rather typically Teutonic efficiency, he could not abide their somewhat sloppy administration. Although the Department of External Affairs frequently sympathised with him, Joe Walshe, suggested that "this latest protest should be ignored". Mollenhauer was told that he would have "to work the 'trial and error' system with his correspondence as no assurance can be given in respect of matters subject to censorship".

Of course, the German commander continued to complain about delays and also about the retention of personal items, such as the camera which had been taken from Arthur Klanke when he was first arrested. In addition, he demanded the return of Alfred Heinzl's camera after it was confiscated when he was caught violating camp regulations by taking photographs in the German compound.

Ironically, however, it was the British who caused the camp authorities most embarrassment in regard to the retention of their belongings. Covington, Ricketts and Barnett were out on parole near the landing slip at the Curragh on 21 July when an Irish air corps plane landed. They went over to speak to the pilot, who chatted with them and allowed them to see his fancy helmet with its built-in radio head-set. The men noticed Cowper's name inside the helmet. The Irish had no right to use any internee's equipment, and this was particularly true in Cowper's case because he had escaped, and his helmet should have been returned with his personal belongings. The internees protested formally, and this led to some recrimination between camp authorities and Army Headquarters.

The adjutant general in Dublin demanded an explanation as to how the internees had been allowed to approach the aircraft and see the equipment; in reply, McNally complained that the pilot should not have been wearing Cowper's helmet in the first place. The air corps, for its part, explained that headgear with earphones and a microphone was in short supply. On 4 June it began using three confiscated British helmets, while the air corps tried to purchase them from the British, along with the Lockheed Hudson aircraft in which Cowper and his colleagues had landed. The plane was indeed purchased and reconditioned, and Shaw, Welpy and Todd had the added frustration of watching their own planes flying over the camp. But Army Headquarters ordered that henceforth the internees should not be allowed to approach any aircraft at the Curragh.

In spite of this new restriction, the gradual relaxation of parole conditions continued. There were three types of parole. Camp parole, in accordance with which the men were allowed out in military uniform but had to remain generally within the precincts of the Curragh Camp. On local parole they could go outside the camp area, but only when dressed in civilian clothes, and then they had to remain within a radius of ten miles of the camp. Special parole was accorded in specific circumstances, which were gradually extended in the coming months. Initially it was used to allow the internees make quarterly visits to their diplomatic representatives in Dublin. In early 1941 monthly visits were permitted. In 1943 the pretence that the visits were primarily to visit the legations was dropped and they were allowed to go to Dublin once a week without having to make prior arrangements with their legations. Over the next two years the remaining parole restrictions were gradually eased.

During July 1941 Ward asked that the twelve-hour parole allowed to married internees to remain with their wives until ten-thirty at night should be extended so that they could spend the whole night together. This was duly conceded. They could stay with their wives three nights a week, provided they remained within the triangular parole area bordered by the three nearby towns. Married NCOs were allowed to sleep with their wives two nights a week. At first Ward and Midgely had to report back to the camp by eight o'clock in the morning, but this was later extended to noon. By then all the others were allowed to remain out until eight in the morning, so the internees basically had the right to sleep where they wished within the parole area.

The German internees were entitled to the same hours, but Mollenhauer insisted on the implementation of a differential system in accordance with which his permission was needed for officers to stay out later than four in the morning, two o'clock for senior NCOs, one o'clock for other NCOs, or after eleven-thirty on week nights and one o'clock on weekends for other ranks.

Despite their orderlies and their segregated dining and recreation rooms, the Allied officers did not have that many privileges over their non-commissioned colleagues. Chuck Brady, who was a sergeant when he was interned, learned after some weeks at the Curragh that he had received a commission which was back-dated to the previous March when he had left Canada.

"I accumulated a fair bit of back-pay," he wrote, "and I threw a most expensive party." He found the commission made very little difference to his life in the camp. His fellow Canadian and crew-mate, Sergeant Paul Webster, remained his closest friend, but he noted that the commission "did open a few more doors to the Gentry of Ireland".

Once they were accorded the right to visit private homes in June 1941, the Allied officers were in particular demand with what remained of Ireland's ascendancy element, as well as some wealthy people involved in the horse-racing scene. They were invited to meals at Ballymore Eustace House, Bennettstown House, Brownstownhouse, Castletownhouse and the homes of retired British officers like Captain Darby Rodgers at Ifield Lodge, or Captain Jack Daley at Rushmore, Co. Wicklow. These invitations were usually for the officers only, which may well have led to a certain amount of resentment on the part of some of the NCOs, though they at least had the benefit of the extra food. "Because of so many eating out at friends," Fred Tisdall explained, "the supply was good for those eating at the camp."

The Allied officers did so much socialising at first that Maffey's staff became concerned about reports of the men drinking too much and generally misbehaving. His office asked the Irish if there was any truth to the reports. Viewing the request as "very urgent", the Provost Marshal asked McNally "for the matter to be discreetly investigated and observations forwarded as soon as possible".

Commandant Dominick Mackey, the head of military intelligence at the Curragh, reported that there was little substance to the rumours:

> Although the British officers do take a drink or two no complaints whatever have reached me or the APM Curragh on their conduct as officers and gentlemen. They are on the whole very well conducted. The only incident which came to my notice indirectly was contained in a letter written by Sergeant Todd, British internee, when he referred to an incident at the house of Mrs Reeves, Athgarvan, where FO Ward was staying with his wife. The extract:
>
> "Mrs R. was telling me that she wants to see more of me and Bill Ricketts up there now for she has given our officers the boot. Seemingly Mr Ward and a few others had turned

> the place into a hotel and Mrs R. told me that they were treating her like a bar maid waiting to serve them in a pub. Of course, that's not good enough. But remember, darling, that they are officers and gentlemen of the RAF, while we are only non-commissioned officers. Well Mrs R. made the table jump six inches at tea one evening when she dropped the bombshell – that shook them.
>
> "I never would have told you all this for I usually mind my own affairs, had it not been for the fact that Mr Ward rather injured my pride yesterday and I shall never forgive him for it. He gave us all a lecture about how an NCO should behave in the presence of an officer and what we should do and what we should not do to him. I know what I would like to do, but what got my rag was that in all my service, I have never once been disrespectful to an officer and I have been in twice as long as he has....
>
> "The whole trouble is that Mrs R. put her foot in it when she told him that the majority of our NCOs were gentlemen and that she preferred them to him."

Observing that Todd may have exaggerated the incident, Mackey nevertheless noted that Ward and his wife had since moved house.

The internees were frequently invited to dances, but Ward and Mollenhauer were anxious that their men should not attend the same function. They were afraid of loose talk about fraternising between the enemy internees, and had already been embarrassed by such rumours. According to one report some of the English internees had helped the Germans overcome language difficulties while shopping in Dublin. Of necessity they frequently had to travel on the same bus to Dublin, but there was no truth about them going shopping together. What had happened was that the English internees were helping out the Poles and some bystanders mistook them for Germans.

Visitors to the cinemas at the Curragh were often surprised when the lights came on after a show to find a row of grey uniformed *Luftwaffe* airmen on one side of the hall and a row of blue uniformed RAF men across the aisle. On a couple of occasions internees from each side turned up at Protestant services and word got out that they had sat "side by side", but the idea of sitting next to Nazis even in church was too much for the Allied internees. Hence a system was devised by which the first side to apply for permission to attend any function would be granted the sole right to attend it. The system worked well at first, though there was a hiccup in early September when German and Allied internees found themselves at the same Red Cross dance. Later the system fell into disuse as the various internees became accustomed to ignoring one another.

All the men were free to join local clubs. Several of the Germans joined the Newbridge tennis club, as did four of the Allied internees. Other Allied airmen joined the golf club, or the Newbridge rugby club, where three played on the first fifteen; three men played on a local soccer team. Others enjoyed riding at some of the nearby stables, where they were allowed to exercise the horses. One of the English sergeants had his own hunter which he rode in some point-to-point meetings, and three of the Allied internees hunted with the Naas Harriers. Bud Wolfe, the camp's lone American, used to turn up in Western attire and raised many eyebrows in those staid circles as he charged ahead of the field in his cowboy hat, riding with a one-handed style that shocked members of the hunt.

At the camp the internees formed teams of their own. The Allies had their own tennis, cricket, soccer and table-tennis teams, and these played Irish army or local community teams, as did their German counterparts. But the German and Allied teams never played each other. On the few occasions when German and Allied internees did meet in individual competition, the rivalry was intense. The Allied table-tennis team was invited to play a Newbridge club when, on the night of the match, they found to their horror that two Germans were playing with the local club.

"I drew one of them as my opponent," Ros Tees recalled. "Although I am usually a good loser, I was thoroughly chagrined when I lost to him. It was like losing the war!"

"Sport was perhaps the only outlet for those deep periods of mental depression that used to come on from time to time and we took every opportunity for exercise," one of the men wrote in 1944. "Fortunately facilities were excellent and the Irish Army gave us access to most of their fields and sports clubs. From their point of view it aided our security by contenting us physically and mentally thereby lessening our desire to escape. That we termed psychological security, and on some of the internees it had the desired effect."

John D. Kearney, the Canadian High Commissioner, presented the men with a tennis table and equipment. He also sent Canadian newspapers and magazines to the camp. When the Canadians visited Dublin, he organised free passes for them to certain cinemas, but he still kept a certain diplomatic distance from the men. Unlike the British representative, Kearney was slow to visit the camp personally and did not report on conditions there until specifically instructed to do so by his government. Yet, because of his hospitality in Dublin, the Canadian internees were convinced he was more concerned about their welfare than Maffey was about their British colleagues.

"There is no question that John D. Kearney did all he could to make life better for the Canadians," Brady recalled. "I think it fair to say we Canadians felt that at least our representative in Éire was concerned for us and, without placing his position in jeopardy, did all he could for us."

"He was like a real father to us," Calder wrote.

Brady's own father, who was born and reared in Dublin, had emigrated to North America in 1908 and served in the Canadian army during the First World War. Thus Charles Brady had several Irish relations, and he naturally sought them out. Shortly after being interned he visited his father's sister and her family in Dublin, but he quickly became disillusioned with his relatives, who turned out to be avowedly anti-British, if not pro-German. "I was more than shocked to hear my cousins tell me that I was fighting on the wrong side; they were convinced that London was in ruins and that the glorious Germans would soon rule England," he recalled. "I left very quickly and never contacted them again!"

With the approach of Christmas 1941 it was decided to give the internees an extra day in Dublin for shopping. The Allied internees then asked for two consecutive days so they could stay in the city overnight and attend a hunt ball at the Gresham Hotel. Commandant Guiney endorsed the request, but it was refused by Army Headquarters, leaving the men probably even more frustrated than if they had not been accorded the extra day in the first place.

Most of the men had already had their two days in Dublin by the time the New Zealander, Bruce Girdlestone, was interned on 22 December. "The first week was a miserable seven days," according to him. He had suffered cuts and bruises when crashing. While waiting for those to heal he went for long walks about the Curragh. He described events to his mother:

> On the twenty-ninth we had our Christmas dinner. A huge feast was prepared and Stanley [Kerniewski], our Polish sergeant, prepared a Polish menu. It was a terrific night. We toasted the King, our allies, and later on the Irish, but in a different sort of way. Towards the end of the evening I went outside into the compound and heard the Germans next door singing in perfect harmony a number of their Christmas hymns to a piano accompaniment. Back in our bar the lads were strongly swinging out on "Salome" and "My Name is Jimmy Hall!" Although there was not the slightest semblance of harmony, we certainly were enjoying ourselves. I thanked God for the democracies and slipped away to bed with the cry of "all's well" being relayed around the gun-posts.

The Lone Wolfe

THE WHOLE PAROLE system was placed in jeopardy in December 1941 when one of the Allied internees failed to return to K Lines after signing out on parole, or so camp authorities contended. The man who went missing was the camp's lone American, Roland "Bud" Wolfe.

A member of the RAF's famous Eagle Squadron, which was made up of American volunteers, Wolfe, who was born in McGehee, Arkansas, had been interned on 30 November 1941. At the time the United States was not yet in the war, not officially at any rate.

Wolfe had only been in the Curragh a couple of days when he formally offered to give a blanket parole. "I was a member of the Eagle Squadron whose members do not swear allegiance to the King or his country," he explained. "They are more or less just working for hire." If released, he declared that he would go home and take no further part in the war against the Axis powers. "If I can do this I shall be able to continue my civilian flying and have a profession after the war," he continued. "If I remain here there will be nothing I can make a living at when this war is over."

Before the Irish could respond, the United States entered the war. This killed the idea, although his mercenary arguments would probably not have appealed to de Valera anyway. Even the Allied internees, who would use just about any ploy to escape, thought that the 22-year-old Wolfe had gone too far. This probably influenced the British attitude to the escape which he attempted within a fortnight.

On the morning of 14 December 1941, camp authorities informed Ward, as the senior Allied officer, that Wolfe had not returned after signing parole the previous night. Ward assumed that Wolfe had absconded in hope of getting back to his home in Ceresco, Nebraska, and telephoned Maffey's office to report what he believed was a serious parole violation. But when Wolfe reported to his unit at Eglington Air Base in Co. Derry that afternoon, he contended that he had escaped legitimately.

Maffey requested that Wolfe be returned immediately to the Curragh in order to straighten matters out, and the American minister agreed. "On the basis of information which the British Representative then possessed, I entirely concurred," Gray wrote.

The young airman was ordered back to the Curragh. He was probably the only American of the whole war, or indeed of any war, who had to return to a prison camp because his superiors had reservations about the manner of his escape.

Wolfe maintained that he had signed parole at ten minutes past nine on the night of 13 December, but that after going out, he had immediately returned, and by re-entering the camp had fulfilled his parole obligations. "I was then automatically off parole," he explained. Consequently, he said, he was free to escape minutes later when he was allowed to leave without being asked to sign another parole form. The guards had possibly been confused; he had already signed two parole forms that day, and was now going out for a third time.

Gray and Colonel John Reynolds, the American military attaché, visited the camp on 4 January 1942 to investigate the affair. "Col. McNally received us most courteously as did Capt. Fitzpatrick, the officer directly in charge of the internee camp," Gray reported afterwards. "He gave us every facility to see whomever we wished of the internees alone. It was evident that Col. McNally had been placed in an extremely difficult position. He is a fine officer with a great humanity and understanding as well as force and executive capacity. Under instructions from his government he has tried to make the internees feel rather as guests than as prisoners, and the internees testify to his kindness and sense of justice. They have enjoyed most complete freedom of movement under a very liberal parole system and it is natural that Col. McNally should feel that his good will has been ill requited by tricks that infringe on the spirit of parole."

After talking with Wolfe and Ward, the American minister decided to take the matter further. He secured sworn depositions from Wolfe and Ward concerning events of the evening of 13 December. Wolfe had personally indicated that he returned to the camp on the night in question "on the chance of getting away with a trick, which has apparently been discussed for a long time as the most probable means of escape", Gray wrote to McNally. In view of the commandant's "unfailing kindness and sportsmanship towards them", the American minister opined that the idea of using such a method to escape "did not appeal" to him, but that the internees were nonetheless under an obligation to try to escape, so if Wolfe's story was true, he should be freed.

Gray was certainly not the best advocate. His arguments tended to undermine the young airman's case, because if Wolfe had returned just to "trick" the guards, as Gray contended, this would have been a parole violation in itself, because he was under an obligation not to do anything to further an escape attempt while on parole.

On the day in question, Wolfe explained in his affidavit, a colleague from Eglington Air Base – Pilot Officer M.E. Jackson – called at the camp to deliver Wolfe's personal belongings. At about four o'clock in the afternoon Wolfe signed parole and left the camp with Jackson to go to a Naas hotel, where they had dinner and some drinks. They returned to the camp at about eight-thirty, and his parole was automatically cancelled on re-entering the compound.

Forty minutes later Wolfe signed another parole form and went out again. "Immediately after passing through the outer gate of the compound with Mr Jackson I mentioned to the outer guard that I had forgotten something in the compound which I wanted," Wolfe testified. "I left Mr Jackson at the outer gate and re-entered the compound. I was then automatically off parole. I went as far as the main hut and then turned about and went out again to join Mr Jackson. This time I did not sign a parole to pass through the gates. Thus as my previously signed parole was void and I did not sign a third, I made a legitimate escape when I passed through the gates a third time."

None of the internees had seen Wolfe return, but Jackson had and he provided sworn testimony supporting Wolfe's story. "We got just outside the outer gate past the guard, and Mr Wolfe asked me to wait there for him, saying that he would be right back," Jackson testified. "He then re-entered the camp, passing through both guarded gates. I saw him enter the living quarters. About two or three minutes later he came out again and was allowed to pass through the guarded gates. He did not stop at the building between the two gates where he had the two previous occasions signed parole."

"After leaving the camp," Wolfe continued, "I caught a bus with Mr Jackson and proceeded to Dublin, where I stayed at a hotel. The next morning I took the 10 a.m. train to Belfast. That afternoon I proceeded to my unit at Eglington, Co. Londonderry. I reported to my commanding officer there and stayed at the station for a day and a half." He was then ordered to go to Belfast to report to the air officer commanding the RAF's 82 Group in Northern Ireland. "After the conference with him," Wolfe added, "I was ordered back to B internment camp."

Wolfe insisted that he had merely seized the opportunity of leaving the camp without signing parole. Ward swore that the internees had often discussed this possibility, and said he would never have telephoned Maffey had he known Wolfe's side of the story.

The camp authorities were prepared to accept that such an escape would have been legitimate, but the guards denied that Wolfe had returned as he stated. McNally promised the guards "entire immunity from blame" if they admitted to making a mistake, but they stuck to their story and produced the uncancelled parole form. Of course, this proved nothing, as far as the internees were concerned, because the forms were not normally given back to the internees.

The competence of the guards in relation to the Wolfe affair was called into question a fortnight later when one of the German internees, Konrad Neymeyr, simply vanished from G Camp. It was thought at the time that he had escaped by tricking the guards at the gate. Gray and Maffey tried to exploit Neymeyr's escape, when they wrote to de Valera in a joint appeal to secure Wolfe's release.

"The view that the sentries can be tricked is strengthened by the circumstances that even after the warning was given by the escape of Pilot Officer Wolfe, German internees succeeded in tricking the sentries into permitting one more to pass out than who had signed the parole book," the two diplomats argued. The Wolfe affair was essentially a conflict of evidence between two officers, on the one hand, and two enlisted men on the other, and the diplomats felt the officers should be given the benefit of the doubt. Describing Wolfe as a man of above average intelligence, they contended he would hardly have violated parole in such a blatant fashion, because he would have known he would be sent back in disgrace.

"If Wolfe and PO Jackson had planned to contrive this story beforehand, they would have arranged to plant some evidence to show that Wolfe had in fact returned and entered the building after having passed through the gates on parole," Maffey and Gray contended. "The weak point in his story, to wit, the lack of conclusive evidence that he did in fact again return, thus contributes to the probability that his story is true. This is, it was a sudden recognition of the exploitation of an opportunity long considered but not arranged for on this occasion."

If this was the weak point in Wolfe's story, it was an even weaker aspect of the case put forward by the diplomats, because the American minister had already stated in his letter to Colonel McNally on 10 January that Wolfe "did return on the chance of getting away with a trick".

Under the circumstances, de Valera thought it unwise to overrule the army authorities. But he did request that parole forms should henceforth be signed in the presence of an officer of the camp staff and that the cancelled forms should be returned to the internees.

The American Connection

Following the United States' entry to the war in December 1941, Roosevelt and Churchill decided to station American troops in Northern Ireland, where they could complete their training while British troops already stationed in the area could be used elsewhere. It was also hoped that the replacement of British troops by Americans would further help to improve Anglo-Irish relations.

The troops began landing late on the evening of 26 January 1942. Maffey informed de Valera of their arrival and pleaded with him not to object to the landing. By not consulting the Dublin government beforehand, however, the United States had essentially repudiated the Irish government's claim to sovereignty over Northern Ireland, and de Valera seized on the occasion to make another of his perfunctory denunciations of partition. Although the Irish people harboured no hostility towards the United States, he emphasised that he had a "duty to make it clearly understood that no matter what troops occupy the Six Counties, the Irish claim for the union of the whole national territory and for supreme jurisdiction over it will remain unabated".

Gray resented the allusion to the American troops as an army of occupation. In a letter to Roosevelt that day he advocated that the president should retaliate with an embargo on all petroleum supplies to Ireland, and he added that Britain should cut all coal deliveries.

"Why should coal be rationed in Britain yet exported to Éire, or why should gasoline that we need be sent to Éire?" Gray asked. "It is not coercion; it is simple justice."

Within hours there was an example of why the British had been unwilling to pursue such a stringent policy. Sergeant

Salvatore Walcott, an American serving in the Eagle Squadron of the RAF, landed his Hurricane fighter at Collinstown (now Dublin airport) on the afternoon of 28 January. He was detained overnight and Captain Frank Fitzpatrick was sent from K Lines to escort Walcott to the Curragh, but de Valera interceded and instructed that the young airman should be released and his plane refuelled so that he could fly away next day. De Valera was able to justify this decision to the Germans on the grounds that the Swiss had recently repatriated the crews of three *Luftwaffe* planes which came down in Switzerland while on training flights.

But Gray was not placated by the benevolent attitude adopted towards Walcott, nor did he change his attitude even when he learned in March that Ireland had been secretly co-operating with the British since the start of the war, and that the extent of that assistance went beyond what even Gray felt might "reasonably have been believed possible". In the coming months the Irish would secretly adopt an even more benevolent attitude towards the Americans.

With the American troops in Northern Ireland, de Valera could relax, as the danger of the Germans being able to divide the country on the partition issue was virtually eradicated. During the remainder of the war his government was confronted with only one diplomatic crisis, which concerned the presence of Axis diplomats in Dublin in the period running up to the D-day landings in Normandy. And that whole affair, which will be discussed later, was merely a ruse provoked by the Americans with an eye on likely postwar developments.

During the nine months following the arrival of American troops in Northern Ireland, all Allied survivors from forced landings in Ireland were promptly released, with one temporary exception on the evening of 24 April 1942. In K Lines, the internees had begun to wonder at the absence of any new Allied internees, when they heard that a man named Montgomery was being interned. "We looked forward to his arrival and speculated how he had come down in Éire," Girdlestone recalled.

> Covey, always the optimist, said that he hoped it was Sir Bernard and, oh boy, what would happen then. Montgomery

was duly escorted in, a young Pilot Officer with a handlebarred moustache that put even Covey's to shame.

The man was from Cheshire, and his real name was not Montgomery at all, but Donald Kennedy. He had landed his Tomahawk trainer about two miles from Arklow earlier that day. He found the barbed-wire compound intimidating.

"My God, I hope that I won't be here in this hole long," he said.

"Brother," said Covington in a mock American accent, "I've been here so long that I'm almost a Catholic, and if the Irish continue to plaster this bloody camp with blasted barbed wire I'll be staggering out of here a teased out old bastard with a bloody Irish brogue!"

Next morning Covey came rushing into my room. Something definitely had happened because Covey usually only runs on two occasions, during escaping attempts and a surprise opening of the bar.

"Girdle, old boy," he shouted, "Montgomery is gone!"

During the night Wing Commander Malcolm Begg, the British air attaché, had collected him at K Lines and taken him to Northern Ireland. Kennedy had clearly been on a training mission, so he was freed in line with the precedent set by the Swiss. The internees, however, concluded that Dublin had been compelled to change its internment policy following the entry of the Americans into the war. They believed the United States had threatened de Valera with "reprisals if any American Air Force lads were interned", according to Girdlestone. "Britain, on learning of America's stand, acted similarly and de Valera gave way."

While there was an element of truth in that, it did not happen the way the internees thought. The American threat was merely implied. The British and Americans knew that confronting de Valera would only get his back up, and in any case Gray had been so open about his views that the Irish leader did not have to be told about the likely reaction of the American minister if any Americans were interned. The British were able to use this to their own advantage.

Irish authorities adopted the attitude that they would release any Allied airmen in circumstances where publicity could be avoided, or where it could be shown that the planes had not been on combat missions. Many of the aeroplanes which strayed into Irish air-space were merely being delivered from the United States, while others were being flown without any armaments by trainee pilots. Begg advised the RAF to instruct all air crews, not on training flights, to pretend they were on rescue missions if they had to land in Ireland. They should say that they were "engaged in air-sea rescue operations in response to an s.o.s. from an unidentified aircraft believed to be German", he suggested.

The true nature of the helpful attitude adopted by the Dublin government only became apparent over a period of months, during which Gray continued to send alarmist reports to Washington. His unease was intensified by stories about the activities of Hempel and Thomsen. They had been acting suspiciously, holding meetings with prominent republicans like Dan Breen, who was widely credited with having started the Irish War of Independence back in 1919, and General Tom Barry, who was probably the most effective field commander during that struggle. On 8 May 1942 Gray wrote to Roosevelt:

> Certain information has come to me which suggests or might suggest that the Germans mean to move in here next month. The German minister has been in Cork where he entertained twice a former gunman and IRA leader, Tom Barry, and another well-known pro-German, Seamus Fitzgerald, a port commissioner who has just been fired by the Government.
>
> In Dublin, Thomsen, the Secretary of the Legation, has been entertaining at the Gresham Hotel Dan Breen, a former IRA gunman and present deputy from Galway, known to be pro-German and suspected of being on the German payroll. He also gave a party in a private room for some members of the Italian Legation and several pro-Axis Irishmen. They had a lot to drink, and late in the evening began to say: "Let us drink tonight. Next month it will not be so happy."

The actions of Hempel and Thomsen may, of course, have been designed merely as a veiled threat to keep the Irish government from making too many concessions to the Allies. Their activities were hardly secret. When Hempel went to Cork, for example, he was followed by an escort car with Special Branch detectives; when he met Tom Barry, the Corkman lost no time in telling his German visitor, whom he had never met before, that he intended to inform de Valera of their conversation. Hempel had no objection. He explained that he simply wished to know what Barry's reaction would be to a British or German invasion of Ireland.

Many years later Barry explained that he told Hempel the Irish people would resist any invasion by either country as "they could not see any difference between German imperialism, which had ruthlessly destroyed small nations, and British imperialism". Nevertheless Barry was impressed by Hempel, whom he believed to be a "real friend of Ireland".

Hempel actually spoke in reassuring terms about his British counterpart. "You Irish," he said, "should thank God for Sir John Maffey, who undoubtedly is a restraining force on bellicose Churchill."

"It was clear to me then," Barry recalled, "that the greatest danger of invasion came from the USA, urged on by the scoundrel, Gray."

The American minister did indeed still harbour illusions about compelling de Valera to join the Allied war effort. Even though he considered the Taoiseach a "malign genius" who was "blind to handwriting on walls and deaf to the rumbling of approaching catastrophe", Gray contended in a letter to Churchill on ll May 1942 that there was still a chance de Valera could be forced into aligning with the Allies, because he had "bowed to events in the past and probably will again".

On 6 July 1942 an American DC 3 transport with 15 uniformed soldiers on board landed at Rhinanna, Co. Clare, after getting lost on a flight from Iceland to Prestwick. They thought they were over either Scotland or England. They were on their way, they said, "to take part in the second front offensive which is imminent." Presumably this was a reference to the forthcoming landing at Dieppe, which took place the following month. Although the Americans were told that they were under arrest, they did not take this injunction too seriously, and neither did anyone else at the airport. After two hours the American consul arrived from Cork, and found everyone in a "happy-go-lucky" mood. He took some photographs of Irish soldiers and their charges. The Americans were given a meal and were put up for the night by the Irish army, before being allowed to leave next morning after their plane had been refuelled.

The following week there was a curious incident when a twin-engined RAF bomber made a forced landing on Ballyness strand, Co. Donegal. The airmen had no idea where they were and proceeded to destroy their aircraft. Ironically, one member of the five-man crew, Sergeant J. McFeeley, was from nearby Letterkenny, and his family still lived there. They had clearly been on a combat mission, but they were taken to the border anyway. McFeeley's father later remarked that he wished they had been interned, because at least his son would have been safely out of the war.

With the approach of winter and the deterioration of flying conditions, Gray was once more concerned about the possible internment of American airmen. As American war factories got into full production an ever increasing number of aircraft were delivered to Britain and there was a marked increase in the number of American planes getting lost over Ireland. Air Vice-Marshall Harold S. Kirby, the ranking RAF officer in Northern Ireland, told Gray in October 1942 that 16 American bombers had recently been lost for a time over Ireland and that two American pilots who came down near the border had been rescued and taken to Northern Ireland by "a plain clothes squad, which the Irish authorities wink at". Kirby, who was a Canadian, added that it was "inevitable that American pilots will come down and be interned and American planes confiscated".

"This luck cannot last," Gray warned the State Department. "While the right to intern can not well be questioned, it would be unfortunate to accept internment without protest." He felt the United States should make it clear to the Irish that interning any member of the American forces would be viewed as an "unfriendly act" seeing "that practically all Éire's sea borne supplies are protected by United States' patrols". The United States could retaliate with an embargo on coal, petrol, steel, wheat and chemical supplies to Ireland. "I know inside me that this is simple justice," Gray wrote to President Roosevelt, "but I haven't the ability to frame the formula that you can, which will cover the case."

As the matter was being considered in Washington, the Irish interned another Allied airman, Sergeant Jan Zimek, a Polish pilot whose RAF Spitfire came down near Oulart, Co. Waterford, on 31 October 1942. With the exception of Kennedy's few hours at K Lines back in April, Zimek was the first and indeed the only Allied airman interned from 35 different Allied landings during the year. He was really – as will be seen later – something of a peace offering to the Irish army, which was annoyed over the surreptitious activities of MI9, the British escape organisation.

On instructions from the State Department, Gray consulted the United States ambassador in London, John Winant, who saw little need to raise the issue about American airmen at the time. "Why not let sleeping dogs lie?" he asked.

"I told him that I had no desire to stir up the Irish situation," Gray wrote, "but that if American planes were grounded on Éire soil, the crews would be interned as of course and the material seized, following a precedent which the British had established, unless we took a different attitude. I said I thought it was an unwise thing for the American Government to assent to the British precedent without making the record clear as to its considered views." Gray added that Maffey believed anything the Americans might do on the issue would also help Britain.

At Winant's suggestion, Gray talked to Major General Russel J. Hartle, who was in charge of American forces in Northern Ireland. "From the military viewpoint, he could see no objection to exploring the question with Irish authorities, and that it would seem to him that a somewhat stronger line taken by us would tend to induce more favourable action toward the British," Gray reported. At this, Winant abandoned his own reservations, and Gray was instructed by the State Department to approach the Irish Department of External Affairs informally.

"American planes which may come down in Ireland will ordinarily be on training or transit flights and not at the time engaged in any hostile activity nor on any hostile mission," the State Department advised Gray. "It is evident that they are not on their way to bomb Germany. They are in a very different category from German planes which come down in Ireland. In view of the distances from Germany and German occupied areas, it cannot even remotely be supposed that such German planes were merely lost on their way on peaceful flights. On the contrary, their very presence over Ireland or Irish jurisdictional waters is conclusive proof that they are engaged in hostile operations either against the United Kingdom or its shipping or against Ireland itself."

Gray put the case to the Department of External Affairs on 30 November 1942. "I asked Mr Walshe if his government was prepared to recognise, in principle, the distinction between such non-combatant transport or training flights and flights which were manifestly combatant," Gray reported. "He said his government was prepared to recognise this distinction and suggested the terms operational and non-operational as better expressing the nature of the two classes of flights."

After discussing the matter with the Taoiseach, Walshe wrote to Gray: "In practice our attitude of friendly neutrality towards the United States results normally – in so far as aircraft and their crews are concerned – in internment of only such crews as are on operational flights. After full consideration of the matter, I am inclined to think that the existing relatively satisfactory situation should be left as it is. New and formal regulations or agreement are more likely to create difficulties than lessen them." In short, the Dublin government had been pursuing the policy desired by the Americans throughout 1942 and would continue to do so, but wished to keep the whole thing on an informal basis.

Although Allied airmen were instructed to say that they were on "non-operational flights", the pilots of five of the next six American planes which came down in Ireland failed to do so, but all 40 of those on board were released anyway. The only one who said he was on a training mission, Lieutenant Vernon Yahne of Mitchell, South Dakota, had got lost and did not know where he was when he landed on the racecourse in the Phoenix Park, Dublin. He was actually busy making preparations to set his plane on fire when he was stopped by local people. The plane was dismantled and moved to Baldonnel, where it was re-assembled and from where a British pilot flew it to Northern Ireland.

On 23 December a Lightning fighter landed with its wheels up on the beach at Ballyvaughan, Co. Clare, after the pilot, Lieutenant Broadhead from Stroudsburg, Pennsylvania, got lost on a flight from Eglington to Liverpool. He was put up by the local member of the Irish parliament and remained with him as a guest for dinner on Christmas Day.

The other four planes had a total complement of 38 men, including four generals, who were on a Flying Fortress which crash-landed near Athenry, Co. Galway, shortly before noon on 15 January 1943. The generals included Lieutenant General Jacob Devers, the American commander of the European Theatre of Operations; Major General Edward H. Brooks, and Brigadier Generals J.M. Barnes and C.D. Palmer. They were en route from North Africa to a conference in London.

They had had a fairly eventful flight. Over the Bay of Biscay they had been attacked by a German fighter but managed to shoot it down. They had subsequently become hopelessly lost and were running dangerously low on fuel when the pilot put the plane down in a field near the Agricultural College in Athenry. It just happened that the army was on manoeuvres in the area at the time. Pending instructions from Dublin, the Americans were disarmed by troops of the 1st Battalion of the Western Command, an Irish-speaking battalion. While the troops spoke to the Americans in English, they spoke to one another in Irish.

"Gee," one bemused American was heard to exclaim, "these guys really know their codes!"

When told that they were not being interned, the Americans began talking freely. After a meal at a local hotel they, and what belongings they could take with them, were transported to the border in two trucks and a convoy of cars. Almost 14 hours after their crash, they crossed the border at Beleek.

The *Irish Independent* tried to publish details of the crash but was blocked by the newspaper censor. One local girl caused a bit of a stir, however, when she wrote to an aunt in Britain:

> Willie, Brendan and all the LDFs were off like lightning and took the crew prisoners! There were three Generals, two Brigadier Gen. majors [sic] and I don't know what else, just arriving from Tunis for a conference in London, and the poor simps thought they were in Scotland... The lads of the village brought them into the town and got a meal for them at the hotel, while suitable transport was arranged for "a flying leap" for the border. All the lads got oranges, bananas, champagne, lemons and all sorts from them. Willie got a grand revolver and some sort of coat that inflates in water. Only that the under carriage got caught in a stone wall and tore off they would have been killed as there is a wood a few yards further on. The whole County Galway is or has been arriving to see the sights.

As the letter was being sent to Britain it had to pass through the Irish censor, who forwarded it to military intelligence, where the mention of the revolver sparked an investigation, much to the embarrassment of some of the army personnel. It turned out that three of the men had held on to revolvers. They claimed the Americans had given them the guns, but Army Headquarters was sceptical, to put it mildly. The guns were duly confiscated, and the chief-of-staff fired off a blistering rebuke to the battalion commander.

Within a matter of days Hempel learned of the crash and the release of the Americans. He even heard rumours that General Dwight D. Eisenhower had been on board. He demanded an explanation from the Department of External Affairs.

Freddy Boland naturally denied the Eisenhower story. "The way rumours travelled around here was simply extraordinary," he wrote. "There was always the possibility that some of them were put around for the expressed purpose of causing difficulties to our neutrality." The plane, he explained, was a mere transport for high-ranking military personnel, who were released because they were on "a non-operational flight".

It was probably in view of Hempel's uneasiness over the incident that the five-man crew of an RAF Wellington bomber were interned a few weeks later, but the crews of all 77 of the other Allied aircraft which landed in Ireland from then until the end of the war were quickly and quietly let go. "Under the circumstances," the Canadian High Commissioner wrote, "the meaning of the words 'non-operational fight' has, sometimes, been stretched almost beyond recognition." The whole argument was merely a "convenient fiction" to allow Ireland to help the Allies, according to Churchill's son Randolph.

Instructions were issued to American pilots to avoid Ireland, if possible, but to land there rather than risk a forced landing in Northern Ireland. Once they landed they were to guard their plane until the American military attaché arrived at the scene. They were to co-operate with Irish authorities, but to supply only minimal information, and not talk to the press. In addition, they were advised to emphasise: "We are on a non-operational flight."

Behind the scenes more extensive secret co-operation was being arranged. In January 1943 Joe Walshe of the Department of External Affairs offered to authorise secret contact between G2 and American intelligence – the Office of Strategic Services (OSS), which was the wartime forerunner of the Central Intelligence Agency (CIA). The Irish handed over a staggering amount of material, including all military intelligence gleaned from German personnel captured in Ireland. The co-operation was such that Carter Nicholas, the head of the Éire desk at OSS headquarters in Washington, visited Dublin in September 1943 to sound out the Irish government about the possibility of having Irish diplomats in occupied Europe spy for the Americans. De Valera gave his blessing for an arrangement whereby the OSS formulated questions for the Irish representatives in Berlin, Rome and Vichy. These were forwarded by the Department of External Affairs, and replies were sent to the OSS. Thus, in effect, the Irish diplomats were acting as American spies.

"A neutral power must extend no aid or assistance, in any way whatever, to either belligerent," J.M. Spraight wrote in his seminal book, *War Rights on Land.* "There is no half-way house between belligerency and neutrality." Describing de Valera's policy as "neutrality" was therefore absurd, because essentially he gave the Allies all the help he could. It would have been more accurate to describe the policy as "determined non-belligerency".

Churchill would have contended, of course, that de Valera had been less than helpful, particularly in refusing to allow the Allies to use Irish ports. Prior to the fall of France, however, the British did not need Irish bases, and afterwards they soon realised that the Irish were right in contending that bases in the south would be useless to the Allies. Because the shipping route via the south of Ireland was too vulnerable to attack from German planes and U-boats based in France, all Allied shipping was routed around Northern Ireland, where the Allies already had bases. In the summer of 1943, when Gray tried to persuade Washington to ask for facilities, the American chiefs of staff made it clear that they had no use for bases in the south. Such facilities would only be a liability to the Allied cause, they concluded.

De Valera had actually become so helpful that Maffey and Kearney, the Canadian High Commissioner, tried to persuade him to release their men who were already interned. The Taoiseach was willing to comply, but he insisted that he would also have to release the German internees. This was too much for British intelligence, which felt that the Germans, having been in Ireland for so long, would be too valuable to their own forces. Maffey, therefore, changed his approach and concentrated instead on getting the Irish to apply the non-operational argument retroactively. He contended that only 13 of the Allied airmen then interned had been on operational flights.

At the end of September 1943 de Valera agreed to free most of the men, but, before releasing them, it was first necessary to move them away from the Germans in the Curragh to a new internment camp being prepared at Gormanston, Co. Meath. It was a measure of the munificence of the Irish approach that the camp's lone Frenchman was included among those who had supposedly been on a non-operational flight, even though he had shot down a German bomber over Ireland. Presumably he was released because he had been in "hot pursuit" of the German plane when he entered Irish air space.

"As a matter of interest to our High Command," Maffey informed the Dominions Office, "it might be pointed out to them that operations off Éire may now be conducted on the assumption that no risk of internment exists."

Pure Bull

COVINGTON MADE ANOTHER of his solo escape efforts on 7 January 1942. This time he had some help from one of his Canadian colleagues.

Noticing that some civilian workmen in the camp had left a ladder unattended between the inner and outer barbed-wire fences, Covington asked Jack Calder for help. With the workmen due to knock off for the day within ten minutes, he suggested that Calder distract one of the guards. Acting as if he intended to go out on parole, Covington entered the parole cage while Calder started talking to the guard at the first gate.

"He said he wanted to do something about a telegraph," the guard later testified. "He had a paper in his hand."

While the guard was talking to Calder, Covington jumped on the second gate and began climbing it. Corporal H. Langford, the guard on the other side, reacted quickly.

"I drew my gun and told him to get back," he reported. Covington jumped down and raised his hands over his head.

"Don't shoot," he pleaded.

"I told him not to move," Langford continued. "He turned his back to the gate and didn't move for about two seconds until Pilot Officer Calder ran to the gate and shouted, 'Run, Buddy. He can't shoot you.'"

As Covington made towards the ladder, Calder started to climb the second gate as if he were going to follow suit, so the sentry had to remain at his post. Langford fired two warning shots in the direction of Covington, who dropped to the ground.

"Keep going," some of the other internees roared from inside the compound. "He's only firing over your head."

"Leave him alone," Calder shouted.

"Don't chase him," someone else cried. "He's dangerous."

Covington grabbed the ladder, quickly scaled the outer fence and made off across the Curragh on foot.

Unfortunately for him the shots alerted the camp, and two off-duty soldiers cycling down the Kilcullen road saw the whole thing. They gave chase, enlisting the help of four other soldiers on the road, and caught Covington before he could make it to the tree-lined area bordering the plain. But the young Englishman did not give up easily. The six soldiers had to drag him back, as he made two further efforts to get away.

After visiting the camp Sam Boal, an American correspondent, embellished Covington's escape attempt in an article in *The New Yorker* magazine. After stating that the English pilot refused to discuss how he got out of the camp, Boal proceeded to give a colourful account of Covington hiding all night in a tree while camp guards combed the ground beneath him. Boal wrote:

> He hasn't much to say about his wait, except that he recalls a large red cow which kept wandering to and fro under the tree. He thinks that the presence of the cow must have kept away the guards, who may have seen it as a perfect symbol of rural calm and rectitude. The cow, however, was to betray Covington, because at dusk, after he had spent twenty-one hours in the tree, a young Irish girl came out into the field to milk it and as she milked she looked up and saw Covington. "I felt a bloody ass," he explains, "but what could I do but smile down on her, like a damn silly moon?"
>
> The girl set up a clamour and the Irish guards came running up and led Covington back to the camp, to the great dismay of his fellow-internees, who regard the escape of one of their number as a community triumph.

Although the article made interesting reading, Boal's story about the tree and the cow was sheer fantasy or – to use the American vernacular – pure bull!

On 22 January, two weeks after Covington's unsuccessful attempt, the camp guards were faced with an embarrassing situation when Konrad Neymeyr simply vanished from K Lines. He had been seen by the guards at around six o'clock, but at ten-thirty that night they noticed he was not in the camp and had not signed out on parole.

Neymeyr had booked seats for himself and eight others at one of the camp cinemas that night. Although the others turned up, he did not. An inquiry concluded that he must have got out without signing parole amid some confusion at the gate. That evening more than 20 of the Germans tried to leave the camp at the same time. The first seven passed through the gate as about 16 others crowded around the parole hut. There had been intense activity throughout the day as the guards had been tipped off that the British were going to try a break. Guiney happened to be just outside the gate talking with Mollenhauer, when he heard Willi Krupp being told to get back.

"Krupp!" Captain Fitzpatrick snapped, "it's not like any of the Germans here to do a thing like that."

The internee had been trying to get out without signing parole, but he duly went back and signed out.

Unlike the Allied compound, no barbed-wire cage had been erected around the parole hut on the German side. "It is the rule," an embarrassed Guiney explained, "to give the least possible inconvenience to the German internees, due principally to the fact that their conduct has been very good and that they take exception to any undue restrictions. The Germans up to now," he added, "have never made any genuine attempt to escape and they always gave to understand that an escape on their part would be futile as they could not leave the country."

As Krupp had been one of Neymeyr's crew, the guards assumed that Neymeyr must have slipped out during this confusion. "In my opinion," Fitzpatrick wrote, "this incident is a reprisal for the alleged breach of parole by PO. Wolfe, as the Germans were very much hurt at the fact of PO. Wolfe not getting punished."

Neymeyr later said that he knew nothing of the Krupp incident. He insisted that he had slipped out through the fence, not the gate. "I got out of the camp by crawling through the barbed-wire fence," he explained. But, some 50 years later, he met one of the Irish officers and admitted that he had slipped out the gate in the confusion. He made it to Dublin, where he was helped by an army officer with IRA sympathies to stow away on board the SS *Lanarone*, bound for Portugal. He did not realise, however, that all Irish ships had to call at a British port for fuel and a navicert. A sailor discovered him shortly after the ship got underway and when the ship put into Cardiff the captain turned Neymeyr over to the British authorities. He spent the rest of the war in a British POW camp, where there was no parole and the food compared unfavourably with that in the Curragh.

Neymeyr was the only German to escape from Ireland during the war. There were later some sensational reports of Neymeyr making unfavourable comparisons between the POW camp and K Lines, but though his new conditions in Britain did indeed compare unfavourably, he never wrote to anyone at K Lines. They did learn, probably through Hempel, of his incarceration. Military intelligence was rather disturbed about Hempel's sources of information.

"Did you hear Neymeyr has left us, sir?" Mollenhauer telephoned Hempel the morning after the escape.

"Yes," the Minister replied. "I heard it first thing this morning." G2 had a tap on his telephone but apparently never found out how he first learned of the escape.

When, in response to the Wolfe affair, de Valera suggested that the cancelled parole forms should be given to the internees on returning to the camp, he advised that the guards should "be constantly on the alert for all ruses that may be adopted, especially at the time the internees are departing or returning from parole". As it was, the Allied internees were considering various ways of exploiting parole to escape. They experimented with acids and disappearing ink, but all to no avail. Such tricks would have been a parole violation, but the cardinal rule for the Allied airmen was simply not to get caught.

The way that seemed to hold out the best prospect of success was to somehow steal parole forms and smuggle them out to the men on parole. After the form was signed at the window of the parole hut, the guard handed it to the officer in charge, who recorded the details in a parole book and then placed the form on one of 26 jibs arranged in alphabetical order on the hut wall. When the airman returned, the guard at the window called out the name, and the officer on duty recorded the details and removed the form.

Despite de Valera's request, the guards generally retained the cancelled parole forms, except if specifically asked for them by an internee. Wolfe made a practice of demanding his form, and he had an unexpected piece of luck on 15 April 1942. At the time there were forms for Webster, Wolfe, Wakelin and Welpy on the "W" jib. As Wolfe returned from parole, Kelly, the officer in charge, took down Webster's by mistake and handed it to the guard in the duty room who, in turn, gave it to the guard at the window, who passed it on to Wolfe. Three different guards handled it without noticing the mistake, a debacle which lent credence to Wolfe's contention that he had indeed tricked the guards when he had escaped before Christmas.

Webster had initially signed out on parole at three o'clock in the afternoon, but returned later to sign out until two o'clock the following morning. The officer noted the particulars in the parole book but did not bother to take Webster's initial form off the jib, with the result that there were two forms in his name. It was the second valid form which was handed to Wolfe shortly afterwards. He took it, waited for five minutes, and signed out again on parole himself. Thus there were now two forms in his name – the one that he should have been given earlier and the latest one. Army authorities later surmised that Wolfe located Webster and gave him the form, which stated that parole was terminated once the form was "returned to the signatory". There was no mention of where or by whom it should be returned, hence technically Webster was immediately relieved of his obligations.

When Wolfe returned to the camp that night, Kelly retrieved the parole form he should have returned the first time and he recorded that Wolfe was 45 minutes late, but he still did not suspect what had happened. It was only when Brady returned to the camp without Webster that Kelly suspected something might be wrong, because the two Canadians were usually together. On cross-checking the forms on the "W" jib with the parole book, he discovered his mistake.

By then Webster was on his way to Northern Ireland. A friend drove him to Dublin, where he joined American and British soldiers returning to base. On the way a British officer, in civilian clothes, tried to draw him into conversation, but the young Canadian, preoccupied with the danger of being caught, failed to respond. The officer became suspicious and had Webster arrested once the train crossed the border, but, of course, he had little difficulty explaining his suspicious behaviour at that point.

The camp authorities protested that there had been a parole violation. "The British internees are playing fast and loose with the parole privilege," Guiney complained to McNally. They were sure Wolfe had violated parole in helping Webster to escape, but they could not prove it.

Unfortunately the story had a rather tragic ending. Webster rejoined his unit and was quickly back in action, only to be shot down and killed in the Allied landing at Dieppe four months later.

The Big Punch-up

Following his internment in mid-December 1941, Grant Fleming took over from his fellow Canadian, Ward, as the senior officer of the Allied internees and instilled a new vigour and determination into various escape plans. He and Girdlestone shared a room together and their determination to get out was infectious.

Fleming had come all the way from Calgary, Alberta, to join the RAF and he was determined to get back to where the action was as soon as possible. Given the circumstances of his arrival in Ireland, it was hardly surprising he had no desire to stay. Seven members of his crew perished in Galway Bay, and when he made the shore he was naked and exhausted. The only thing he had on, he later said, was a gold watch and somebody stole it. "His dislike of the Irish started from that moment," according to Girdlestone.

The latter, who crash-landed on the northern tip of Donegal five days later, was even further from his home in Wellington, New Zealand. "The Irish captain in charge of the escort, on learning that I was a New Zealander, gave me a discussion on Irish history all the way down to Co. Kildare," Girdlestone recalled. "He gave a summary of the past thirty years in Éire, of Sinn Féin, the Easter Rising, and the Black and Tans. Most of it was firey, extremely so.

"I read every book about Irish history I could lay my hands on, to discover why the country had adopted such an unreasonable and unorthodox attitude towards the war and against England," the New Zealander continued. There were no nationalist heroes for him. He simply could not understand Irish nationalism, which he equated with a narrow-minded and Roman Catholic philosophy. To taunt the guards, he hung a portrait in his room of Oliver Cromwell, who had massacred Irish Catholics in Drogheda.

In January 1942 Fleming began working on an escape plan which ultimately involved all 33 of the Allied internees. Their task was formidable, because things had changed greatly since Mayhew was first interned. Initially the camp had been surrounded by a ten-foot-high barbed-wire fence, but now there were four such fences. The first was simply stranded, with guards patrolling between it and the next fence. There were gun-posts on each corner of the camp, but fears of the guards shooting live ammunition had been dispelled by what had happened during Covington's recent break.

"They now know that they cannot be shot while attempting to escape," Guiney warned Army Headquarters. "Therefore I am of the opinion that it will serve no useful purpose in future having the police armed with revolvers, and I recommend that all policemen should carry batons and be given permission to use them should the occasion arise." He also asked for twelve extra guards to be drafted into the camp. Colonel McNally, who was "in entire sympathy", suggested that the guards should be given "definite authority to use these batons vigorously in the case of an attempted escape". This was duly authorised while the Allied internees were planning their break.

Their plan was to cut their way through the first fence with wire-cutters and to overpower the guards on patrol. They then had to figure out a way of getting over two 14-foot-high fences of thickly coiled barbed-wire, set eight feet apart. Fleming's plan was to build special two-part ladders that would have one part 16 feet high, with a second ladder about nine feet long hinged at the top. They would lay the longest part against the second fence and swing over the other part so that it formed a bridge between the second and third fences, the two coiled barriers. They also planned to use the roof of a sentry box and a duckboard to cross the double barrier. They were confident they could just roll over the outer stranded barbed-wire fence by using mattresses.

They already had the mattresses and they smuggled some wire-cutters into the compound. A friend on the outside secured enough steel strips, in two-and-a-half foot sections, for the ladders; they smuggled these into the camp in their golf bags. The steel strips were hidden under Baranowski's mattress, and the Polish captain was given the task of pretending to be sick. They plied him with drink and had him stay in bed for a week. This was the only way they could feel relatively sure that the parts would not be discovered. The men selected hiding places on the outside in the event of the escape being successful. Fleming, Keefer and Calder planned to use the hay loft in the stable at a friend's estate, and they stored some food there while on parole. Girdlestone decided on a secluded church, and he hid rations in its chimney.

The night selected for the break was 9 February 1942. By pure coincidence, John D. Kearney, the Canadian High Commissioner, telephoned Fleming that afternoon to enquire about conditions at the camp. He had been asked by his own government to report on the welfare of five Canadians interned there. It was indicative of the way the Canadian diplomats had been avoiding the internment issue that Ottawa was unaware that there were actually nine Canadians interned at the time. Fleming said nothing to cause Kearney to doubt that conditions were anything but satisfactory. Camp rules were lenient and the health of all the men was excellent, he reported. They were housed in well-heated quarters, had plenty of good food and were being well treated. "The boys have no complaints and appreciate the treatment but find life boring."

During the afternoon "the boys" bolted the steel strips together to form two hinged ladders, and organised themselves into various groups, each with specific tasks. There was a diversion party armed with flash-bombs and smokescreen material; its aim was to distract the guards' attention from the east fence where the escape bid was to be made. This group was also assigned the task of securing the inside gate to prevent the guards entering the compound proper.

The operation began shortly after seven o'clock in the evening. Three internees approached the parole cage as if going out on parole. Alex Virtue entered first and dropped some money to distract the sentry; he and Tees then made a dive for the gate and began climbing it, while Diaper threw a smoke canister and tied the inner gate shut. Meanwhile the "first-wire gang" was cutting away frantically at the wire of the inner fence in order to get at the three senties on the east side of the compound. The guards were quickly overpowered. One was tied to a post while the other two were knocked flat on their backs and two men sat on top of each of them, pinning them to the ground. The two ladder groups rushed out from beside the huts and raced through the gaping hole, followed by the final group led by Ward.

Initially things went exactly according to plan. The two ladders were erected and the sentry box was dragged to the second fence, where the duckboard was put into position. But then everything began to go wrong. The duckboard collapsed between the wires as did the second part of the ladder of the group led by Fleming. He raced to the other ladder, on which Keefer, Webster, Remy and Girdlestone had managed to cross, but one of the guards began shaking the wire to dislodge the crosswalk and it came crashing to the ground, leaving Fleming entangled on top of the third fence. By the time he extricated himself and jumped to the ground the place was swarming with guards.

Kelly called for help from all available guards, including the reserves from the No. 1 Internment Camp, Tintown. Sergeant Diver raced to the duty room, grabbed an armful of batons and handed them out. The extra guards came on the scene running, some with a baton in each hand, flailing at anyone who got in their way. One of the gun-posts opened up and was blazing away. Although Kearney was told that "only blank cartridges were used", there was some live ammunition. The internees could hear the whistle of bullets going through the air. Between 15 and 20 live rounds were fired, but the firing did not stop even when the guards came on the scene, so it was obvious that they were not trying to hit anyone.

A guard pointed a rifle at Newport's stomach and told him to get back into the compound. "I asked him if he had been instructed in international law," Newport later testified to a military inquiry.

"I don't give a fuck for international law. Do as you are told."

Newport ignored him and began to scale the wire.

"All right, you asked for it," the guard said, levelling his rifle.

Just then Sergeant Diver came over and ordered the guard to fire over the head of Wolfe who was on top of the wire. It was a live round, and at that point Newport decided to back off.

A fierce battle ensued at the outer fence before the internees were literally clubbed into submission. The Allied airmen were particularly bitter about the treatment meted out to Fleming, who was set upon by five guards. "Their whole attitude was one of savage brutality and their shouts expressed a desire for the damnation of England and all Britishers in general," Webster recalled. "The main object seemed to be more to give us a sound beating than to prevent our escape."

Kelly contended that those at the outer fence had resisted strongly. "They were putting up a terrible resistance and had to be dragged to their quarters," he noted. "In my opinion their idea in resisting was to engage the police while the others were getting over the wire and only for the prompt turn out in police and staff, some of them would have got away." He added that the internees inside the wire gathered in a mob and "were very bitter and used very abusive language".

One of the guards who grappled with Fleming complained that the Canadian had "done everything in his power to cause bodily harm", and had tried to roll them into the barbed wire.

Fowler was accused of throwing anything he could get his hands on – sticks, stones and bottles – at the guards around Fleming. "Get away, you dirty rotten Irish bastards," he roared.

Ward, who had a particularly good vantage point from the top of the sentry box, where he remained after the duckboard collapsed, was very critical of the guards. "If the main object was to stop Flight Lieutenant Fleming from escaping they had him at their mercy, by sheer weight of numbers without the use of clubs," he explained. "Apparently this was not their sole object, for when Flight Lieutenant Fleming was beaten off his feet they saw their chance to beat him some more. This time the guards were not satisfied with mere clubs but solicited the aid of a spade and their boots. Never have I witnessed such a cowardly and brutal attack on a defenceless man – a Royal Air Force officer. Up to this moment the fray had been quite clean, but now our anger was at a pitch and many remarks were cast at the guards, which would ordinarily not have been said."

"You dirty yellow Irish fucking bastards," Ward shouted. "What could we expect?"

"You black fuckers," Covington screamed. "Only for us you'd die with the hunger."

"We had two or three guards at our mercy and completely outnumbered inside the compound," Ward recalled, "but outside of being held to the ground, they were never struck."

Calder was particularly annoyed. "I shouted through the fence that unless the beatings stopped we would use pieces of the ladder to slug the guards inside the fence."

One of the guards said Midgely lifted his fist and threatened him. "I would put you, you green bastard, through the ground."

"Shower of cunts," roared Todd, singling Kelly out for particular abuse. "There goes Kelly, the dirty yellow rat."

"They're a nice lot of dirty fuckers you have out there," Ward snapped, giving Kelly a Nazi salute. "Did you see the clubbing and slugging that your men were doing out there?"

"Yes," Kelly replied, his hair messed up and face flushed. "I'm proud of them. You should all be treated like that."

When the fighting died down Calder was in the area between the fences, and he refused to move back into the compound when asked to do so by one of the guards. "I'm not going for a while yet," he said. "I'm pretty damn sore."

"You're just going to start more violence if you stay here," the guard explained. "You know these men don't like the English."

"I'm not English," Calder said. "I'm a Canadian. But I'm proud of fighting beside the English, if that's what you're getting at."

"Then your ambitions can't be very high," the guard replied.

When it was over most of the internees were a sorry sight. Their clothes were in tatters and they were a mass of cuts and bruises, both from the barbed wire and the batons. Six of the men needed hospital treatment, as did one of the guards, who had been hit in the face with a stone. The six included five of the men who managed to make it to the outer fence, together with Calder. They refused to sign out on parole in order to receive medical treatment, so they were taken to the military hospital under heavy escort. On reaching the hospital, the escort massed around the rear door of the ambulance. Seeing a chance to escape, Girdlestone and Fleming slipped through the thin partition into the driver's cabin and bolted out the door with the guards hot on their heels. After a short chase they were cornered in a cul-de-sac and captured. They were dragged away by guards who held the prisoner with one hand and punched them with their free fists. An officer looked on.

"If the journey back to the ambulance had been much further than four hundred yards," Girdlestone wrote, "hospital treatment would have been doubly necessary."

Fleming asked to speak to the officer, but was told to "shut up", much to his indignation. He heard one of the guards say, "The fucking bastard, I wish I had broken his damn neck."

All of the injuries were superficial. Even after the hammering Fleming had received, the only thing that needed attention was a half-inch laceration on his left forefinger. Remy had a slight scalp wound on the back of his head, Girdlestone had abrasions on his finger, wrist, right knee and face, while Keefer had abrasions on his thigh and wrist. According to the medical report the various abrasions were "almost altogether caused by barbed wire".

The internees deeply resented the manner in which Fleming was beaten. Colonel McNally tried to cool tempers by visiting the men in their mess afterwards, but this led to some further ugly scenes. Tees and Fowler said they were struck by a guard in the mess and other guards taunted them to come out and finish the fight. McNally had to order the guards to go outside the wire. When he and Kelly went to meet the officers in their anteroom, both Remy and Baranowski struck Kelly. In the case of the Pole, the assault was totally unprovoked because he was not even in the camp when the break was attempted.

Kelly behaved in a dignified way and did not try to retaliate. "I felt more humiliated by their language towards me in front of my own NCOs than the blows which I received from them in the officers' anteroom without hitting back," he explained.

Kelly was probably singled out as something of a Germanophile because he spoke German, but he actually sympathised strongly with the Allies. He had witnessed the rise of the Nazis in Germany and was not impressed. As a young schoolboy he had been brought to one of Hitler's rallies and given a front row seat. Amidst all the histrionics, he thought that Hitler was trying to be funny and he laughed.

"This is no laughing matter," Hitler roared at him, much to his own embarrassment and that of those who had brought him to the rally. He never attended another. Later he was particularly critical of Chamberlain's appeasement of Hitler because he realised such a policy was doomed to failure. Personally he felt that Ireland should have joined the Allies, but he was a soldier, not a policy maker, and he had a duty to act impartially at K Lines.

The internees' main complaint was that excessive force was used by the guards, who displayed an anti-British and non-neutral attitude. Fleming said he had instructed his men not to use violence, so he placed all the blame for what happened on the Irish. But, of course, the camp authorities saw things in a different light.

"If Flight Lieutenant Fleming was seriously saying that he had issued orders against the use of violence towards the guards," Guiney concluded, "it would appear that the internees regarded this attempted escape as some kind of game. In that event it was rather a pity that they did not inform the other side of the rules under which they contemplated it should be played. As it is they can hardly complain that the guards came on the field with a different viewpoint as to the code to be observed."

The guards probably used strong language and "may not have been too polite in their methods, particularly towards the end of the incident", Guiney admitted. "But," he continued, "if only a fraction of the reports made by the military policemen are accurate, it can hardly be held that the internees themselves were altogether on the side of the angels."

The injuries to Keefer would seem to support this view because there was no question of his being ill-treated; even Fleming acknowledged that "Keefer was treated reasonably well when the guards heard he was a Canadian".

Guiney thought it particularly significant that "Fleming was treated only for a cut finger. This hardly bore out the picture of a man clubbed, kicked, and attacked with a spade," he argued. "Similarly the other internees who succeeded in crossing the wires appeared to have escaped rather lightly in the matter of injuries considering the treatment they claimed to have been meted out to them by the guards."

Although feelings ran high in the camp for the next few days, the internees made no effort to enlist the help of their governments to protest against their treatment until Army Headquarters in Dublin ordered that all parole be suspended on 12 February 1942. Fleming then telephoned Maffey to inform him of the situation. The British representative sent Wing Commander Begg down to the camp to investigate matters and visited the camp himself a couple of days later.

The Canadian High Commissioner had hoped to accompany Maffey but postponed his visit at the latter's suggestion in order not to give the appearance of being overly concerned. It was not until 18 February that Kearney visited the camp. Following discussions with the men, he concluded they would not have been as bitter if someone had managed to escape. The High Commissioner suggested to Colonel McNally that it would be best all round if as little as possible were made of the whole affair. Instead of holding a formal military court to investigate the various complaints, it would be better if only an informal inquiry were conducted. He also proposed that certain guards be transferred from the camp and a limited form of parole be reintroduced immediately.

On 20 February Maffey and Kearney discussed the affair with de Valera, who promptly agreed to recommend the restoration of limited parole. He explained he was anxious that "every facility and comfort, not incompatible with international duties, be accorded the aviators", but he was reluctant to make any commitment on the question of transferring any of the guards because, he explained, he did not want to interfere too much in military affairs. Slight injuries were bound to occur, he said, especially when the guards were surprised by smoke bombs, which had obviously been smuggled into the camp in violation of the conditions of parole.

The wire fences around the Allied compound were further strengthened and a conference of representatives from the departments of Defence and External Affairs was held in the Taoiseach's office, with de Valera presiding, on 23 February. He warned that Maffey and Gray had made it clear that such means as *ruse de guerre*, bribery and intimidation were legitimate tactics for the internees to use in trying to escape, so he called for a strong guard at the camp at all times, but he stressed that the authorities should take "the utmost precaution to ensure that none of the internees is shot".

Before allowing the re-introduction of parole, McNally asked for permission to have the Allied compound searched thoroughly. This was agreed and Guiney was authorised to use "all reasonable force" if the internees resisted. During the search – which netted three wire-cutters, two nippers, a bit, screws and improvised ladder rungs – the Allied internees played soccer among themselves, and Girdlestone, undeterred by the recent fracas, seized the opportunity to try to sneak out of the camp. Noticing that the guards on duty were watching the action on the field, he slipped away and crawled under the wire by the fence that divided the Allied and German compounds. The light was already bad as the long winter evening was approaching, so the game soon broke up.

Girdlestone lay motionless until after dark. The camp was lit up and there were lights by the fence, but these were on the German side, with the result that they cast a short shadow out from the fence where Girdlestone was hiding in the middle of a concertina of barbed wire. He managed to crawl through the barbed wire to the corner of the compound where he met a heavy mass of wire about ten yards from the outer perimeter. He had to move very slowly because there were guards near by and, unfortunately for him, it was a very still night. After some hours one of the guards heard something by the iron fence. He and a colleague investigated, but the grass inside the wire had grown very long and Girdlestone was able to conceal himself. One of the guards suggested it must have been a fox and they left, but 20 minutes later the other guard made a more thorough search, during which he found the New Zealander.

"All right, Corporal!" Girdlestone exclaimed. "I was only playing a joke." There was no need to sound the alarm, he said, as he extricated himself from the wire and returned to his hut.

Next morning the men, with the exception of Baranowski, were allowed out on parole again and things quickly returned to normal. The internees found, however, that some of the Irish children had a new game. Instead of playing cowboys and Indians, they were now playing Irish guards and British internees. "It was not good for our badly damaged egos to notice that few of the kids wanted to be internees," Girdlestone noted.

WHO'S BOSS?

WHEN THE CANADIAN High Commissioner visited K Lines for the first time on 18 February 1942, he was immediately struck by the fact that the German compound did not seem as heavily fortified with barbed wire as the Allies' section. Mollenhauer had done so much complaining that army authorities were still slow to act against the Germans.

While the German internees were generally very good in observing parole, they had no compunction about violating the camp's censorship regulations by mailing letters while on parole and receiving mail at addresses of accommodation. After Neymeyr's escape, however, the Irish authorities began to take a more serious view of such violations, fearing that things might get out of hand.

A further disturbing incident occurred in the early hours of 15 February 1942. One of the German internees, *Unteroffizier* Josef Emmerich, had too much to drink at Osberstown House, near Naas, and when it was time for him to return to the camp, he asked the owner of the bar to drive him into town where his bicycle was parked. The owner refused and Emmerich left in a huff and, according to the owner, borrowed his car without permission. The police were immediately notified. At about three o'clock in the morning a Garda stopped Emmerich on a bicycle in Naas and tried to question him.

"I am a German and you have no right to question me," he replied. "I will report you to the German legation." Emmerich became "very aggressive" when the Garda said he was investigating the theft of a car.

"How dare you speak to me," he said. "Take you hand off my bicycle." At that point he hit the policeman's hand which had been resting on the handlebar. Then, with the Garda shouting at him to halt, Emmerich rode off and went straight to the police station and complained that the Garda had assaulted him.

According to the Garda on duty at the station, the internee was most insulting and aggressive. "I will report you to the German legation," Emmerich shouted repeatedly, demanding that he be driven back to the Curragh. The civic authorities gave serious consideration to pressing a number of charges against him – including theft of the car, drunken driving, driving without a licence or insurance, assault and obstructing a policeman doing his duty – but in the event they decided not to proceed.

"If breaches of this kind are allowed to go unpunished," Army Headquarters warned that a serious situation could arise. Irish officials decided it was time to assert their authority over the German internees. Less than two weeks later, on 28 February, Ernst Lorra and Georg Sigl were caught in Dublin while on local parole, which did not entitle them to leave the Kildare area. Camp authorities reacted by withdrawing their parole privileges for two weeks, much to the indignation of Mollenhauer, who complained that the Irish were usurping his authority.

"I deny to any person apart from the German *Wehrmacht* the right to punish a German soldier," Mollenhauer wrote to McNally. "They are only subject to German disciplinary law and were it not for the fact that the above measures were taken, I would have dealt with their action. Quite apart from the fact that I, as Senior Officer of the Camp, should have been informed and given the reasons orally or in writing by the person who imposed the punishment."

He was particularly resentful of what he believed was discriminating treatment. In recent weeks much more serious parole violations by Allied internees had not been dealt with as severely. Wolfe, for instance, had been confined to camp for only five days after he was adjudged to have violated parole in going to Northern Ireland, and the Allied internees as a whole had only been confined to camp for 13 days after their punch-up with the guards on 9 February. Lorra and Sigl had only gone to Dublin to meet some people and there was no question of their violating parole as part of an escape attempt. "Above all," Mollenhauer wrote, "I consider the amount of punishment grossly unjust and can only compare it to the different treatment of the British internees. Even if the offence were so as it is alleged it is a mere trifle in comparison to the happenings at the last British attempted escape, especially the assaults against the Guards personnel [*sic*] and the fact that they brought into camp implements for escape while on parole."

Mollenhauer certainly had a valid point, and Hempel protested on his behalf to the Department of External Affairs, which found itself in a predicament. Freddy Boland blamed the Minister for Defence for not taking a realistic view of the whole internment situation. "At the root of all our difficulties about military internees at the Curragh," he said, "lies the tendency of the Minister for Defence to think of them as being in the same category as prisoners of war or persons interned under the Offences Against the State Act [under which members of the IRA were interned]."

Despite protests from the Department of External Affairs, the Department of Defence was making no apologies. "The fact that no punishments were imposed by us in previous parole incidents," the secretary of the Department of Defence explained to his counterpart at External Affairs, "was due to reasons of policy or expediency (e.g. in the Wolfe case you asked us not to punish him in view of representations you had received) or difficulties of proof but never because we felt we had not the right to. In the present instance, there was no doubt. The men were found in Dublin." Mollenhauer's complaints were ignored, and in March another German had his parole cancelled for a week after he was caught sneaking out of the married quarters of the military barracks in Kildare, which were out of bounds to the internees.

Kurt Kyck had been visiting his girlfriend and future wife, Elizabeth White, who lived with her parents in the barracks. Her father was a sergeant in the Irish army who had served in Germany with the British army of occupation following World War I when he met and married Elizabeth's German mother. Kyck looked on the White's quarters as a home from home, but he had been formally refused permission to visit the barracks back in September 1941. After some narrow escapes at the gate, the latest of which had been only the previous night, the military police established a stake-out to catch him on 26 March 1942.

Mollenhauer again resented the disciplining of one of his men. He had still not received an answer to his previous complaint, so he asked Hempel to protest once more to the Department of External Affairs.

"What caused so much trouble in these cases was that when Mollenhauer made representations, he got no reply to them," Walshe wrote to his counterpart at Defence. "Any reply was better than not making a reply at all." It was an ironic piece of advice in that his department had earlier suggested that a letter of protest from Mollenhauer should be ignored.

In a way there was a certain air of contentment amongst the Germans, whose complaints were mainly about improving conditions. They organised educational classes and had a self-imposed daily routine to sustain morale, whereas the morale on the Allied side was generally very bad, except where they were working on escape plans.

"Our boys, rightly or wrongly, feel that if they organise classes it might be interpreted as acquiescence of their lot, whereas they want it known that they are doing all they can to rejoin their units," Kearney maintained.

"The German internees next door realised that they were in a foreign country, a state of mind that never existed with us, and they settled down with typical Teutonic thoroughness to their internment," Girdlestone observed. "I guess if we were in Germany as prisoners-of-war we could have settled down to our detention just as the Germans did in Éire. But the fact that we were in an English-speaking country made our position seem ludicrous."

While the Germans may have been more resigned to their fate, it did not mean they were any more satisfied. In fact, the reverse was true. They made very few attempts to escape, with the result that they were all the more resentful of petty restrictions. Mollenhauer asked for permission to fly the German flag in honour of Hitler's birthday on 20 April 1942, but this was refused. He went ahead and told his men to fly the flag anyway, and this led to an incident with the guards. When the Department of Defence tried to make an issue of the affair, the Department of

External Affairs again advocated turning a blind eye. "We have the right to impose penalties, without any reference to the senior internee officer," Boland wrote. "In our view, however, there may be a distinction to be drawn between the question of the existence of the right to punish and the question of the extent to which it is wise to exercise it."

Some months later Mollenhauer was complaining of further discriminatory treatment following another Allied escape attempt in August 1942. This time he complained that the crew of the German bomber which crashed near Tramore, Co. Waterford, were transported to the Curragh on 23 August 1942 in an open truck, while recaptured Allied airmen were returned in the comfort of a saloon car. "Please explain," he wrote to the camp authorities, "why the crew of *Hauptmann* Berndt was brought from Co. Waterford to the Curragh in an open lorry while recaptured British internees were being comfortably conveyed in a 'Ford V-8' and although I had already strongly complained when *Hauptmann* Muller came here in a lorry."

The Irish were not really discriminating against the Germans in this case, and certainly no insult was intended. Using the truck was merely a practical means of conserving fuel; there was a tremendous shortage of petrol in the country, and it was strictly rationed and confined largely to people engaged in emergency or security services. It would have been a waste of petrol to transport the men in a convoy of cars and, by the same token, it would have been equally extravagant to return lone Allied internees in trucks. However, when it came to standing up for his men or defending his right to act as their spokesman, Mollenhauer was not deterred by the fear of offending Irish sensibilities. When he protested that the new internees were questioned at the camp by military intelligence before he was allowed to speak to them, the Department of External Affairs was taken aback by the "decidedly impertinent" tone of Mollenhauer's protest. "Indeed," Walshe wrote, "it calls for a sharp reply." But he realised that the controversy could have been avoided if G2 had exercised a little common sense and interviewed the men before they were transferred to the Curragh. "No excuses would be necessary, if a little extra efficiency on the G2 side could be achieved, even at this late stage, in dealing with belligerent internees," he wrote.

Army Headquarters was worried not so much at the validity of Mollenhauer's complaints as the need to play down the incident, in case the Germans might learn the real story behind the shooting down of their plane. The JU 88 bomber commanded by *Hauptmann* Gottfried Berndt had been on a mission to attack shipping in the Irish Sea when it was spotted from the look-out post at Carnsore Point. It was sighted shortly afterwards off Clogher Head, Co. Louth. These sightings were duly reported by radio and the messages were picked up in Northern Ireland. Three RAF Spitfires took off from their base in Kilkeel, Co. Down, to intercept the German aircraft.

A bitter struggle ensued as the three fighters chased the bomber down through the heart of Ireland. One of the Spitfires, piloted by a Pole, Boleslaw Sawiak, was shot down near Rathoak, Co. Meath, at nine o'clock in the morning, and died shortly afterwards in hospital. The German plane, with its right engine out and a damaged rudder, proceeded down over Kildare, Kilkenny and Waterford before it was again intercepted by the two remaining fighters. In the following exchanges the right engine caught fire.

Hauptmann Berndt decided to make a forced landing. The crew, consisting of *Leutnant* Paul Stoermer, *Oberfeldwebel* Karl Hund and *Unteroffizier* Josef Reiser, began dumping their ammunition and loose implements for the landing, which was effected with considerable skill. The only casualty was a hen killed on the ground by flying debris and a heifer some two miles away that was somehow shot through the leg. A woman also claimed that slates were knocked off her roof and a hole made in her porch, but a neighbour dutifully informed G2 that the hole had been there the previous Sunday.

Had Mollenhauer known about the real circumstances leading to the shooting down of Berndt's aircraft, he would undoubtedly have had a lot more to say.

Escape Fever

THE MASS BREAK-OUT attempted by the Allied internees in February 1942 really tested the Irish guards, and Guiney feared the possibility of trouble breaking out simultaneously at K Lines and Tintown, where republican internees were held. He noted that "it is not outside the bounds of possibility that a joint arrangement could be made on these lines". He was particularly worried about the possibility of the IRA and the Germans acting in collusion with one another in a joint escape bid.

Although camp authorities apparently dismissed the prospect of the IRA and the British internees co-operating, this was not altogether unlikely, especially when the internees in B Camp were led by a determined Canadian like Fleming. He toyed with the idea of enlisting IRA help after he was approached by Michael Burke, an IRA member who offered to spring Allied pilots if they paid him for each pilot who got away. At the time the cost of training a pilot was estimated at £10,000, so Burke felt the British would pay generously. He promised to get the IRA to attack K Lines as a diversion for a simultaneous escape bid by IRA internees at Tintown.

Burke certainly had the credentials to organise the proposed break. He had helped three IRA internees to escape from the British camp on Spike Island in 1921, the only successful escape ever from the island. But while it was one thing for MI9 to conspire with sympathetic Irish nationals to help Allied internees to escape, it was something altogether different to have the internees conspire with the pro-German IRA and possibly help members of the IRA to escape from Tintown. Fleming was uneasy about the trustworthiness of his IRA contact, so nothing ever came of their talks.

Instead, on 17 August 1942, Fleming led another mass break involving 18 men. Initially it was intended that 14 would take part; the others were not told of the plan. The 14 went to a movie that evening and then returned while most of the camp were out on parole drinking at a nearby pub. Four who had stayed in the camp joined in. It was an ideal night for a break – dark, overcast and windy with rain expected.

Calder and Wolfe spearheaded the escape bid. At eleven o'clock they approached the parole cage as if going out on parole. Wolfe went first, pushing a bicycle. As he approached the first gate he stopped, bent down and began to adjust his bicycle clips.

"Jack, you go ahead," he said, "I won't be a minute."

When the sentry opened the inside gate, through which only one man was permitted at a time ever since Calder helped Covington in the previous escape bid, Wolfe threw his bicycle into the opening so the guard could not close the gate. Then Wolfe and Calder overpowered him while their colleagues rushed out of the mess and through the gate. Covington inserted a corkscrew into the keyhole of the parole hut, so those inside were unable to enter B Camp from the hut. Fleming, Tisdall, Keefer and Girdleston had four metal curtain rods, taken from the showers, and used them to prise the third gate off its hinges. The startled guard did not have time to overcome his surprise before the gates came crashing down on him, effectively taking him out of the picture.

"The alarm bells were really going to town," Girdlestone wrote. "Whistles were blowing, the gun posts were opening up and the combined noise was rather a contrast to the stillness of ten seconds ago. Everybody was shouting. We were shrieking with glee because we never realised the gates would fall so easily; the Germans next door were crying out words of encouragement, I think to us, and the Irish were shouting to each other because it made them feel so much more efficient. It was only a second or two later that we were tearing for the outer wire." Some of the internees had brought rugs which were placed on top of the outer barbed-wire fence so they could roll over the obstacle.

Meanwhile Calder and Wolfe were still wrestling with the first guard. In his anxiety to get away Calder gave the sentry a tremendous shove and sent him hurtling into the barbed wire. Wolfe was caught off balance, went into the wire with the sentry and became entangled, ended his chances of escape.

Nine of the men managed to scale the outer fence before extra guards came rushing in. The other nine made it to the outer wire, before they were overpowered by the guards rushed to the scene. Calder, Tees, Tisdall, Remy, Wolfe, Ricketts and Todd were taken at the outer fence. Welpy hid in a turf shed, but was discovered after about a quarter of an hour. Covington managed to hide in one of the gun-posts for longer before he was found. As he was marched back into the compound, he retrieved his corkscrew from the keyhole of the parole hut.

A full-scale search for the escapees was promptly begun. The whole Curragh camp was roused and the area cordoned off. Patrols were also sent out and roadblocks set up. Stanislau Kerniewski, the Polish sergeant, was the first to be recaptured when he ran into a patrol at around one o'clock in the morning. Much to the amusement of the soldiers, he tried to bluff his way out by telling them in his broken English that he was coming home from work. It was indeed an odd hour to be coming from work, but the good-natured Pole – looking down at his hands and feet, which were a mass of cuts from the barbed wire – explained he was "a butcher coming off a night shift". The soldiers were amused but not at all fooled.

Baranowski and Brady were caught about an hour later when they ran into the cordon. Some of the men on parole were also arrested as they returned to the camp oblivious of the escape. They protested indignantly that they were on parole, but they ended up spending the night in cells in the local Garda station just the same.

Duncan Fowler walked all night; by morning he was tired and hungry. He had been advised if he needed help to go to the largest house he could find, because there was a good chance that the owner had been wealthy when the British ruled Ireland and, consequently, would be more sympathetic to the British cause than the average Irishman. Fowler duly picked out a large house and knocked at the door.

"You know who I am?" he said to the owner.

"Yes."

"I am tired and hungry and I wondered if you could help me."

"Just step in here," the owner said. "You have caught me at a rather bad time. My wife is upstairs with a doctor in attendance. She is about to give birth. But I'll go to the kitchen and see what I can get. You wait here and, if you are afraid I won't come back, there is a trap door out of the conservatory over there and you can slide out that way."

The owner returned a short time later with a glass of milk and some bread and butter. He explained it was all he could get without arousing suspicion among the kitchen staff. The whole vicinity had been alerted and the army had already searched his grounds.

"If you go down to the barn," he said, "you can have a sleep. I have called the man that works for me and I sent him off on a mission that will take most of the day."

After resting for some hours, Fowler set off on foot in the direction of Dublin. It was dusk when he reached the outskirts of the city, but he was spotted by a patrol and taken to a Garda station for questioning. At one point he was momentarily left alone and he made a dash for freedom, but was caught after a short chase.

All but four of the escapees were caught within 24 hours. Girdlestone managed to stay at large for five eventful days. He spend the first night hiding under a hedge about two miles from the camp, unable to make further progress as the cordons were in position. Next morning the entire area was searched, but the soldiers overlooked his hiding place. In the evening there was heavy rain and the cordon was withdrawn, so he was able to make his way to a friend's house, soaked to the skin but in tremendous spirits.

His host told him the house had already been searched and a Garda, who had been stationed outside for most of the day, had been withdrawn at nightfall. Feeling that the strain of hiding a fugitive was too much for his friend's wife, who was in the last stages of pregnancy, Girdlestone decided to move on the following night. His friend made arrangements with a member of the Escape Club to pick up Girdlestone at a spot some miles away. After dark the friend rowed him across a river near the house, and the New Zealander set off for a barley field three miles distant. In the morning he was picked up at the rendezvous in a car driven by Dicky Ruttledge of the Escape Club and driven off in the direction of Dublin.

On the way they stopped at a pub and were stunned to find two uniformed Gardaí inside when they went in. Unable to turn around and leave without arousing suspicion, they ordered a drink and Ruttledge talked to the policemen, who explained they were "keeping a look-out for the boys from the Curragh". Ruttledge bought them a drink and he and Girdlestone moved on.

They had lunch at Ruttledge's home, where Girdlestone read in the daily newspaper that all but four of the escapees had been recaptured. That afternoon Ruttledge's wife accompanied Girdlestone on a bus into Dublin to bring him to a friend's house where they thought he would be safe. In the city they got a taxi to the man's house, but on pulling up outside Girdlestone noticed two men approaching the car. Assuming they were detectives, he told the driver to go on immediately, leaving the two men standing in their tracks. Ruttledge's wife was stunned by the incident and Girdlestone admitted he was "scared stiff". They made their way to the home of an elderly lady whose son was a colonel in the British army. They explained the situation to her and she willingly put Girdlestone up for the night. Ruttledge decided to move him to the border as soon as possible.

At about four-thirty the following afternoon Ruttledge and Dr Hugh Wilson called for Girdlestone in the doctor's car, but as they drove out of the driveway a car pull out of a lane down the street and began following them. Wilson tried to lose the pursuing car in the narrow Dublin streets but was unable to. At times the cars were travelling at frightening speeds through the Dublin slums, until they drove into a cul-de-sac. Girdlestone jumped out and took off on foot. He was able to get about a 300-yard start on the police detectives who followed him as he jumped over fences and ran through backyards, until he finally took refuge in an outdoor lavatory at the back of one of the tenement buildings.

The lavatory was attached to a woodshed, but the wall dividing them stopped short of the ceiling, so he was able to slip over the dividing wall into the woodshed, which was padlocked on the outside. Within about five minutes he heard the police search the lavatory and then come round to the door of the woodshed, but on finding it locked they left.

The area was surrounded and the tenements searched, but still the police overlooked the woodshed, where Girdlestone waited until after dark. Before venturing out he put on a pair of dirty old overalls that were in the shed. He crept through the backyard of the tenement and then out to the street, where he began whistling the tune "Galway Bay". "There were police patrolling outside," he wrote, "but they were looking for a well dressed man with a springly step, not a shambling, dirty idiot, clad in overalls whistling an Irish tune.

"I felt fine," he continued. "I just couldn't get over my luck. The convenient architecture of the WC and the overalls. I went down to a fish and chip shop and ate a huge greasy meal." Girdlestone spent the night under a hedge and tried to head north in the morning, but found patrols at some crossroads.

"I turned back to the city and had breakfast in a small tea shop near the docks," he recalled. "There, I chatted with the only customer and found that he was a mate aboard an English ship, sailing in the morning. I guess I should have chanced my luck and told him who I was but he was obviously Irish and as I knew all shipping was diligently searched on leaving Dublin, I didn't risk it."

Leaving the tea shop Girdlestone decided to make for the home of a friend, who he was sure would hide him for a few days. While he was crossing a street in the centre of the city, a car pulled up behind him and he suddenly found himself surrounded by five guards from the camp. "Mr Girdlestone," one of them said, "we've got ya."

Vic Newport was the first of the escapees to make it to Northern Ireland; he had help from a retired British army captain. Fleming and Keefer crossed the border on foot on 28

August after being hidden by a friend for eleven days. They were arrested as suspicious characters by members of the Royal Ulster Constabulary, but, like Webster, they had little difficulty explaining their reasons for sneaking across the border.

Back at the camp, Girdlestone was dejected over his recapture, but there were still some eventful happenings in store. On his first day back he was lying on the grass in the August sunshine talking about recent events with Calder when he noticed that a medical orderly, who had been coming to the camp to treat the internees for cuts suffered from the barbed wire in the escape attempt six days earlier, bore a striking resemblance to Kerniewski. This, he thought, might afford a splendid opportunity of springing the Pole.

Girdlestone and Calder rounded up six others and they lured the orderly into Covington's room, where they overpowered him, gagged him with a towel, and stripped him. He fought vigorously when they were relieving him of his trousers but was hopelessly outnumbered. Kerniewski was found and the orderly's uniform fitted well, except for the hat which tended to fall over his eyes. The Pole strolled off towards the gates, carrying bandages in one hand and a dish in the other. What had started pretty much as a lark seemed suddenly to have a chance of success.

Indeed the effort might have been successful had it not been for the Pole's happy nature, because on reaching the guard at the second gate Kerniewski gave a broad smile, revealing his wonderful set of gold teeth which had become famous throughout the area. His glittering smile gave the game away immediately.

"There was nothing else to do but exchange the clothes back again," according to Girdlestone. "The orderly vowed never to set foot inside the camp again!"

Although the effort had failed, Albert Dalton was more fortunate a few days later. Returning from the swimming pool with Masterson, Barnett, Diaper and Jefferson in the early afternoon on 29 August 1942, Masterson entered the parole cage first and was given Dalton's parole form by mistake. He duly signed Dalton's name and while Barnett and Diaper filed into the cage, he managed to signal Dalton to clear off. The guard at the gate heard Dalton ask Jefferson to bring in his towel and then saw him cycle away. Masterson then gave Dalton's form to Ward, who had again become the commanding officer following Fleming's escape. Ward made arrangements for the form to be delivered to Dalton, who was thus relieved of his parole obligations.

Camp authorities contended, however, that he had violated parole because he did not return to the camp and sign in again, as provided for in new forms issued after Webster's escape. However, though the parole forms had been altered to provide for the internees to sign them on their return to the camp, the conditions still merely stipulated that "the period of parole will not be regarded as terminated until the signed form has been duly returned to the signatory". The conditions of parole did not specifically state that the internee would only be relieved of his parole on receiving the form from a guard at the camp.

Dalton's escape from the area that afternoon was greatly facilitated by the crowd attending a race meeting at the Curragh. The camp guards were left looking for the proverbial needle in a haystack in trying to find him among the huge race crowd.

Complaints and Concessions

IRISH MILITARY INTELLIGENCE had a very good record on security matters and this was recognised by both the British and American services. Following the arrest of Wilson and Ruttledge while trying to drive Girdlestone to the border, the Escape Club was broken up. The Irish had in fact been aware of its existence for some time and put most of its members under surveillance on learning of the break from the Curragh.

Under instructions from London, Maffey talked to de Valera on behalf of those who had been arrested for helping Girdlestone. His "office had no connection with the Escape Club", but Maffey explained that it was difficult for him "to maintain an attitude of 'complete disinterestedness' regarding these individuals, as they had been led into the mess as tools of a British organisation". He added that the problem could "have been avoided if I had been taken into the confidence of the Éire Government at an earlier stage".

The Escape Club was actually involved in much more than simply helping internees across the border. It was a kind of fifth column ready to help British forces, and Maffey was afraid of the implications if all this became public.

"I gather," Maffey reported, "that the ramifications of the plot are wide and deep and therefore, unless I press upon the Éire Government such reasons as I can urge for refraining from a Grand Inquisition with pains and penalties to follow, a possible chance may be lost of averting serious result over a wide field." But de Valera adopted a firm attitude; he was under pressure from the security forces who resented this British interference. And the situation was being made particularly difficult by loose talk by "these conspirators". They had been saying "that they had nothing to fear as I would have supplies cut off from Éire if a finger were laid upon them," according to Maffey, who was embarrassed by the reckless talk.

Maffey tried to persuade de Valera to drop the case by arguing on the following lines:

> There was nothing to be gained and much to be lost by imposing further penalties in the present case. He would realise that my position was very difficult when Éire citizens in a sporting spirit fell in with suggestions coming from a British quarter, even if I were in no way a party to them... In the assistance rendered to the internees there was nothing sinister, nothing un-Irish, not even necessarily anything pro-British. The matter wanted looking at from a human angle rather than from the political angle. Enough had surely been done to produce the deterrent effect which was required.

Late that afternoon, on 31 October 1942, an RAF Spitfire on a training mission landed near Oulart, Co. Waterford, and de Valera ordered the internment of the pilot, Jan Zimek, a Pole. He was the only Allied airman to be interned in 1942. Maffey tried to argue for his release.

"I made the most of training flight and other arguments but," he reported, "Walshe asked me not to oppose a decision which was Mr de Valera's personal decision in the light of difficulties confronting him as a result of the Wilson case and also increased IRA activities."

The Taoiseach consulted with Colonel Dan Bryan, who had taken over from Archer as head of G2 during 1942, about the prosecution of Dr Wilson of the Escape Club. Ruttledge had skipped bail and fled to Northern Ireland, and now de Valera wished to know if the military would resent it if Wilson was not jailed. Colonel Bryan had no strong feelings on the matter, so when the case did come up, Wilson was fined £300 and sentenced to two years in jail, but the sentence was suspended pending his future good behaviour. Maffey's office paid the fine, and the whole thing was quietly forgotten.

As winter approached, morale in the Allied camp, which had risen during the summer months when there was plenty for the men to do, began to wane. Ward was again in charge, but he lacked the enthusiasm which Verity and Fleming had shown for escape, and this did little for the morale of the younger airmen determined to get back to the war. They resented Ward's apparent complacency.

"He proved useful at typing if nothing else," one wrote sarcastically. "When he took over command of the camp after Grant Fleming escaped, his letters to the British Embassy were models of correct service phraseology. We did not find him at all useful in our escape plans ..."

If Ward lacked the burning enthusiasm of some of the younger men, it would have been understandable. He was a married man with children, and may well have had enough adventure in his 17 months of war. In fairness to him, it should also be noted that Maffey urged Ward to keep things quiet at K Lines in the light of the on-going Escape Club affair. The British representative explained that he was working behind the scenes to secure their release, and Ward should try to keep the men as content as possible. To help pass the long winter nights Wing Commander Begg, the British air attaché, procured some of the latest movies about the air war such as *Target for Tonight*, *Coastal Command*, *Next of Kin* and *Dangerous Moonlight*. These were all banned by the censor, but special permission was given for private showings at the Curragh provided they were "exclusive to British internees".

The frustration of the Allied internees was caused largely by the incongruity of their situation. Since Kennedy's release in April, they had heard that "hundreds of Allied airmen were being slipped over the border and back to the war". As a result the internees felt that they were little more than "window dressing" to keep the Germans happy. "We were to stay as evidence of internment for the German Legation and the anti-British Irish," Girdlestone explained. "If either of these two groups heard of the surreptitious filtering of British and American airmen over the border and back to the war, the resulting uproar would be terrific. We were told to keep quiet and not to escape."

Mollenhauer believed that the location of K Lines at the Curragh afforded preferential treatment to the Allied internees. They had no language barrier and there were numerous people in the vicinity who were born and reared as British subjects. Many of them, or members of their families, had spent their working lives in the service of the British Crown, and they had a natural affinity with the Allied airmen. Ireland did have a small colony of German people, but they were centred in the Dublin area, which the German internees could only visit once a month. He therefore requested that they be moved to a new camp nearer to Dublin, and he tried to exploit a situation in October 1942 following an incident involving a number of local people near the Grand Hotel, Newbridge. According to Mollenhauer, four of his NCOs – Krupp, Emmerich, Herbert Schulze and Max Galler – were subjected to an "unprovoked assault and serious insult".

"You are not in Germany now," a passing soldier heard one of the locals say, but he did not know how the brawl began. The Gardaí arrived on the scene and found it necessary to restrain Krupp physically. Mollenhauer formally complained that a Garda had "bodily touched *Feldwebel* Krupp" and he demanded an explanation from the Garda sergeant who accompanied the two constables to the scene.

When his letter was ignored, Mollenhauer protested to McNally. "I must urgently request the Army authorities to secure our safety and freedom from insults – as well as the apprehension of and criminal procedures against the attackers," he wrote. "Otherwise we should have to take self-defence and self help."

The army authorities were not inclined to look favourably on what they felt were Mollenhauer's incessant complaints, and on the question of touching a German, he displayed a sensitivity which the Irish found rather offensive. When, some time later, Fleischmann was caught in the act of discussing escape plans while on parole, the intelligence officer who caught him emphasised his point by grasping the internee's arm, much to the indignation of Mollenhauer, who demanded that the army should have Fleischmann's jacket cleaned because, he contended, it had been contaminated by the soldier touching it.

In December the internees were again given two days parole for Christmas shopping in Dublin, and the German minister managed to obtain an extra concession for Ernst Muller, who was allowed to stay overnight at the German legation in order to attend a dinner party. This set a precedent that the Irish authorities were soon to regret.

On Christmas Day Mollenhauer arrived in the parole hut carrying six bottles of wine and a cake that he asked Kelly to deliver to Ward as a gift from the *Luftwaffe* to the RAF. When Kelly presented the gift, Ward reacted indignantly. He refused to accept it and made some very derogatory references to the Germans, but Kelly placated him and persuaded him, in the spirit of the season, to reciprocate by sending back a couple of bottles of brandy that well-wishers had sent to the Allied internees. Even if it was a rather grudging gift, it was one of the few friendly gestures that the Allied airmen ever made towards the Germans. On the other hand, Kelly felt that the German gesture was indicative of the respect the *Luftwaffe* officers had for their RAF counterparts, while they held the Irish army in little more than contempt.

In January 1943 Hempel asked for permission for Georg Fleischmann to spend a night at the German legation, but this was refused by army authorities on the grounds that the Minister for Defence had given permission for Muller's visit on a once-off basis.

"Hempel took this rather amiss," Frederick Boland of the Department of External Affairs noted. The German minister complained he was "doing his best to make things easier for the internees", for whom a night in Dublin was a particular treat. He was trying to relieve the monotony of internment by inviting the officers to join other Germans at the legation for dinner, but if the internees had to be back at the camp in time they had to be in the city centre by nine-thirty to catch the last bus to the Curragh, which simply did not leave them enough time to attend the dinner party. If necessary, Hempel was prepared to send Fleischmann back by taxi, but he felt this would be needlessly expensive. He hoped to have each of the officers to dinner in turn, but if he had to hire taxis it would be necessary to have three or four at a time and this would tend to undermine his aim of providing them with a break from the camp.

There was "an element of reasonableness" to Hempel's request, according to Walshe. "His object in inviting the officer internees to the parties at all is, I think, the laudable and well intentioned one of trying to cheer them up and remove some of the complaints they make." The Department of External Affairs sympathised with the Germans and asked General MacMahon to reconsider the Fleischmann case, because it was "unreasonable and inconsiderate" to require Hempel to send the men back by car or taxi when they could go back by bus with just three hours extra parole.

The Department of Defence relented in this instance, but balked a few days later when one of the Allied internees sought permission to travel to Dublin four days a week in order to attend Rathmines Technical College. It was decided, however, that the internees would henceforth be permitted to visit Dublin four times each month instead of once, as had been the case for the past two years.

During 1943 Mollenhauer continued to demand that the German internees be moved to a new camp. On 5 April he made a formal complaint that one of his men had been assaulted by an Allied sergeant outside the Grand Hotel in Newbridge. Ward contended, on the other hand, that the Allied sergeant in question – Jan Zimek, the Pole interned the previous October – had actually been the victim; that he was tripped by one of the Germans and had not even retaliated. Zimek's subsequent activities, however, raised questions about his behaviour on the night.

On 16 May 1943 there was an incident at a dance in Newbridge. The German Willi Krupp and the Pole Stanley Kerniewski were talking together at the back of the hall when Zimek came over and criticised Kerniewski for speaking to that "fucking German" when the Germans as a whole were treating the Polish people as an inferior race.

Afterwards, according to one account, Krupp and four other Germans followed Zimek out of the dance-hall, and one of them supposedly struck him from behind. When he tried to retaliate, the other Germans restrained him. No doubt the scrap was typical of many such incidents outside dance-halls throughout the country that night, and certainly did not warrant being turned into an international incident. But two weeks later a more serious matter involving the 25-year-old Zimek occurred at a dance on 1 June. After dancing with a local girl, Zimek asked her to sit with him. Before she could sit down, however, one of the Germans, Otto Jaeger, asked her to dance. She refused, much to Zimek's delight.

"You did not dance with Jerry," he said. "That was right."

During the night they danced together several times and she agreed to have Zimek see her home, but they became separated on leaving the hall. The next time he saw her she was walking down the street with another girl, followed by two German NCOs, Karl Hund and Josef Reiser, with their bicycles. The Germans started talking to the girls as they reached the outskirts of the town. As Zimek passed them on his bicycle the girl waved to him to carry on, but the idea of being dumped for a German was too much for him. He turned and began cycling around them in circles. The girls became frightened.

"We were afraid," the girl who had been with Zimek explained. "I have never seen any men or boys acting in this manner previously."

As the girls walked off, Zimek collided with Hund's bicycle and fell to the ground. The Pole became quite abusive, calling them "fucking Germans", according to Reiser, who said Zimek was about to strike out but Hund, a proficient amateur boxer, landed first with his right fist. Zimek fell and struck his head on the road. As he lay there unconscious, the two Germans dragged him to the side of the road and left him.

Some of the Allied internees, who were drinking in the Central Hotel, learned what had happened and went to the scene, where they arranged to have a car take Zimek to the Curragh military hospital. A fractured skull was diagnosed and he was moved to Sir Patrick Dun's Hospital, Dublin, where his condition quickly improved, though he remained extremely irritable.

Fearing that the incident would lead to serious trouble between the Allied and German internees, McNally now supported the idea of establishing completely separate internment camps. Until the tension died down, he restricted parole so that each set of internees was allowed out on alternate days. This was soon modified to daily parole until six o'clock in the evening, with parole thereafter for each side on alternate evenings, until things returned to normal.

Hempel renewed his call to have the German internees moved to another location. Maffey, too, called for the camps to be separated and he asked for Zimek's release, because the Pole was threatening to kill Hund when he got out of hospital. "There is obviously a good case on all counts for getting him out of the country without delay, and I hope this course will be followed," Maffey wrote. Otherwise, he warned that Zimek would cause trouble not only between the German and Allied internees but even among the Allied internees themselves.

Freddy Boland agreed. He told de Valera that the doctors were afraid Zimek was likely to "do himself a serious injury," if returned to the camp. The Department of Defence made it clear that it "would be glad to be rid of this Pole", with the result that de Valera agreed to hand him over to the British on "compassionate" grounds. Zimek was transferred to Northern Ireland on 3 July 1943. His release set a precedent for three others to be let go on compassionate grounds in the following months. In addition, the Zimek affair went a long way towards persuading the Irish authorities to split up the German and British camps, but not in the way the Germans had hoped.

THE CALDER CAPER

AFTER THE DISAPPOINTMENT of failing to escape in the break-out of August 1942, some of the men did a lot of socialising. Calder became friendly with a local girl named Anne, who was home on leave from the WRENS (the British Women's Royal Naval Service), and embarked on an elaborate escape attempt with her help. His plan was to feign madness in order that he would be transferred to hospital without signing parole. Anne agreed to help him and Dr Wilson loaned him some medical books and advised him on the symptoms of a mental breakdown. He also coached Calder on the questions he would have to answer to deceive the medics. The only other person who knew of Calder's scheme, which was intended to take several months, was Bruce Girdlestone.

The 27-year-old Calder withdrew socially and began to write a book, which surprised no one since he had been a journalist before the war. He had served for a time as a sports reporter on the *Daily News* in Chatham, Ontario, before joining the Canadian Press wire service. During five years with the agency in Montreal and Toronto, he rose to take charge of the Ontario sports desk in Toronto.

While in Britain before his internment, he contributed a number of articles to Canadian newspapers. One concerned a visit to Windsor castle shortly after his arrival. He was on a routine tour along with 54 other airmen from various parts of the British Empire when they were suddenly invited to have afternoon tea with the Royal family. As the senior Canadian officer present, Calder introduced his own colleagues and then observed the proceedings with the careful eye of a trained newsman, knowing he had a good story. He noted the King mentioning that the beautiful flower-beds in the castle's garden were being turned into vegetable plots because Britain needed to grow as much food as possible. The Queen talked about the family's pre-war visit to Canada, and Princesses Elizabeth and Margaret chatted with the men. Pilot Officer Hugh Miller of Windsor, Nova Scotia, playfully asked the girls whether they preferred the traditional red coats of the Royal Canadian Mounted Police, or the blue uniforms of the RCAF.

"Oh," the young future queen replied tactfully, "I don't know." But her younger sister was more forthright.

"I like the red coats best," Princess Margaret said.

"Even better than the air force uniforms?" asked Pilot Officer Bob Mitchell of Estevan, Saskatchewan.

"Well," she replied, "they're brighter, aren't they!"

The account of that royal meeting, which Calder filed with Canadian Press, made front page news across Canada, as did his account some weeks later of a daylight bombing raid on Brest to attack the German battleship, *Gneisenau*, which was in dry-dock in the French port. It was Calder's first daylight raid and his report was carried prominently not only in Canadian newspapers but also in the United States. It was reputed to be the first eyewitness account published in North America of a bombing raid as seen from the air by a participant.

The raid was not particularly successful, as none of the three planes in the formation managed to hit the battleship. "I saw the bombs bursting slightly to the left and beyond the target," Calder wrote. "At least we had helped to mess up the docks." The raiding party was, however, officially credited with shooting down three enemy aircraft and "Slapsie Maxie", their New Zealand leader, was awarded the Distinguished Flying Cross. "We were shot up slightly," Calder noted, "but no one was hurt."

Later he wrote of the events leading to his internment for the influential Canadian journal, *Maclean's Magazine*. Now with so much time on his hands, it seemed quite natural he should write a book. Part of his plan was to refuse parole and spend most of each day writing. Every afternoon at about four o'clock he would take a break and go for a run around the compound before returning to his typewriter. Then at meals he would often get into heated arguments with Girdlestone. These were, of course, staged but they were very convincing, and it was not long before Calder's anti-social behaviour was attracting the attention of both his colleagues and the guards.

By June 1943 he was ready to implement the final stages of his plan. It seemed a good time to play on the humanitarian feelings of the Irish authorities, as they had been particularly amenable to approaches on compassionate grounds in recent weeks. Not only had Zimek been released, but on 12 June they allowed Wakelin two weeks' parole to visit his mother in England following the death of his father. Ten days later Ward was given a similar parole to visit his wife, who was ill in England.

Calder had prepared for the final implementation of his scheme by bolstering the seriousness of his writing. He submitted five more articles to Canadian Press. These articles, which began appearing in newspapers throughout Canada during June, infuriated some of his colleagues, who resented his depiction of the camp as a virtual holiday resort. They were "almost living the life of Riley", he wrote. The *Toronto Star* actually headlined its article: "Interned Canadian Fliers Live Life of Riley in Eire."

"Because of parole conditions, a reasonable plenitude of good food and excellent recreation facilities, our internment is in striking contrast to usual prisoner-of-war treatment," he wrote. "So friendly are some Dublin merchants that we are able to maintain a first-class bar in the camp. We may bring in as much food as we can buy. It would be a luxurious way of living through the war, for we remain on full pay. Those who want to may study for post-war activities."

Of course, it was ridiculous to describe conditions at K Lines as "luxurious", and his colleagues could not understand him depicting the place in this light, because this would likely weaken British and Canadian pressure on the Dublin government to release the Allied airmen. Moreover the men resented the manner in which Calder played down their disgust at being interned and presented an understanding, if not sympathetic account of what was happening in Ireland. His description of the attitudes of the Irish people was balanced. He noted, for instance, that James Dillon, the deputy leader of the opposition, was the only Irish politician to call on the Dublin government to join the Allies, but his efforts had been ineffective.

"The main result of his words," Calder wrote, "was to stir up anti-Irish feelings abroad, where he was widely quoted." At home his brave stand had a negative impact. He was forced to resign not only as deputy leader of his party but from the party itself.

Calder related how the Allied internees had been tormented by the German celebrations in the early months, but that this had begun to change in the autumn of 1942 when the tide of battle turned in North Africa. "We smuggled fireworks into our quarters," Calder wrote. When the news broke of the victory at El Alamein and Montgomery's counter-attack, the internees set off their fireworks. "The young Nazis have never had a chance to reply to the hullabaloo we raised that night."

News of the Allied successes was generally welcomed in Ireland. "I have found," Calder explained, "great relief at the fact that the Axis is being hammered at last."

"Rightly or wrongly," Chuck Brady recalled years later, "many of us felt that until the victory at El Alamein, many Irishmen felt that Germany would win the war and that they were playing it cosy, but after that turning point, as well as the American entry into the war, their belief changed and it certainly appeared that we were looked upon more favourably."

Calder had ulterior motives in writing the articles. They bolstered his notoriety, and in a very subtle way drew attention to himself and his peculiar behaviour during recent months. The time had come to implement the final stage of his plan. He arranged for his girlfriend to send him a letter breaking off their relationship on the grounds that he was more interested in his book than in her. The letter was really for the eyes of the army censor, who was expected to inform the camp commandant; he apparently did because the commandant openly expressed concern about Calder's condition.

On the night of 25 June 1943 as a guard was making his rounds Calder flew into a rage. He threw his typewriter on the floor and stomped on it before grabbing his manuscript and tearing it into shreds. Then he dissolved into tears.

"Even I was awed at the display," wrote Girdlestone, who knew it was only an act. He actually had a copy of Calder's manuscript hidden away.

Calder had studied the Irish temperament and concluded that it consisted of a mixture of deep sentimentality and excitability. During the months he was supposedly slipping into his mental depression, he was playing on the sentimentality, and now the time had come to play on the excitability.

The guards were genuinely concerned when he seemed to go on a tremendous drinking spree. In the course of three days he emptied three bottles of brandy at a rate that he might have drunk them. He washed out his mouth and brushed his teeth with brandy. His breath was foul and his drunken displays convincing. At the end of the second day, Girdlestone told Brady and Harkell, whose help he needed, what was actually happening. They were amazed. They had been completely taken in by Calder and were convinced he was going mad. After they mastered their amazement, the New Zealander went over the details of what they were to do the following night.

Shortly before midnight on the third day of Calder's spree, as Brady and Girdlestone were involved in a card game in the officer's anteroom, Harkell – whose room was next door to Calder's – burst in excitedly.

"Mr Calder!" he said. "Something's the matter with Mr Calder!"

The men rushed out and found Calder writhing in mock pain on the floor, his mouth covered with iodine stains. The guards had been alerted by the commotion, and Girdlestone ran to the fence and shouted to them that Calder had tried to commit suicide. The captain of the guard took one look at Calder and called an ambulance, but Girdlestone argued that there was not enough time and asked that Calder be taken to hospital immediately in an army truck. Calder was carried from his room and placed full length on the floor of the truck, and the captain of the guard suggested that Girdlestone should accompany him to the hospital. The New Zealander signed out on parole and hopped on to the truck.

On reaching a tree-lined area on route, Girdlestone asked the driver to stop as Calder wanted to get sick. The driver duly obliged and the guards helped Calder down. He suddenly gave a mighty heave and tried to bolt, but one of the guards managed to hold on to him long enough for his colleague to regain his balance and together they overpowered Calder. Girdlestone, not daring to give any active assistance, could only look on helplessly. The guards immediately became suspicious, but Girdlestone contended that the Canadian was having some kind of spasm. They continued to the military hospital, where Calder was treated with an antidote for the iodine. Next day, at the suggestion of Kearney, the Canadian High Commissioner, he was moved to Sir Patrick Dun's Hospital, Dublin, where he continued to feign depression.

Although warned that Calder's effort might be part of an escape attempt, the report of his actions was so convincing that Kearney was not sure. He pretended, however, to be convinced that the airman was trying to kill himself and asked the Department of External Affairs to release Calder on humanitarian grounds. One of the last things the Irish wanted was the bad publicity that would inevitably follow if their most famous internee should commit suicide, and they readily agreed to his release. Calder was moved to hospital in Britain on 1 July 1943, and, as he told his family, he had more trouble convincing the British doctors he was sane than he had in persuading the Irish that he was mad. Some of his colleagues never forgave him for the false reports he had written of camp life. Leslie Diaper, one of those who had baled out with him over the Clare coast in October 1941, was still bitter more than four decades later. "Calder was a journalist," he snapped when asked about him. "And like all journalists, he was a liar."

Within a week of his transfer Calder was discharged from hospital and allowed to rejoin his unit. He was quickly back in action, but as he returned from his sixth mission his plane crashed into a mountain in Scotland. He was the lone survivor. A young woman pulled him from the burning wreckage, and for some days his life hung in the balance as doctors deliberated on whether or not it would be necessary to amputate one of his legs. This did not prove necessary.

Calder spent several months convalescing at the Royal Victoria Hospital in East Grinstead, where he wrote another widely circulated article – this time on the medical treatment that Canadian airmen were receiving. He turned the first sod for a Canadian wing being added to the hospital and caused some embarrassment in Ireland by giving an interview on the BBC World Service in which he admitted taking part in a bombing raid after his release from the Curragh. Hempel duly learned of the interview and exploited the fact to obtain concessions for the German internees.

After nine months Calder was fit enough to return to active duty, and he began flying combat missions in July 1944. "I'm happy to be into the thick of things again," he wrote to his mother. "We shall be working very fast and hard." But he also anticipated having leave "to see a good deal more of these islands than I have seen already. I have been fortunate in that respect haven't I?"

Within a few days his plane received a direct hit from anti-aircraft fire while on a bombing mission over Hamburg. With the plane in flames, the English pilot ordered the crew to bale out.

"Jack had some difficulty in leaving the aircraft," the pilot recalled, "but I myself saw him clip his parachute on and leave. I followed him out. Unfortunately," the pilot continued, "we were over the coast and the wind blew us out to sea." While the pilot had his seat-type dinghy on, he recalled that navigators never wore them while they were bombing and that "Jack was not wearing his when he baled out".

"Whether Jack landed in the sea or not," the pilot wrote to Calder's parents after the war, "I could not say, but there having not been any news of him would seem to suggest that. I made many enquiries through the Red Cross and various sources whilst I was in the POW camp, but the answer was always in the negative."

Calder was probably already dead when his mother received her last letter from him, which was mailed a few days before the fatal mission.

"If I should go 'missing'," the young airman concluded, "I would want you to be very quiet about it – particularly when the newspapers phone – because I probably would be walking back to you. And if I should fail to get clear, I would want you to think of me walking towards you anyway, for that is what I would want to be doing. There is no death, you know."

The Tunnel and the Move

While Calder was working on his escape plan, Girdlestone and Remy started on a scheme of their own. They decided to dig their way out.

In the past some tunnels had been attempted from the mess, which was the only hut built into the ground – all the other huts were raised and the underneath of each was lit at night. The Irish guards checked the mess regularly though, and each effort was discovered before it really got going.

Girdlestone and Remy decided that they would try digging from one of the raised huts. They thought up a scheme to screen the two-foot-six-inch gap between the floor of the hut and the ground. They thought that if they could position a dog kennel underneath the hut, they would cut through the floorboards and work through the kennel into the earth.

The first step was to acquire a dog. Colonel McNally, the camp commandant, was an enthusiastic breeder of gun dogs, so Girdlestone began to show a keen interest in them and managed to acquire a pup as a present. The New Zealander and his French colleague then brought Covington and Brady in on the scheme. They made sure the dog got in everybody's way, so there was no suspicion when they asked the guards to build a kennel for it. The kennel fitted under the hut all right, but after cutting the trap in the floor of Covington's room, the men found to their disgust that the spacing between the floor joists was too narrow to allow a person pass through.

Undeterred they asked for the kennel to be moved instead to a lean-to bicycle shed attached to the hut. As the dog was only likely to prove a nuisance at this stage, they gave him away, but left the kennel in place until the guards became used to its presence. In early February 1943, they began digging the tunnel under the kennel. They bought a barrel of Guinness stout from the bar and took it over to Covington's room, where the non-drinking Remy watched impatiently as his colleagues drank the contents. After dismantling the wooden crate and burning its staves in the stove, they used the bottom as a manhole cover for the mouth of the tunnel.

It was a measure of the distrust existing among the Allied internees that those digging the tunnel felt it necessary to keep it secrect from their colleagues as much as from the guards. As a result they were only able to dig at lunch- and tea-times because the other internees used the shed too much at other times during the day. At night the frequent checks by the guards made digging too risky. They rigged up a crude warning system to tell the digger when someone was approaching the shed. Remy's room overlooked both the camp gate and the bicycle shed entrance, so a string with a stone attached to it as a pendulum was run through eyescrews from the hut to Remy's room. A couple of tugs on the string swung the stone against the shed and sounded a warning.

Work on the tunnel continued during March. On St Patrick's night the internees had a birthday party for Brady at Osberstown House, and during the party Covington announced his engagement to a local girl, Noleen McMahon. Brady had hardly got over the party when he was rushed to Sir Patrick Dun's hospital for an emergency appendectomy. He told "such a rosy story" of his treatment by the nurses that "all of the boys were keen to experience it". Two of the English sergeants went in for minor treatment and, "not to be outdone", Midgely went in to be circumcised, according to one of his colleagues. It was certainly a rather novel way to meet the nurses, if that was his real aim.

Covington's marriage plans ran into a bit of a snag in the following days. Like many of the internees, he equated Roman Catholicism with the narrow sense of Irish nationalism on which he blamed his internment, so he was not willing to have a Catholic wedding, whereas his fiancée's family insisted that their daughter be married in a Roman Catholic church.

"Covey was definitely not going to have a Catholic ceremony," Girdlestone recalled. "On the eve before the wedding, we took four of our sergeants down to Nolie's house. While Covey chatted to the parents, we sneaked out Nolie's luggage through her bedroom window and she spent the night with some pro-English friends." Next morning, 3 May 1943, the couple were married at the Church of Ireland in Ballysacs, and they had a reception afterwards in a Newbridge factory. "The wedding caused great consternation to the entire Catholic community which believed that unless a priest is present at a mixed marriage, the couple are living in sin!" Girdlestone continued. The internees believed it was as a direct result of Covington's wedding that the Roman Catholic Archbishop of Dublin spoke out on the danger of mixed marriages shortly afterwards.

In the midst of these activities the work became so strenuous for the four officers that they invited three British sergeants – Harkell, Ricketts and Reid – to join them. The new men were enthusiastic and the work proceeded apace. They dug down several feet and then turned horizontally towards the nearest fence, keeping true direction with a compass and measuring their progress with a length of string. The digging was interrupted first by Covington's marriage and again after the incident between Zimek and the Germans. With the curtailment of parole it was too risky going into the tunnel, especially when they were anxious to keep the secret among the seven of them. In the long run the incident had an even greater consequence in that it, more than anything else, persuaded the authorities to separate the German and Allied internees. Those involved in the tunnel project had to work with the added pressure of knowing that all their efforts would be for nothing if they did not finish before being transferred.

As the tunnel got longer, the diggers began to have difficulty breathing. They could not construct air vents because the ground above them opened into the compound, so they had to devise a system of pumping fresh air to the end of the tunnel. Covington tried to construct a pipe by using cylindrical cigarette tins, but this proved ineffective, so they decided to attach bellows to a garden hose and pump the air in that way. Procuring the hose and the bellows, however, was no straightforward matter: if they purchased a hose in the locality the guards would undoubtedly learn of it. In the end they decided to steal one. The task proved more difficult than they had expected.

"There is so much rain in Éire," Girdlestone wrote, "that one wondered whether or not the angels had their bathroom directly overhead. Garden hoses were therefore extremely rare."

Eventually they saw a hose in the back-yard of a house in Newbridge. "That night," Girdlestone continued, "we broke into the yard and slipped away with the hose, cut it into portable lengths and smuggled it into the camp as we returned from parole. Now we only needed the bellows." But the time factor suddenly became critical. On 6 September Wing Commander Begg visited K lines and told the internees they were to be moved to a new camp in Gormanston, Co. Meath, in about six weeks time. He asked the men "not to attempt any breaks, as negotiations with the Irish were developing very favourably" for their release. The men had been hearing that story since the United States entered the war. Covington and Girdlestone exchanged winks and pretended to agree to sit still. But Harkell and Reid were in a different position. They felt it would be foolish to continue if the tunnel endangered the chances of their release, especially when there was no guarantee their escape plan would succeed. "They feared repercussions from the British Office if their part in an escaping attempt were discovered," Girdlestone noted. "Being sergeants, they did not want to defy the British Office."

"Under the present circumstances," Harkell explained, "I feel that the scheme is wrong in principle, in view of what is at stake, and find it useless to try to continue." Nevertheless both he and Reid promised not to reveal the existence of the tunnel to anyone.

"As far as secrecy is concerned," Reid said, "you may rest assured that I will give nothing away."

The following week two more Allied internees got married. Donald Taylor from Lincoln married his fiancée, who came over from Darlington, England, and next day, 14 September, Ros Tees married Eileen Lewis of Newbridge in the Protestant church at the Curragh Camp. The latter wedding afforded the tunnel group their opportunity of getting the bellows.

"It was a large wedding and we all were there in force,"

Girdlestone explained. "The whole Curragh knew about the ceremony. When the festivities were at their height, Covey, Ricketts, Remy and I, slipped away to the local grocery store where we had previously seen some bellows on display. All of us were noticeably bright and hilarious when we arrived in the store which was filled with Irish soldiers, some of them being our guards off duty."

"I say old boy," Covington began, "what about a wedding present for Tees?"

"That is a good idea," replied Remy in his husky French accent.

They began selecting items. Covington picked out an egg beater, Remy bought a tin opener, Girdlestone selected a rolling pin, while Ricketts acted as if he were unable to make up his mind, before settling for the bellows. "The whole store was amused and several people were shaking their heads declaring that the English were always a little mad," according to Girdlestone.

Although Girdlestone and his colleagues had their doubts, Maffey was indeed trying tirelessly to arrange their release. When de Valera insisted that he would have to release the Germans if he released all of the Allied airmen, Maffey had switched his approach and tried to persuade the Taoiseach to apply the non-operational argument retroactively. And he enlisted the help of the Canadian High Commissioner. While the internees were at Tees's wedding on 14 September, Kearney was writing a "most secret" despatch to his government in Ottawa outlining the result of their efforts:

> Mr de Valera informed me that he was taking the necessary steps to transfer all Allied internees from the camp at the Curragh to another camp, but he was having some difficulty in finding a suitable location and material with which to equip it. He also said that he had decided to make the "non-operation flight" ruling retroactive, and, at the same time as the Allied internment camp was transferred, those airmen who landed in Eire and interned while not engaged in operational flights would be released. He told me that, although Sir John Maffey had suggested that all Allied internees be re-

leased, regardless of the circumstances under which they landed in Eire, he did not see how he could accede to this request. I understand that the liberation will take place when the new internment camp, which is to be located at Gormanston, Co. Meath, (a small watering-place about twenty miles north of Dublin) will be ready, which will be sometime next month. Mr de Valera, in the course of his remarks, said that, if and when his action with regard to the release of Allied internees became known to the Dáil and the public, he and his Government would be subject to some criticism, but he regarded his action in the matter as being in accordance with his policy of "benevolent neutrality", and that this was another occasion wherein he had more than stretched a point.

News of their impending release was deliberately withheld from the internees for fear the Germans might somehow find out and scuttle the arrangement by protesting. All the internees knew was that the Allied airmen were being transferred to Gormanston.

"We learned that the new camp would be ready by the middle of October," Girdlestone recalled. "We felt sure that we could complete the tunnel by that time if we worked double shifts, so feverishly we set to work." It was hard work, especially after their numbers had been diminished by the withdrawal of Reid and Harkell, but for the remainder of the week they were spurred on by the thought of the months of work that would be wasted if the tunnel was not finished in time.

Suddenly the proverbial thunderbolt struck. On 18 September the men woke to the sound of digging. Their tunnel had been discovered; the Irish guards were digging it out.

Morale was so low and distrust so rampant in the Allied compound that the tunnel group thought they were betrayed by their own colleagues. "We later discovered," Girdlestone explained, "that Welpy had seen Covey going down the tunnel mouth a few days previously. He had informed Ward, the senior officer, who told the British Office. The Irish were then informed and a quick stop was put to our activities! Incredible, isn't it?

"For three days," he added, "the camp was a grim spot. Even

the guards could feel the tension."

Maffey learned of what had happened and he came down to the camp personally to give the men news he had not intended divulging for some weeks. Twenty of the internees were to be secretly repatriated while they were being transferred to Gormanston Camp. He warned that the information was given in the strictest confidence because the Irish authorities did not want the Germans to know about the repatriation.

There is some confusion about how exactly the tunnel was found. The Irish records indicate that the guards' suspicions were roused when they discovered bags of earth in the Allied compound. Kelly accepted the explanation that these were merely being held as fire extinguishers in case the Germans tried to set fire to one of the Allied huts, but the guards were not so gullible. A search unearthed three half-filled bags of earth in the kennel on 14 September. Kelly then went to Ward and told him that the guards knew there was a tunnel and pleaded with him to disclose its location as it would be found anyway. The two of them had got on well together and Kelly pretended that he was going to be in deep trouble if he did not find the tunnel. At that point Ward presumably did not know where the tunnel lay, but he evidently found out and, following a telephone discussion with Maffey, he informed Kelly. Kelly was amazed at the professionalism of the structure when he saw it the following morning. Irish soldiers proceeded to dig it up while the internees were still in bed.

Despite this incident, the Irish stood over their promise to give "a liberal interpretation to the phrase 'non-operational flight'". When Maffey requested the release of all but 13 of the men, de Valera also agreed to release Remy and Brady as well. Maffey was still not content, however. On 9 October he again tried to persuade de Valera to release all the Allied airmen at one time. If the Irish continued to hold those who had b een on operational flights, he told him, it would eventually become necessary to intern Americans. If that should happen, Maffey warned, it could lead to trouble with the Americans.

"I see," de Valera replied. "This needs thought."

"I feel convinced that previous to this talk the policy vaguely developing in his mind was to avoid interning Americans on some pretext or other but to hang on to our airmen as a shop window exhibit of neutrality," Maffey reported. He tried to hammer home his point in a conversation with Walshe a couple of days later.

"He said he knew perfectly well that, if we interned any American airmen, we might get a very 'bloody' Note," Walshe reported. "I felt I could not let that remark pass, and I said that, if we got a 'bloody' Note, we'd send back a Note more 'bloody' still."

"It was no argument in our eyes for their retaining our eleven airmen to keep the Germans quiet," Maffey insisted. "If other methods were difficult, why not allow the eleven men to escape?" Walshe did not commit himself on this point, but he did give the British representative "the impression that we shall be able to work matters out this way if no better way presents itself".

De Valera's government was actually in a weak position. He had lost his overall majority in a general election in June 1943 and was now dependent on the support of some independent deputies, who were all determined to avoid involvement in the war. He "seemed obsessed by the 'fifty-fifty' neutrality idea," Maffey noted, observing that the Irish leader possessed a "Himalayan obstinacy". When de Valera argued once more that he could only release all the Allies if he also let the Germans go, "I left him in no doubt for the fiftieth time as to the complete unacceptability of any such plan, and I took the opportunity of ramming in for the fiftieth time our grave apprehensions regarding any German in Éire," Maffey reported.

The Allied airmen left the Curragh camp for the last time on 18 October 1943. "There were no tears shed," Girdlestone wrote.

They travelled first to Dublin in a military convoy. Two motor cycles in the lead were followed by a truck of armed guards. The 20 men being released came next, followed by a truck with their luggage, then the twelve men being transferred to Gormanston with their luggage in a fifth truck. A second truck-load of armed guards, followed by a military staff car, took up the rear.

The convoy split up in the Phoenix Park, Dublin. While the others went on to Gormanston, the men being released headed for Northern Ireland. Their families were notified that they had been freed, but were given no details, other than a suggestion that they had actually escaped. "I have to ask that you will treat this information as confidential and do your utmost to ensure that no mention of his escape appears in the press," the New Zealand naval secretary informed Girdlestone's parents.

Girdlestone wrote of the events to his mother. He had managed to have two letters smuggled to her via England while he was interned, but in his other letters he had felt strongly inhibited by the censorship. Now he gave a full account. "There's nothing more to tell," he wrote in winding up his story. "Individually we liked the Irish, with their sentimentality, brogue and blarney, but the wartime intrigue of an internment camp is hardly an environment in which to paint the Emerald Isle red!

"Ireland is a great place to come from," he concluded.

In Gormanston

THE ELEVEN MEN interned at Gormanston were all sergeants – seven English, three Scots and a Welshman. They were what remained of three different crews which had unquestionably been on operational flights. Calder had admitted in his *Maclean's* article that his plane was returning from a bombing mission, so the Irish held on to Browne and Diaper; Virtue, the fourth member of that crew, had been released in September 1943. Fred Tisdall had also admitted in a letter published in the *Toronto Globe & Mail* that Wakelin, Newby, Reid and himself had been on an operational flight.

The remaining five were the crew of an RAF Wellington bomber which came down about two miles east of Waterford in the early hours of 17 February 1943 while returning from a bombing mission over France. They had been lost for some time and decided on a forced landing because they were running low on fuel. One wing struck a tree on landing and the aircraft burst into flames, but everyone escaped serious injury. The crew consisted of two Scots from Edinburgh, George Slater and Eric Ross, and three Englishmen – James Holloway from London, Donald Taylor from Lincoln, and Frank Thomas from Newton-Lee-Willows, Lancashire. Their initial internment probably owed much to the fact that they arrived just a few weeks after the release of the American generals who had crashed at Athenry. Hempel had complained about that, and the crew of the Wellington were given as a kind of peace offering to the German minister.

The internees at Gormanston were accorded a parole area extending to a ten-mile radius from the camp, which allowed them scope to explore an area that was new to them. They were also permitted to go to Dublin once a week. Most of the men just signed out each day until eight o'clock the following morning; since they could sign out again immediately, it meant that they really only had to report to the camp each morning. The married men – Browne and Diaper – could stay with their wives until eleven o'clock three mornings a week. Eric Ross was given permission to attend classes at Rathmines Technical College in Dublin two days a week and he, Slater and Reid joined Drogheda Rugby Club and won places on the club's first fifteen. They played in all the club's home games and were given special parole to travel to Dundalk for a vital cup match.

Yet the internees did not even wait to settle in before they began scheming to escape. Thomas and Taylor moved to get out on compassionate grounds, like Calder and Zimek before them. Thomas complained of suffering from violent headaches, which a specialist doctor attributed to an injury received in crashing. On 11 November 1943 Maffey asked that Thomas be invalided out of the country. De Valera agreed and the airman was released on 26 November.

Taylor's scheme was to feign a mental breakdown. He refused to shave or bathe and he frequently barricaded himself in his room, where he complained of seeing threatening shadows. A psychiatrist suggested Taylor's "removal to hospital for mental observation as soon as possible." He was turned over to the British authorities at the border next day, 25 January 1944.

Ross was also released on compassionate grounds a few weeks later after he broke his ankle while playing rugby. Maffey had jumped at the opportunity to ask for the airman's release so that he could be treated at a military hospital in Northern Ireland, but the Irish initially felt competent to deal with such a straightforward medical problem. Maffey's case was strengthened, however, when the bone was set improperly and the ankle had to be broken again for resetting the following week. Tisdall, the senior Allied internee, reported that Ross was very perturbed, and Maffey protested to the Department of External Affairs. This time de Valera intervened to secure the airman's transfer to Northern Ireland.

The other internees tried to tunnel their way out of Gormanston. Reid, who had been involved in the tunnel at the

Curragh, set about using his expertise, and was quickly active in planning two separate tunnels in the new camp. The first was discovered before it really began.

On 12 November while all of the men were out on parole, two Irish captains searched their rooms and discovered a 15-inch-square trap cut in the floor of a built-in closet in Newby's room. The two captains also found hand spades in the rooms of Reid and Taylor. The following week they checked again. This time they found Newby's German shepherd guarding the locked closet, but the officers were able to force the dog to retreat by shining a torch-beam in his eyes. They discovered that the internees had started excavating and had dug down about a foot and a half. The hole was covered with a wooden frame with sods of earth placed on top.

Captain T.J. Ringrose got permission from Army Headquarters to allow the men to continue as it would "keep them off other ways and means of escaping". The guards were ordered to keep an eye on the progress of the tunnel and to intervene before it got too far. As they checked one night, in the near darkness they disturbed a thread left on the door. The internees knew at once the guards were on to their tunnel; they continued to use it as a diversion while they began working on a second.

On 3 February 1944 the guards found that a four-foot-square trap-door had been cut in the floor of an unoccupied room in the internees' sleeping quarters. This room was always locked, but the men had somehow acquired a key. There was no dog to protect this opening, and on examining it closely the guards found a thin tread, which they carefully replaced afterwards. The finding was reported to Army Headquarters, which gave permission for the guards to follow the same procedure as before. They watched from their vantage point in the internees' dining-room, as Browne, Holloway, Wakelin and Slater worked on the tunnel late at night. By the end of March the internees had dug about a quarter of the way to the fence. Within a month they were so close to completion that the perimeter guards could hear their digging. Army Headquarters decided it was time to call a halt. At 2 a.m. on 1 May a small search party barged into the hut. They found Reid at the opening; Holloway was in the tunnel. They had a kit bag to hold the earth, dry and wet batteries and a bicycle lamp. It took the guards five hours to fill in the tunnel.

Although this proved a bitter disappointment to the men, they had only a short time to remain at the camp. Following the successful Allied invasion of Normandy on 6 June 1944, Maffey exerted strong pressure on de Valera to release the remaining airmen. Initially the Taoiseach held firm.

"In regard to our interned airmen," Maffey reported on 10 June, "he told me in the most explicit manner that he had re-examined the matter with every desire to be helpful – particularly to me personally – but that he found it quite impossible to give way on this point."

Only the previous month de Valera had won a handsome majority in a general election which he called to capitalise on his domestic popularity following his rejection of the American Note demanding the expulsion of the Axis representatives. Having governed for almost a year with a minority government, he was now safely in power and could not pretend that he lacked the authority to release the remaining Allied airmen.

"Quite unforeseeable complications would accrue if this question produced no more than an impasse," Maffey warned. The British representative was going to London for consultations and he demanded to know exactly where de Valera stood in the matter:

> Mr de Valera paced about the room uneasily and said that as today was Saturday he would not be able to get in touch with his cabinet before my departure. I said that we required to have his answer in London at the latest before early on Tuesday morning. I should expect a telephone message in London from Mr Walshe one way or the other on Monday evening. Mr de Valera said he would arrange this.

The British representative had issued a virtual ultimatum. Unless Dublin released the remaining men, Britain would tighten the economic screws.

"He was obviously badly shaken," Maffey reported. "It is so much for a neutral to think that supplies are a kind of manna dropping as the gentle dew from Heaven. Fortune has spoiled

Mr de Valera by paying him unfailing dividends for his untiring obstinacy." The British representative noted that it was "impossible to forecast" de Valera's decision. "He has the martyr complex and would hunger-strike for a principle. But there are one or two hard-headed men in the Government and we can only wait and see. At any rate the long chapter of arguments and dialectics on this subject is now closed. It may be necessary to give a turn of the screw."

De Valera, however, relented. On 15 June 1944 the eight remaining Allied internees were secretly released and driven to Northern Ireland. The internment camp at Gormanston was closed, though it was opened briefly again to house three German airmen who arrived in Ireland in the final hours of the conflict.

Closing K Lines

Although the Dublin government had tried to keep the release of the Allied airmen in October 1943 a secret, the story soon leaked out. De Valera was questioned about the matter in the Dáil, but he declined to answer in the interest of national security. When Hempel complained to the Department of External Affairs, Boland told him simply that the men had been freed because they had not been engaged in operational duties when they landed in Ireland.

Some weeks later when a German plane made a forced landing near Portroe, Co. Tipperary, Hempel asked that the seven-man crew should be released on the grounds that they had been on a non-operational flight, but his request was rejected. Walshe noted that the plane must have been carrying explosive because, when the crew destroyed it, the resulting explosion was heard some 50 miles away. "It could not be conceived that a German plane would come into such a highly belligerent area as the waters immediately beyond our territory without being fully armed," Walshe noted.

Hempel was just taking a chance. He complained that the Irish government had changed the ground rules in regard to the internment of Allied airmen without notifying him. In the interest of fairness, he thought the German airmen should be released, but the Department of External Affairs did not give him any grounds for hope.

In September 1943, after more than two-and-a-half years in St Brichin's Hospital, Max Hohaus, the only survivor of the six-man crew whose plane had crashed near Durrus, Co. Cork, was released on special parole to spend a month convalescing in the seaside village of Ballybunnion, a popular Irish holiday resort. Since his injuries were such that there was no likelihood that he would ever again play an effective part in the war, the Irish made arrangements to have him returned to Germany as part of a Red Cross swap of maimed Allied and Axis prisoners of war. He was sent to Britain, where he joined injured prisoners being repatriated.

The Irish placated Hempel by making minor concessions on matters like the acquisition of new staff. Back in December 1940 the Germans had tried to increase the size of their legation by transferring some diplomats from the United States, but de Valera had frustrated them. But on 4 October 1943, when Hempel asked for one of the internees as a replacement for his coding clerk, who was seriously ill with cardiac trouble, his request was granted, despite strong objections from Colonel Dan Bryan, the head of G2. Hans Bell of Dusseldorf took up duties at the legation on 10 November 1943, and he was joined some months later by a naval NCO, Horst Huse from Danzig, who acted as doorman.

By then Hempel had learned of the secret release of the Allied airmen during the transfer to Gormanston and he was able to use this to secure further concessions for the men at K Lines. In the past, for instance, the men had been repeatedly denied permission to stay in Dublin overnight, but Mollenhauer's request for a 48-hour parole in Dublin in the run-up to Christmas 1943 was treated more sympathetically.

"These trips to Dublin constitute our only relaxation and distraction in this position," Mollenhauer explained. "Internment, as it progresses, has been to bring harmful mental and physical affects which can be reduced by these visits."

Hempel endorsed the request and let the Department of External Affairs know that he was aware not only of the release of the Allies but also that Calder had returned to active service. When the department checked this, Kearney confirmed that Calder had recently spoken about his exploits on the BBC World Service. Boland concluded that Hempel's request could not be turned down under the circumstances. "The fact that we have released so many British and the German minister is aware of the fact," he argued, "makes it morally difficult to refuse the present request and its refusal might conceivably exacerbate

German feeling over the recent release."

Not only was Hempel able to obtain the requested overnight concessions for the men before Christmas, but he also managed to get special parole for four of the internee officers to move to Dublin in order to attend University College, Dublin, early in the new year. The four, Rudolf Lauer, Eric Kruger, Walter Habich and Arthur Klanke, got a house together in the Mount Merrion area, from where they cycled to the college. Shortly afterwards they were joined by another officer, the Berliner Ernst Muller.

In accordance with their parole conditions, they were supposed to avoid the waterfront and remain within a radius of ten miles from their residence. They were also supposed to remain indoors at their residence between midnight and seven o'clock in the morning and stay away from bars frequented by visiting Allied servicemen, especially the bars in the Gresham, Hibernian and Dolphin hotels. In addition, they were not to associate with people active in Irish or international politics or "do anything that has the slightest political flavour". Each of the internees signed the following typed parole form:

> On being granted leave of absence for the purpose of pursuing a Course of Study at University College, Dublin, I hereby give my word of honour that I will return to my Quarters at the Curragh Camp on the termination of the current College Term; and that while I am on parole I will not make, or endeavour to make, any arrangements whatever, or seek or accept, any assistance whatever, with a view to the escape of myself or my fellow-internees, that I will not engage in any military activities or any activities contrary to the interest of Éire, and that until I am returning to the internment Camp, I will not proceed more than ten (10) miles from my place of residence in Dublin, namely Frankfort, Mount Merrion, Blackrock, Dublin.

On New Year's Day 1944 the internees awoke to the news of the rescue of more than 150 German sailors by the Irish ship, *Kerlogue*. Anxious to meet and talk to the sailors, Mollenhauer asked to be allowed to visit them in Cork, or at least talk to the senior officer on the telephone. His requests were rejected, in part because the authorities feared he might stir up unrest. The

Irish had enough on their hands on the diplomatic front without allowing the *Luftwaffe* internees to take a hand in things.

Maffey, having failed to get the Irish government to compel the *Kerlogue* to stop at a British port after rescuing the sailors and before proceeding to Cobh, was insistent that the Germans should be interned and not allowed to roam about Ireland. He impressed on de Valera that "a German in Éire is a menace to England, while an Englishman in Éire is no menace to Germany." Hempel, on the other hand, wanted the sailors treated as distressed seamen and released. The Irish were in a delicate position, and things were not helped by Mollenhauer, who caused a minor diplomatic incident over the refusal to allow him to contact the sailors in Cork.

"*Hauptmann* Mollenhauer has been very difficult to get on with," Commandant Mackey of G2 reported on 8 January. "With his acute sense of his own importance and his superiority complex and a complete absence of humour, he is not at all liked even by his comrades in the camp." To make matters worse, the intelligence officer added that the German commander "looks upon consideration and kindness as a sign of weakness and so imposes further".

When Mollenhauer kicked up a fuss and got into a heated argument with McNally, McNally accused him of being "insubordinate". Hempel protested to the Department of External Affairs that McNally's accusation was unwarranted. The secretary of the department took the complaint seriously enough to formalise it in an exchange of notes.

"You told me," Walshe responded incredulously to Hempel, "that Captain Mollenhauer held the view that he was not 'subordinate' to the Military Authorities and that he could not, therefore, be regarded as 'insubordinate' however reprehensible his conduct might be. If this were accepted, it would lead to an intolerable situation in which all discipline and order would be undermined. We could not for a moment countenance Captain Mollenhauer's contention."

The controversy was really indicative of the strain developing between Mollenhauer and the army authorities. The whole affair had really nothing to do with practicalities; it was a question of mere semantics. Hempel and Mollenhauer were not contending that the internees were immune from Irish law, nor that they had a right to ignore Irish authorities, but that they were not subordinate to the Irish military. "Everyone, whoever he may be," Hempel wrote, "has to obey the police regulations without on that account – at any rate in German, and as far as I can judge also in English current language – becoming a 'subordinate' for the police."

The Irish army was acutely embarrassed when in the midst of this controversy a number of soldiers attacked *Hauptmann* Muller as he returned from parole on the night of 12 January. It was a particularly cowardly attack by three Irish soldiers on the slight, five-foot five-inch German officer. He was not liked by the Irish soldiers, who considered him an arrogant little Nazi. Mollenhauer protested vehemently and as a result the soldiers were court-martialled and received harsh terms of imprisonment. One was sentenced to twelve months' hard labour, while the others got six and four months each.

The dramatic increase in the number of German internees following the arrival of the sailors posed some serious security difficulties. Even with the removal of the Allied internees from K Lines, there was not enough room to house the sailors there. The camp authorities had felt their security was being stretched to the limit at the Curragh when there were just 70 Allied and Axis internees; now there were three times that number of Germans. It was decided to construct a new camp adjoining Tintown, where IRA internees were held. The sailors were to be given some weeks to settle into the new camp and then the *Luftwaffe* internees would be transferred there also.

Mollenhauer promptly complained about the proposed site of the new camp, with the result that Hempel asked to inspect the area. Anxious to assure themselves that everything was proper, de Valera and Traynor visited the camp in advance of the German minister. These inspections complicated things for the Irish army and did nothing for McNally's already strained relations with Mollenhauer. The army authorities refused to allow him to visit the new camp, but this refusal was personally rescinded by de Valera after Hempel made representations.

Mollenhauer was horrified at conditions in the German compound at Tintown when he visited it on 21 February. "To say I was astonished is putting it mildly," he wrote next day to his girlfriend and future wife, Paula Mecklenberg, who was living with her parents in Dublin. "Primitive is the best way of putting it. It lacks the most essential comforts. The walls are not painted, insufficient sanitary accommodation for the men, the rooms are not divided. One cannot speak of beds. There are only 15 centimeters high from the ground, walls damp, the ground wet and muddy, mildew on the boards, the men must eat from iron utensils."

His letter led to further problems when the military censor took exception to the account and refused to forward it. Having given what he believed was a legitimately critical account of conditions, Mollenhauer resented the high-handed attitude of the censor, motivated more by his sensitivity to criticism than by any security considerations. After all, Mollenhauer would be able to give his girlfriend exactly the same account in person on his next weekly visit to Dublin.

Thoroughly annoyed by Mollenhauer's attitude, Irish authorities were delighted when they learned from Hempel that *Kapitaenleutnant* Joachim Quedenfeld of the *Kerlogue* was going to take over as the commanding officer of the *Luftwaffe,* as well as of the naval internees, once the men from K Lines were moved into the new camp. In March, with this move, K Lines was completely shut down.

SEAMEN IN DISTRESS

IT WAS 26 minutes past ten o'clock on New Year's Eve when Valentia picked up a message from the Irish freighter *Kerlogue*:

> Proceeding Cobh expect arrival 2 a.m. tomorrow morning. Have on board 164 seamen survivors, seven men seriously injured, one man dead. Please instruct port control Cobh that I request urgent medical assistance. Have no food, water or clothing. Kindly telegraph my owners the circumstance.
> Thomas Donohue, Master.

"Will do everything possible for you," Valentia replied. The *Kerlogue*, a 142-foot-long steamer of 335 gross tons, owned by the Wexford Steamship Company, was returning from Portugal with a cargo of oranges. "Soon after leaving Lisbon, the weather became worse," according to one of the crew. "We found ourselves in a ship little larger than an ocean-going tug, ploughing North well out in the Atlantic with the decks awash and rolling heavily."

On the morning of 29 December, when the *Kerlogue* was 362 miles south of the Fastnet Rock and 340 miles west of Brest, a German Focke Wulf Condor aircraft approached the ship and signalled by lamp: "S.O.S. Lifeboats." The captain changed to a southerly course and followed in the direction of the plane. Soon a second Condor appeared and it marked an area by dropping flares. Within a quarter of an hour the ship's ten-man crew found themselves in the midst of a horrific scene.

"The sea was dotted for miles around with men," the first officer recalled. "As rafts rose on the crest of giant waves we could see men on them and others clinging to them. Here and there, there were bits of wreckage with one man, two men and three men hanging on. At first we did not know whether they were

British or German, whether they were survivors of a torpedoed or bombed merchant ship or whether they were warship personnel whose vessel had been sunk in a naval action.

"Then through my glasses I saw that one man was still wearing a naval cap. In the gale the ribbon ends were flying straight out. They were long ribbons, larger than those worn in the British navy. I knew then that the survivors were Germans and German naval personnel at that."

The first survivors were taken on board at 11.45 a.m., and the *Kerlogue* continued to pluck men out of the sea until nine o'clock that night.

"Some were terribly injured," the first officer explained. "All were suffering from shock and exposure. We hauled up some of them with a hook through their clothes. We did not know whether they were alive or dead. Their faces and hands were blue from exposure. They must have been in the water for hours.

"For ten hours we circled around picking up a man here, two men there, half a dozen more from a raft," he continued. "There seemed no end to them. Soon the ship was black with the survivors. They were everywhere."

Fourteen survivors were jammed into the bridge. The passageway was so crammed that no one could pass, while others sat or stood on the companion-ways. There were 57 in the engine room, which was so crowded that the engineer was unable to move across it and had to signal to the rescued sailors to handle instruments that were out of his reach.

The condition of the injured was pitiful. There was no doctor on board and the medical supplies were quite inadequate. Donohue had the worst of the injured put in his cabin and the crew's quarters. Two men died, and the ship paused to bury them at sea; another died on board on 31 December, but his body was brought to Cobh.

"Food, water and clothing were our greatest worries," a crew member recalled. "We shared whatever clothing we had but most of the Germans were practically naked. We broke open the cargo of oranges to keep them alive."

The behaviour of the survivors was most correct. Early on one of the officer asked Donohue to bring them to La Rochelle, Brest or some Spanish port, but he replied they could discuss the matter when the picking up operation was completed. Then he told the officer that he had to head for Ireland because he had a perishable cargo.

At midnight the captain recorded in his log: "Moderate swell, rough sea, rolling and pitching, giving all possible aid to wounded."

The *Kerlogue* was supposed to head for Fishguard, as all Irish ships had to put in at a British port for a navicert, but, in deference to his passengers, Donohue made straight for Cobh. He deliberately maintained radio silence for as long as possible in order to avoid being ordered into a British port. Indeed after he had sent the message to Valentia, the Admiralty radioed from Land's End ordering the ship to proceed to Fishguard, but the crew claimed they were so busy helping survivors and keeping the ship going that they never heard the message.

Back in April 1941 the *Kerlogue* had towed the *Wild Rose* of Liverpool with its crew of 13 into Rosslare after it had been attacked by German bombers, but now the crew of the Irish ship had very good reason to fear the British. Only nine weeks earlier two RAF Mosquito fighters had attacked the ship in broad daylight about 130 miles south of Ireland. The two planes were actually from the 307 (Polish) Squadron, and their pilots had not recognised the Irish tricolour or the word "ÉIRE" painted on the side of the ship. They reported the ship was flying a French flag with "EMPO" written on the side. It was a tragic mistake. Four members of the crew were injured, including Donohue's predecessor, who sustained permanent spinal injuries. The British refused to accept responsibility for the attack, contending that the ship was off course, but they did agree to make *ex gratia* payments to the injured. Now the crew had no desire to tangle with the British again.

Alerted by Valentia, military and medical personnel were standing by at Cobh. A Motor Torpedo Boat (MTB) set out from Haulbowline with doctors on board. They met the *Kerlogue* off Flathead little over an hour before docking. The doctors went on board and twelve German ratings transferred to the MTB to relieve the congestion on the ship.

While all this was going on, Maffey called on Walshe at one-thirty in the morning to protest at the *Kerlogue* not putting into a British port. "Maffey was very excited and somewhat dictatorial in his attitude," Walshe wrote to de Valera. He demanded that the *Kerlogue* be instructed to proceed to Fishguard at once, or else hand the Germans over to a British destroyer.

"The suggestion to send them on to Fishguard, which would involve another ten hours agony, could hardly be entertained," Walshe explained. "It would not redound to the credit of either his Government or ours if we treated these victims of a sea battle with such cruelty." Maffey then asked for an assurance that the Germans would, at least, be interned in Ireland.

"I replied that I felt certain that that was the intention of the Taoiseach," Walshe reported. De Valera, for his part, had already given instructions that everything possible should be done through the army and the Red Cross to succour the survivors on landing.

The crew of the *Kerlogue* had been too busy keeping the ship moving and the injured alive to ask the sailors what had happened to them. The interrogating was done after they landed in Cork by Major General Michael J. Costello, the officer commanding the Southern Command, and his ranking intelligence officer, Commandant Florrie O'Donoghue. The senior German naval officer, *Kapitaenleutnant* Joachim Quedenfeld of Flensburg, spoke quite freely when interviewed, as did the other two surviving officers – *Kapitaenleutnant* Kurt Nitz and *Leutnant* Heinz Soltow.

The survivors had been part of the crews of a destroyer *Z27*, which had set out from Brest, and two MTBs, *T25* and *T26*, which had sailed from St Nazaire as part of a flotilla to escort a blockade runner. They were spotted by a British reconnaissance plane and attacked some hours later by two British cruisers, HMS *Glasgow* and HMS *Enterprise*, which routed the Germans without much difficulty. The battle was over in little more than an hour.

While in Cork, the men were anxious to write home, and in just a couple of days 322 letters were presented to the military censor. These provided a considerable wealth of intelligence material, not only about the battle and its aftermath but, more importantly, about conditions on the continent. The information was shared with Allied intelligence.

After the destroyer had been abandoned, the cruisers closed in and fired from close range to make sure it went down, much to the disgust of the men on the liferafts, who began singing the German national anthem. They then gave three cheers. In the heavy seas the rafts were flooded and the men had to sit up to their chests in water. By morning nearly half of them had vanished. According to the letters, many of the men just toppled off deliberately rather than continue the struggle to stay alive in the cold December conditions prevailing in the Bay of Biscay.

It was actually warmer in the water than out of it, according to Quedenfeld. They found that their ordeal under fire had been nothing compared with the effort now needed to survive. In letter after letter survivors mentioned that they were sustained during the tortuous hours before the arrival of the *Kerlogue* by their determination to see their wives, parents and girlfriends again.

Hempel visited the men in Cork, and afterwards made a presentation of a silver cup with an engraving of the swastika, German eagle and "Bay of Biscay" to Donohue. He also wrote him a letter of thanks for saving the lives of the German sailors. "I wish to express to you and to your crew my profound gratitude as well as my high appreciation of the unhesitatingly valiant spirit which has prompted this exemplary deed worthy of the Irish tradition of gallantry and humanity," he wrote.

In contrast with the various members of the *Luftwaffe* who were questioned at Collins Barracks earlier in the war, the naval people were quite open. Quedenfeld took a liking to Major General Michael J. Costello, whom he described as "a great story teller". Part of General Costello's military training had been in the United States back in the 1920s, and there is no doubt that he sympathised strongly with the Allies; indeed, at one point in the war, the American minister suggested to President Roosevelt that Costello should be invited to take over the Irish government in the event of the United States deciding to invade Ireland. Now Costello made copious notes of his interviews with the German commander, and these were passed on to American intelligence by the Department of External Affairs.

Quedenfeld had joined the German navy eleven years earlier after a stint in the merchant marine. In February 1942 he was involved in the famous Channel dash when the battleships *Schornhorst*, *Prince Eugen* and *Gneisenau* made their dramatic run through the English Channel. He served in the Mediterranean during the North African campaign and had only been in the Bay of Biscay since November. He talked freely about the effectiveness of the French resistance, the attitude of the French people to the British and American bombing of targets in France, and the relative ineffectiveness of this bombing compared to the sabotage of the Resistance. He also spoke about Germany's allies – praising the fighting qualities of the Finns and Hungarians while being bitterly critical of the Italians and Rumanians.

He talked optimistically of winning the war in Russia in the next six months. "We will kill them all," he said. But it was apparent he was more hopeful than confident. "If we cannot stop the communists, no one else can," he insisted. "After Berlin, it will then be London. It will then be too late for the English to be sorry."

Commandant Florrie O'Donoghue of G2 formed the opinion that Quedenfeld "was not a fanatical Nazi", and Costello agreed. Major General Costello noted, for instance, that Quedenfeld "probably represents the old naval school". He rarely gave the Nazi salute. In fact, he never gave a "Heil Hitler" salute until after the German minister gave the example: on the night of Hempel's arrival in Cork there had been much of this saluting. Although it had been continued by the NCOs and men, O'Donoghue noted there was a noticeable decrease on the part of the officers after Hempel's departure.

Quedenfeld seemed to know very little about Ireland. He thought the Irish people as a whole sympathised with the British while de Valera and the IRA were friendly towards Germany. "Quedenfeld had no real conception of the IRA," Costello reported. "He seemed to think a section was represented in the Army while another section was free to engage in the bombing campaign in England. He was surprised to learn the Irish government had members of the IRA interned."

The other men, many of whom were only teenagers, were a largely dispirited bunch. "These men have never known victory," O'Donoghue noted. "None of the men seemed to be content that they had done their duty. No *esprit de corps*." They were, however, effusive in their praise of the *Kerlogue* and her captain in their letters home. In addition, they were almost ecstatic about the food in Ireland:

> We got as much meat at one meal as you would get in a week. As far as food goes, I have never eaten better. We get more than ever we got, even in peace time.
>
> The food here is beyond all praise. I don't exaggerate when I say that we get twice as much to eat as on board, meat in large portions, white bread, and good butter, fresh milk and five cigarettes daily.
>
> I have never seen anything so friendly as the Irish. The food is simply marvellous, as you may imagine, a lot of ham, eggs and meat and simply marvellous.

Another wrote that they were getting five times as much food daily as they had been getting at home. "I could wish that you were as well of as I am," he added.

As a result of the kindness and good nature of the Irish soldiers, the young sailors concluded Ireland was pro-German and well disposed towards Hitler. And they seemed to accept the prospect of internment for the duration of the war with equanimity. "For us the war is over for a while," one wrote. "We have certainly had enough of it to be satisfied."

Quedenfeld wrote about being continually invited by Irish officers to their mess and having a very nice time with Costello, to whom he expressed being "very thankful" for having seen to it that the men would be comfortable in the Curragh. Quedenfeld put up no resistance to being interned, even though he and his men had clearly been rescued on the high seas as shipwrecked sailors.

Word quickly reached the Curragh, where the other internees were excited at the news. "I suppose," Rudolf Lauer wrote to a girlfriend in Dublin next morning, "you've heard the exciting news about the German invasion in the South of Éire. Imagine this brave Irish ship picking up 164 of our sailors out of the icy-cold waters. It's a good job indeed." He was aware of the situation under international law, but from the outset he had doubts about whether it would be applied.

"I wonder whether they'll be sent home after treatment and relaxation," he continued. "According to international law they should I think because they are definitely shipwrecked. But still I wonder."

On 25 January 1944, the new camp at the Curragh was opened, and the 153 men who were fit enough to travel were transferred there. The others, who remained in hospital in Cork, were transferred in the following few weeks.

The Naval Camp

The new camp adjoining Tintown, which housed some 500 IRA internees, was opened on 24 January 1944 when *Leutnant* Heinz Soltow and five NCOs were transferred there from Cork. Quedenfeld and 146 others followed next day, while the remaining men stayed on in Cork for varying periods of convalescence.

They were a bit of a curiosity at first. Most were dressed in black woollen suits that had been provided by the Red Cross; some had managed to salvage leather boots, which they wore with the pants tucked in. "They came marching down the main road singing 'Erica' as only the Germans can sing a martial air," one Irish soldier recalled. "Most of the camp turned out to see them. Soldiers instinctively stood to attention and saluted as they passed." Their marching and singing songs like "Hamburger Lied", "Erica", and "Anna Maria" on their way to the swimming pool became a highlight at the Curragh. The Irish soldiers set up a "Help the German Sailors" fund to assist the naval internees, who seemed very badly off. They hosted the internees to the cinema, invited them for a drink in the canteen and collected items like brushes, soap, polish, darning needles and razor blades on their behalf.

Living conditions in the new camp left a lot to be desired. "The place as a whole is much too wet and does not appear to become any drier," Quedenfeld complained. From a health standpoint he argued that it was "imperative to make a change", because some of the sailors were suffering from rheumatic pains as a result of their long hours in the water. Now those pains were "aggravated by the dampness" of the camp which, he contended, was only suitable as a temporary holding station. He also objected to housing ratings in big dormitory huts with 30 to 35 men to a room. Putting that many together would inevitably lead to disagreements.

"A soldier in internment without sufficient occupation would be easier to disagree with than a soldier doing service and living in freedom," Quedenfeld argued. "It must be insisted on that not more than twelve men be placed in one room. In German barracks not more than six men occupy one room."

To make matters worse it was also planned to transfer the airmen from K Lines to the new camp, which was going to be too cramped to house them in the manner to which they had become accustomed. The German commander suggested leaving the *Luftwaffe* people where they were and moving the sailors into the old Allied compound at K Lines; this would allow the *Luftwaffe* some independence and at the same time permit him, as the senior officer, to regulate "all matters of importance". He offered to put his men at the disposal of the Irish army to prepare the former Allied compound for the transfer, but Lieutenant General Daniel McKenna, the Irish Chief of Staff, did not want Germans working with Irish soldiers for fear they would influence them.

As was mentioned earlier, Mollenhauer was horrified at conditions in the German compound at Tintown when he visited it on 21 February. The gloom of the place was added to by new arrivals. The naval internees who had remained in Cork to recuperate found settling in at the Curragh particularly difficult, as did the *Luftwaffe* internees after they were transferred there in March. While in K Lines the officers had been provided with Irish army orderlies, as there were no German privates to do menial duties, but the orderlies were withdrawn following the transfer to Tintown as there were naval ratings now available to undertake such tasks. This naturally created some difficulties, but there were even greater problems over the parole hours.

Luftwaffe internees initially enjoyed the same parole hours as they initially had at K Lines: officers were permitted to stay out until eight o'clock in the morning and NCOs did not have to return until five o'clock. All naval internees, on the other hand, had to be back at the camp by midnight. "In such circumstances," Quedenfeld complained, "I, as a senior officer, get less leave than a *Luftwaffe* NCO." The Irish response, however, was not to extend the hours of the sailors, as the German commander wished, but to restrict the airmen to the shorter hours. Henceforth all internees had to be back by midnight, except on one night a week when the NCOs had an extra half-hour and the officers could stay out until 2 a.m. This gave rise to an understandable sense of grievance on the part of the interned airmen.

"Now the *Luftwaffe* leave has been reduced to the same terms as that of the navy," Quedenfeld complained. "This is very hard on them and they consider it a punishment which has not been merited since their conduct has been above question. Personally I can't understand why since the beginning of their internment a difference has been made between the *Luftwaffe* and the navy."

There were no time limits in the formal regulations set by Army Headquarters. The parole hours were at the discretion of camp authorities, who regularly extended local parole for late night parties when individual internees asked in writing for an extension. What Quedenfeld was really looking for was the right to grant these extensions himself.

"Leave it to me and I will see it is not abused," he wrote. "This will give me more scope for the management of the camp."

But the problems concerning parole arose against the backdrop of what was probably the greatest crisis of the war, as far as the Irish people were concerned. On the day that Mollenhauer visited the Tintown camp for the first time, 21 February 1944, the American minister handed de Valera a formal diplomatic Note demanding the expulsion of the German and Japanese representatives from Ireland on the grounds that they posed a threat to the lives of Americans taking part in the forthcoming invasion of Europe, which was still some three months away.

In the days before the D-Day invasion, the Allies engaged in a range of deceptions to fool the Germans, such as deploying a phantom army based in south-east England and employing General Sir Bernard Montgomery's famous double in Gibraltar to give the impression that he was preparing to invade southern France. In the case of Ireland there was a quite different ruse – the infamous American Note was really just a political ploy to discredit de Valera in American eyes. The note was deliberately worded to provoke his refusal, so that the Americans could depict him as being indifferent to the lives of American soldiers.

The scheme had been suggested by Gray, as part of a plan to ensure that de Valera would not be able to enlist American support for his efforts to end partition. Northern Ireland provided bases for American preparations for D-Day, and Gray was determined to contrast this with what he felt was the Taoiseach's selfish indifference. Initially Gray proposed that President Roosevelt should ask for bases in such a way that de Valera would inevitably refuse and Belfast's co-operation could be contrasted with Dublin's refusal, but this scheme was blocked by the American military. The American Joint Chiefs of Staff, who were convinced the bases would be of no use to them, opposed taking any chance of de Valera's agreeing to hand over the facilities, because the Allies would then become obliged to divert men and equipment to defend them. Gray next suggested that Washington should ask for the recall of the German minister and Japanese consul from Dublin. He told Maffey that the request was deliberately worded to provoke de Valera's refusal. "The American line is to play for the answer 'No'," Maffey reported. "Mr Gray, who has just left my office, tells me that that is what his President wants."

The OSS, however, informed the State Department that it was happy with the security situation in Ireland. The Irish had provided "full co-operation with the British and with us in security measures, and liaison with respect to counter intelligence and affirmative intelligence", the OSS official explained. At Britain's request, de Valera had compelled the German legation to surrender its radio transmitter, with the result that the only means of communication with Berlin open to Hempel was by a cable to Berne that passed through London. The British could cut Dublin off from the continent at will, but they were not really concerned about that. They had broken the German codes and were feeding the legation with misinformation and then monitoring Hempel's reports.

Some of the internees did prove quite useful to Thomsen at the German legation in picking up tit-bits of information from Irish workers returning from Britain. "The information supplied," according to John P. Duggan's *Neutral Ireland and the Third Reich*, "covered items ranging from factory locations and troop concentrations to accounts of the effects of *Luftwaffe* raids." But it was doubtful that any of this information was of use to the authorities in Germany. In *The Deception Planners*, Denis Wheatley recalled how his section fed Hempel with bogus "information from people who purported to be Nazi sympathisers", then looked on with satisfaction as the Germans forwarded the false information "in all innocence".

"We could be sure, in fact, that Germany would not be much more effectively represented in Dublin by Hempel than Greenland is by the Polar Bear," Maffey assured his own government.

De Valera was therefore taken aback when Gray handed him a Note essentially accusing Ireland of acting with callous indifference towards the Allies. The Note concluded by demanding "as an absolute minimum the removal of these Axis representatives whose presence in Ireland must inevitably be regarded as constituting a danger to the lives of American soldiers and to the success of Allied military operations".

"As long as I am here Éire will not grant this request," de Valera replied. "We have done everything to prevent Axis espionage, going beyond what we might reasonably be expected to do and I am satisfied that there are no leaks from this country. For a year and a half you have been advertising the invasion of Europe and what has got out about it has not been from Éire. The German minister, I am satisfied, has behaved very correctly and decently and as a neutral we will not send him away."

De Valera suspected that his government was being set up as a scapegoat in case anything went wrong with the D-Day landing, and his fears were increased when Robert Brennan, the Irish minister to the United States, telegraphed that officials at the State Department had told him that if the diplomats were not expelled, "the punishment would be, not invasion or any other measures, but the angry curses of millions of American mothers, many of them Irish".

The Taoiseach had already authorised the most extraordinary

intelligence co-operation with the Americans, and if they were really worried about security, there were secret channels though which their fears could easily have been alleviated. Over the years Gray had been thoroughly indiscreet, but he seemed to be threatening to reach a new low when he told American reporters that, for security reasons, it was not possible to tell what was known about the activities of the Axis agents in Ireland. This was highly confidential information which had been given to the Americans in line with the secret co-operation agreement.

Walshe protested vigorously to Ervin Marlin, the OSS's agent-in-charge of Ireland. "I said that if any information which we gave to him in confidence, as part of our secret arrangement for securing the safety of American interests in this country, were used for the purpose of trumping up a case against us, there would be a catastrophic breach, not only in the friendly relationship which had been established between our two Intelligence Services, but also in the wide relations between the two Governments, which naturally required a considerable degree of trust in each other."

De Valera sent Walshe to London with an offer to implement whatever security measures the British and American intelligence people desired, short of expelling the Axis representatives. As a result of the visit, a secret conference between the British, American and Irish security people was arranged for Dublin in early May. Among the things considered were the intensification of radio security, co-operation between the Irish coast-watching service and the RAF in Northern Ireland to prevent Axis agents being dropped by aircraft, as well as detailed discussions about the surveillance of the German legation, its personnel, and the internees both at the Curragh and at university in Dublin. This included tapping their telephones, censoring their mail and compiling lists of their correspondents. G2 kept an eye on all contacts of the German internees, especially foreign nationals. The addresses of all Irish people who corresponded with the internees were carefully noted by G2, which then had their backgrounds investigated, and the Special Branch was notified to keep an eye on any suspected of having pro-German leanings.

Against the backdrop of exaggerated American concern about

the Germans, the Irish authorities were naturally cautious about the internees. With so many of them allowed to roam about the parole area, the camp authorities felt that they needed the extra influence of being able to control the conditions of parole, because there were already indications that some of the internees were flouting not only camp regulations in matters like censorship, but also the civil law. There had been numerous complaints about the men not having lights on their bicycles at night and there were several complaints that they were stealing bicycles to go "joy riding", or just to get back to the camp. The army wished the civil authorities to prosecute offenders, so it deliberately highlighted offences, even trivial matters like the German seaman, Heinz Karolczak from Dortmund, caught in a bar with 18 local people on St Patrick's Day. All public houses were supposed to be closed on that national holiday, but the law was flouted throughout the country; indeed, St Patrick' s Day was one of the heavier drinking days of the year. The Department of External Affairs adopted a more tolerant approach by turning a blind eye to petty matters, as long as the internees paid for any damage.

Army authorities were irked by such tolerance, and Quedenfeld did not help matters by flagrantly violating camp regulations with a political demonstration on Hitler's birthday on 20 April 1944. After breakfast the internees paraded while Georg Fleischmann recorded the scene on a movie camera and Alfred Heinzl took photographs. The parade was called to attention by Mollenhauer. He turned and saluted Quedenfeld, who addressed the men briefly in German. They sang the German national anthem while one of the internees hoisted the German flag on an electricity pole; then the parade dismissed. The whole thing had taken only a couple of minutes, and was over before the guards had time to do anything about it.

Quedenfeld explained afterwards that he did not ask for permission for the demonstration because he knew it would be refused. "You don't realise what this means to us Germans," he told Guiney. "I am sure you people did something similar while you were interned."

Fleischmann and Heinzl had compounded the flag-raising incident by again violating the regulation prohibiting the use of cameras within the Curragh area. The army wanted to make an example of the two internees, but de Valera asked that the whole thing be ignored. Having spent time in British jails following the Easter Rebellion of 1916, the Irish leader evidently understood and quite probably sympathised with Quedenfeld's feelings in the matter.

But such incidents made the camp authorities more inflexible when Quedenfeld asked that German orderlies and cooks be paid extra or else replaced by Irish army personnel, who had, after all, done nearly all of this work at K Lines. Internees working within the camp were really being discriminated against because they were only paid the allowance which they would have received even if they were not working. Because of their duties, however, they could not avail of the opportunity of earning extra money by joining colleagues working for the Irish Turf Board, cutting peat in the nearby bogs. Quedenfeld's demand nearly landed him in a similar predicament as had his earlier request for the same parole hours as the *Luftwaffe* internees. Instead of paying the men extra, the Department of Finance in Dublin suggested that the allowances of those working in the bogs should be stopped. Fortunately, saner heads at the Department of External Affairs prevailed and the idea was dropped, but the kind of bureaucratic thinking which inspired the suggestion of withholding payment for work in the bog went some way to explaining why many of the German officers felt so frustrated.

"As the sailors integrated with life in the Curragh, their tremendous flair for organisation and improvisation became very apparent," Chris O'Callaghan, one of the Irish soldiers' recalled. "They were given access to unit tailor shops and were soon turning out extremely well cut suits, in rather gay material. The suit jackets had 'Prussian' collars, were belted and rather short in length, approximately the German *Luftwaffe* style. The Irish nicknamed them 'bum-freezers'. Trousers were also of a distinctive cut, very tight about the seat, tapering out into a very wide bell-bottom at the ends. In wartime, utility conscious Ireland, these suits stood out like beacons."

O'Callaghan noted that "there was a distinct correlation between the growth of the stylishly clad Germans and a cooling off by the Irish towards them." The Irish soldiers found that they had no chance with the local girls when the German sailors were around, and as the more industrious of the Germans got money, they began to display a certain aloofness and independence.

Camp authorities used the threat of restricting parole as the most effective means of compelling the internees to observe camp regulations. In the past, British and German internees on parole in Dublin had made a habit of waiting until the last minute before turning up for the final bus to Kildare, in the hope it would already be full and they would not be permitted to board. They could then spend the night in Dublin, but McNally's successor, Colonel Seán Collins-Powell, clamped down on this by refusing to extend local parole hours for those who did not make a serious effort to get on the bus in time. On Saturday, 3 June 1944, four naval NCOs said they were unable to board the bus and did not return to the camp until ten o'clock on Monday morning. They had a statement signed by a Garda superintendent to the effect that the bus was overcrowded. Collins-Powell retaliated by ordering that the internee officers and NCOs no longer be allowed special parole to go to Dublin before nine o'clock in the morning – previously they had been allowed to sign out early at seven o'clock in order to catch the first bus.

Quedenfeld admitted that three of his officers, who had travelled on the bus on 3 June, had told him that the four NCOs could have boarded as there was standing room. He confined the four men to camp for 28 days each, but he took exception to the two-hour curtailment of special parole on the grounds that all the officers and NCOs were being punished for the misbehaviour of a few individuals.

"Such procedure is forbidden in the German Army and I cannot accept the justice of it in this case," he complained. "It should be sufficient when I, as camp senior officer, take disciplinary action in cases of misconduct." This, of course, was a virtual re-run of Mollenhauer's earlier arguments with McNally, and the camp authorities were again determined to enforce their regime. When it became apparent during the summer that the practice of missing the bus had ceased, Collins-Powell authorised the early parole once more. But even after the success of the D-Day landing, the camp authorities showed little inclination to relax the parole hours further. Quedenfeld argued that his officers should have different hours from the NCOs, because their authority was being undermined when they were treated in the same way. "It makes proper discipline impossible when an officer is compelled to be back in the camp at the same time as young NCOs," he wrote to Collins-Powell on 13 June 1944. "The case has arisen that I, as camp senior officer, have had to hasten back in the company of one of my youngest NCOs in order to be back at the camp at 23.59. I would suggested therefore that all officers be granted standing parole until 02.00 so that the cases of breach of discipline can be reduced to a minimum."

Local parole was normally extended for punctual internees upon request, though there were some exceptions. One of the *Luftwaffe* NCOs was refused an extended parole for a party at the home of a local Garda after Commandant Mackey of G2 reported that the internee was having an affair with the wife of the policeman, who was away on temporary duty. In fact, Mackey noted, the internee and the Garda's wife had both been treated recently for venereal disease. With G2 involving itself in such matters, it was hardly surprising that some of the internees continued to circumvent the censorship regulations by posting letters outside the camp and by using aliases and addresses of accommodation to receive their Irish mail. This was not only to prevent the censor reading their personal letters, but to save their correspondents the inconvenience of being investigated by the Special Branch.

The Weber Affair

Conditions in the naval camp were aggravated by disciplinary problems surrounding the mutinous behaviour of a number of internees led by Josef Weber, who had been causing trouble for his superiors even before his internment. About 18 months earlier he had been downgraded to a rating second class. Now in the comparative safety of Ireland the 25-year-old from Essen became outspokenly critical of the Nazi regime in Germany.

While in Cork, Weber had urged fellow ratings to ignore the authority of their officers and NCOs, and he threatened to join the British the first chance he got. At the Curragh he made disparaging remarks about Hitler and the Nazis and got into heated arguments with colleagues. On one occasion it led to blows, and he was brought before a secret court-martial for striking an officer and two sergeants. Under German military law he would have faced the death penalty, but he was unrepentant. He contemptuously refused to recognise the court and at the end of the proceedings broke away from his escort and struck the sergeant holding him. He was sentenced to 21 days solitary confinement in an NCO hut on a severely restricted diet. For two days out of each three he was given only bread and water and had to sleep on bare boards in an unheated room with just two blankets to ward off the mid-winter cold. Every third day he was allowed normal rations and could sleep in a regular bed.

The incident was hushed up for fear the British would make propaganda out of it, with the result that the Irish guards did not learn of the affair for some days. The first indication they had that something was amiss was on the night of 21 February 1944, when one of the guards on duty in the compound noticed "a considerable number" of naval ratings walking up and down with their hands deep in their pockets, their collars turned up and their caps pulled down over their ears. He asked them what they were doing.

They were just annoying their orderly sergeant, one sailor replied. Another said they were trying to frighten the guards, but next day two of the internees explained privately that they had been waiting for Weber to return from parole. Although confined to camp, he had slipped out using a pass secured for him by one of the other ratings. On returning to the camp that night he was surrounded by his colleagues who snatched off his cap, coat and scarf and brought him directly to his hut. They had pounced on him to prevent the orderly sergeant learning he had been out of the camp. In spite of the solicitude of his colleagues the German officers learned that Weber had defied his confinement. Believing this amounted to a blatant challenge to their authority, Quedenfeld turned to the Irish for help and asked for Weber's removal from the camp.

He told McNally of a long list of charges against Weber: leaving the camp without permission, escaping while confined to barracks, having a dangerous influence on the younger ratings, and even of planning to defect. Observing that the obstreperous seaman might "intrigue against Ireland on his outings", Quedenfeld asked the Irish to intern Weber elsewhere for the duration of the war.

"Since I am not in a position to keep this soldier in custody in the camp," Quedenfeld wrote, "I am compelled to make this request. I accept all responsibility." The German minister formally endorsed the request.

Transferring Weber to a prison posed legal problems. The Irish authorities were particularly anxious to play down all matters relating to the internment of the sailors because, of course, as distressed mariners they should not have been interned in the first place. Imprisoning him for the duration of the war would further flout international law, under which the disciplinary punishment of even a prisoner-of-war was not supposed to exceed 30 days. Rather than risk a challenge in the Irish courts, de Valera decided that Quedenfeld's request should be rejected, and Weber was left in the camp.

It was apparent from the letters written by the internees and carefully scrutinised by the military censor, that some of them seemed to have a rather naive outlook on the war. Well into 1944 they still believed that Germany was going to win. They somehow thought that Britain and the United States would eventually join with Germany and turn on the Soviet Union. Letters to the internees from Germany generally avoided war topics, except for news of frequent bereavements or homes being destroyed by bombs, or the letters might mention the writers being interrupted by having to run to bomb shelters during air raids. The Irish censors found the German mail more amusing than informative. They were amused, for instance, to read one letter from a woman informing her husband at the Curragh of their marriage – of which he was somehow not yet aware. Another gave a boyfriend details of the birth of their baby and thanked him for his proposal of marriage. To Irishmen brought up in the restrictive Catholic atmosphere of the time, such happenings seemed extraordinary.

Many of the German internees were woefully out of touch with what was happening at home. The bomb plot on Hitler's life on 20 July 1944 came as a terrible shock to them, who had all taken an oath of loyalty to Hitler: "I swear by God this holy oath: I will render unconditional obedience to the *Führer* of the German Reich and People, Adolf Hitler, the Supreme Commander of the Armed Forces, and will be ready, as a brave soldier, to stake my life at any time for this oath." There was intense activity in the camp after German radio announced that the attempt had been unsuccessful. All of the internees gathered at seven o'clock that evening in their recreation room, where they were addressed for about 20 minutes. Afterwards they appeared resentful as they gathered in small groups.

"They tried to kill Hitler in Germany today," the guards were told.

Rudolf Lauer of Dortmund had been in Ireland almost three years and was clearly upset when he wrote to a girlfriend in Dublin:

> What do you say about these damnable events of the day before yesterday? How that could happen right in the heart

> of Germany will always be a puzzle to me. Oh Lord if those lousy bastards should have succeeded in accomplishing their lousy intentions, all the stupendous sacrifices would have been in vain. How on earth generals, officers that have been brought up with the German army can do a thing like that is unintelligible to me. The first thing that a soldier learns is that loyalty is the backbone of honour. Well, those rascals couldn't even be faithful to their oath to Adolf Hitler. I have no words for that, I feel ashamed about it myself. It's a pity that those traitors were finished off with a decent bullet. They are not worth it. I think there are enough Russian communists in our prisoner of war camps. Perhaps they could apply one of their sick methods to bring somebody from life to death. I wouldn't pity them a bit. Of course there is also a positive point in the whole affair. There is no doubt that there will be no repetition of this business since Heinrich Himmler has been appointed G. in C. of the German home army as well. And he has a good reputation for efficiency. Furthermore every soldier and every civilian has seen that our Lord's blessing was so obviously with Adolf Hitler that there is no doubt about Germany's final victory...

In the aftermath of the bomb plot there was tension with anti-Nazi elements in the camp. Quedenfeld was particularly worried about Weber's influence, so he again asked for him to be removed. "Weber is rather clever, but insubordinate and of base character," he told Collins-Powell. "He is a bad soldier and does not submit to military discipline."

To the more nationalistic officers the outspoken rating was just a communist agitator. "By his fluency of speech, he persuaded a few soldiers of similar disposition over to his side and incited them to open defiance against their superiors," Quedenfeld explained. Fearing that Weber was planning to defect to the British, the commander asked Collins-Powell to jail Weber elsewhere till the end of the war, pending court-martial in Germany "for instigating to mutiny" and assaulting an *Oberfeldwebel*. "Above all," Quedenfeld continued, "it is necessary to prevent him from making any contact whatever with other persons especially with internees, as he will always try to influence them."

Weber, who was transferred to the Curragh military hospital on 25 July after he complained of headaches, was held there for five weeks. On his discharge on 1 September 1944 he was committed to "the glasshouse", as the Curragh military prison was known. The Belfast *Newsletter* reported that the internee was actually sentenced to death by his colleagues, who then supposedly asked the guards for the loan of some rifles with which to execute him. According to the report, the man's life was only spared by de Valera's intercession. It made an interesting story, but it was simply not true.

One Who Couldn't Stay

Once it became apparent that things were going badly for Germany on all battlefronts, morale fell particularly low in the internment camp. Naval ratings complained that they were being given inferior vegetables while the officers got the best of what was on offer. The officers, on the other hand, were themselves complaining bitterly about their fare.

"Our food has deteriorated to an extent that is really amazing for a country of plenty," Rudolf Lauer wrote to his girlfriend. "Once I was told I were [*sic*] a guest of this country, but isn't it a funny way of treating one's guests in giving them constantly rotten and evil smelling eggs and potatoes which are as old as my grandmother.

"For their own reputation the Irish Army should do something about this," he continued. "There are a lot of things which I appreciate and which I am never slow to talk about. I hope you'll forgive me if I hurt your patriotic feelings a little. But it's only your lovely parcel that brought about this explosion."

As a precedent had been set in allowing four of the *Luftwaffe* officers to attend University College, Dublin, as full-time students, others tried to follow suit in order to get out of the camp with its repressive atmosphere. Mollenhauer had been given special parole in June to spend a week in Dublin to sit the first year Arts examinations at UCD, and he was admitted to the second year course when the university re-opened in October. There was a virtual mass exodus of *Luftwaffe* officers as twelve of the 15 in the camp moved to Dublin as full-time students. Kruger, Habich, Klanke and Lauer were joined at UCD by *Luftwaffe* colleagues Mollenhauer, Berndt, Muller, Stoermer, Hollborn, Grau and Stockbauer, as well as the naval officer, Kurt Nitz, and the naval NCO Karl Schwarzkopf. Fleischmann and one of the

Luftwaffe NCOs, Erwin Sack, were also permitted to go to Dublin to attend the College of Technology in Bolton Street. Many of them stayed in groups of three or four in rented houses, and the German colony in Dublin helped to support them. At this time there were 339 registered German aliens in the country. Fifty-two of these were former Austrians and there were 37 Czechs. Many were Jewish and most were anti-Nazi. In fact, 192 were considered anti-Nazi, only 100 pro-Nazi and remaining 47 essentially indifferent. This did not include the five Germans at the legation. The Special Branch kept an eye on the students and their contacts, and people who rented them accommodation were all investigated. The very prurient Special Branch informed G2 that some of the men had amorous involvements with their landladies.

Being internees the men were able to buy duty-free liquor and they exploited this to supplement their incomes. In just one week in December 1944 seven Germans living in two Dublin houses purchased over £352 worth of wine and spirits, even though their daily allowance only amounted to two shillings and two pence each. They had spent more in a week than their total combined allowances for sixteen months.

"I do not think the pay which the internees receive warrants the expenditure of such sums of money on drink, especially when they have to maintain themselves in digs and pay college and other fees," Commandant Mackey complained. He had no doubt the men were reselling the duty-free liquor at a profit which, of course, was "at the expense of the state".

Some of the men at the camp displaying considerable ingenuity making toys and leather goods for sale. They had a workshop with space for about 30 men and tools provided by the Irish army, but there was a chronic shortage of materials. The men could not afford to buy timber. On one occasion four of them stole some materials from a timber-yard, but they were caught before they could use it. They admitted the offence and returned the timber, so the authorities dropped the matter. In the absence of proper raw materials the men had to make do with whatever they could find. They broke up furniture, mirrors and curtain rods, much to the annoyance of Guiney, who complained angrily to Quedenfeld. The latter promised to do what he could to prevent such destruction, but when the weather got cold some of the internees began burning timber from the huts for heating.

While inspecting the camp on 31 October 1944, Guiney noticed that a rafter had been removed, but when he complained about this to Quedenfeld, the latter became quite abusive.

"What do you think I am, a damn policeman?" the German officer asked. "I am not going to go about spying on my men and this would not happen at all if the men were properly treated. I have asked for wood, more lights, we are not getting enough fuel, men are frozen, sitting in their rooms all day without sufficient fire. The *Luftwaffe* in 'K Lines' had plenty of fire but were sent down here to be punished."

At K Lines the airmen had been supplied with coal, but now that the country's coal stocks were seriously depleted, the army was only issued with turf and timber for fuel. The internees had actually been supplied with timber to burn during September when the Irish army had had to do without. Guiney therefore had no sympathy for the Germans in this matter. Indeed, he was so annoyed over the destruction of army property that he took a poor view of Quedenfeld's various requests.

Even though the internees were given a special 48 hour parole to visit Dublin during Christmas the previous year, Guiney objected when Quedenfeld made a similar request for 1944. He also opposed a request for the naval ratings to be allowed to go to Dublin for a day. They had not been eligible for special parole, so they pressed Quedenfeld for permission to visit the city in the run up to Christmas.

"They have approached me very often on this point," Quedenfeld wrote, "and I can very well understand how anxious they are to visit a large town in this country as it is the first time for some of them to be in a foreign country."

Despite Guiney's opposition, G2 had no objections, with the result that both requests were authorised by Army Headquarters. They stipulated, however, that the ratings should travel in groups of twelve and be accompanied by an officer or an NCO.

Quedenfeld and some of his officers were in Dublin on New Year's Eve when German radio broadcast an address by Hitler. It was the first such address broadcast for several months, and it sparked a demonstration in the German compound at Tintown as the internees rushed around shooting off flares and fireworks and throwing stones against the galvanised iron fence separating them from the IRA internees. Some shouted "Up the IRA" and even "Up de Valera" as they smashed the glass covering the notice-board on which the camp's standing orders were displayed; the orders were torn down and strewn about the compound. Some windows in the duty room used by guards were also broken by stones. Much to the irritation of camp authorities, Heinz Soltow – the senior officer in Quedenfeld's absence – took a prominent part in the whole affair.

Quedenfeld later apologised for the incident, which he attributed to high spirits prompted by the men's joy at hearing the *Führer*'s voice after so long. Such scenes were common in Germany on New Year's Eve, he noted, but Mackey reported that some of the *Luftwaffe* told him that the participants would have been given six months in jail if they had behaved that way back home. The total damage done to army property came to just £3, which Quedenfeld paid, and it was decided to forget about the matter. Mackey noted, however, that the fracas did not reflect well on discipline within the camp.

In particular Quedenfeld had set a bad example which probably contributed to the low morale. As mentioned earlier, he had confined four NCOs to camp for 28 days for missing the last bus from Dublin in May, and he sentenced Emmerich to five weeks confinement from staying out overnight in Naas on 15 December 1944. The Irish thought the punishments too harsh, and particularly unfair in the light of Quedenfeld's own conduct. He imposed no sanctions on himself after he missed the bus in August or again in January 1945 when he was more than eight hours late in returning to camp after the New Year's Eve party at the German legation. "I am sorry for having been some hours late yesterday," he wrote to Guiney, "but I did sleep too long after a very hard celebration and I missed my right bus."

With Quedenfeld not acting as responsibly as he might, Irish authorities were faced with the possibility of real trouble once money for the internees ran out. Hempel had been experiencing financial difficulties since early 1944 and had only been able to keep the legation above water by supplementing his intermittent payments from Germany by collecting some of his country's outstanding debts in Ireland, but those quickly began to dry up. Although Ireland owed money to Germany at the start of the war, that situation had been reversed as a result of damage done by German planes mistakenly bombing Irish property. The Irish government insisted that the Germans should pay for the internees in hard currency deposited in a Swiss bank before any more money would be put at Hempel's disposal. In early March 1945 the Department of Defence was informed that a forthcoming double payment being made to the internees was the last money they were likely to receive from their government. Under the circumstances Hempel was anxious that the men should be kept as fully occupied as possible in case they might turn to stealing.

There was little chance of employment before the weather improved enough to permit turf cutting, so the Dublin government decided to set up special classes for the men. Dr Klaus Becker, a German lecturer at University College, Galway, visited the camp to give a talk on Irish folklore, but it was not very well attended. Dr Francis O'Sullivan of the Department of Education gave a lecture on "Education in Ireland" which sparked a lot of interest among the men, no doubt because many were anxious to learn as much as possible about Irish schools in the hope of enrolling in them. Nobody thought much of O'Sullivan's proposal to set up Gaelic classes at the camp. More practically minded civil servants insisted the classes be confined to subjects which would assist the internees making a living upon their return to Germany.

Wilhelm Masgeik, who came to Ireland from Germany in August 1938 as chief engineering adviser to Irish Steel in Cork, offered to lecture to the men. He had passed up the opportunity to return home at the start of the war because he was still under contract with Irish Steel. When the company had to close down in early 1941 due to a lack of raw materials, it was then too late for Masgeik to go back to Germany, so he bought himself a farm. He made himself rather conspicuous on at least one occasion that year while drinking with Henning Thomsen in a Cork hotel. At one point he purchased a bottle of champagne and took offence when the barmaid refused to drink with him. He called the manager and insisted that he dismiss the barmaid. When the manager refused, he threatened to have both of them fired, saying he had friends in high places. As Thomsen was tailed everywhere by the Special Branch, the incident was reported to both the Department of Justice and External Affairs.

In early 1945 Hempel asked Masgeik to move to the Kildare area and hold technical classes in the camp, with the German legation paying his expenses. None of the teachers in the nearby technical schools could teach the internees more than they already knew. Masgeik began his lectures on 5 March 1945 and soon became embroiled in a most extraordinary controversy. He asked for permission to stay at the camp, because he would have difficulty returning to his digs in Newbridge after class, but Guiney said there were "no circumstances" in which a civilian would be permitted to remain overnight. He must have been the only man in all of Europe who was trying to move into a concentration camp at the time. The following night when Masgeik had still not left the camp as midnight approached, the officer in charge – Captain Lawrence Clancy – asked him to leave. Linking Clancy and a sergeant as they walked towards the main gate, Masgeik started name-dropping. He mentioned that he was good friends with Major Generals Michael J. Costello and Hugo MacNeill, as well as former General Tom Barry and Deputy Martin Corry, who was an outspoken member of de Valera's governing Fianna Fáil party. On reaching the front gate Masgeik stopped and warned the two soldiers that he would be getting in touch with his influential friends to protest about the way he was being treated.

"You know you should not have remained in the camp and should have left earlier," Clancy replied.

"If you met friends without money, fellows from your native country, you would like to spend a few bob on them?"

"I grant you all that, but I have got to do my duty and to ask you to leave."

Masgeik admitted that he had been told that he could not stay, but he was now adamant about remaining. "I have no way of getting to Newbridge tonight and I am not going," he declared. "You can lock me up. Nail me up. Do what you wish but I am staying." He turned around and walked back to the camp bar.

"Why don't you make Masgeik behave himself?" one of the guards asked Heinzl next day.

"What can you do with him. He is neither a soldier nor a sailor," Heinzl answered.

Clancy complained to Quedenfeld, who then spoke to Masgeik. About 20 minutes later Masgeik stormed out.

"Captain," he snapped to Clancy, "you did your work well. Since you went to the bloody fucking commander to order me out of the camp, he has done so. And you did it behind my back."

"Yes, I did. The commander is responsible for visitors' conduct and as far as I am concerned, you were his guest and he was the proper person to see."

Masgeik had had too much to drink and he began rambling on about being a civilian who could not be ordered about by a German officer. If he wished, he said, he could have Martin Corry raise the issue in the Dáil and he would sit there for the rest of the night.

"You won't sit here long now," the captain exclaimed, his patience running thin. He sent for a car and got the camp orderly officer to drive Masgeik to Newbridge.

"I am now being removed at public expense, or I should have said at my own expense," Masgeik proclaimed on departing. "I am a rate payer, paying £66 rates this year."

The following week there was another incident. Masgeik had been allowed to stay late because Henning Thomsen of the German legation was in the camp. When it became time to leave, Masgeik demanded that the captain of the guard get him a car as he had been promised a drive by Thomsen, but the latter was now too drunk to drive. In fact, Thomsen had no car either; he had actually made arrangements to borrow Soltow's bicycle to get to Newbridge. Masgeik was offered the loan of a bicycle, but he probably thought if he kicked up enough fuss he would get a drive. Quedenfeld had a heated argument with him in German. Masgeik insisted that as a civilian he would not be ordered about by the military, but the officer in charge of the guard warned him that he would be put out if he did not leave voluntarily. It was gone two o'clock in the morning when he finally left on foot.

Guiney had wished to bar Masgeik from the camp after the previous incident, but he had not been able to get his way. Now, however, Quedenfeld was told that Masgeik would have to be out of the camp by seven o'clock each evening. The German commander had no objections. In fact, he said he would have had him out of the camp earlier if he had known he had the authority to remove him. In the aftermath of the second incident, he was informed by Hempel's office that he had this authority, and he duly told Masgeik as much.

"I spoke to him after my conversation with you yesterday afternoon and he did not like I speaking to him about his general behaviour, so he informed some of the NCOs that he was not coming into the camp again," Quedenfeld wrote to Guiney on 20 March. "He did not even have the manners of saying goodbye to either myself or Lt. Soltow. I am glad he is gone and I do not want to see him again."

More Germans

At one o'clock in the afternoon on Sunday, 11 March 1945, the look-out post on Galley Head, Co. Cork, reported sighting a U-boat off the coast. A couple of hours later two British aircraft were spotted as they searched for the submarine. Shortly before six o'clock in the evening, explosions were heard as the planes dropped depth charges. Nothing else was seen or heard until the early hours of 13 March when those on duty at Galley Head noticed two red flares about seven miles to the south-west. A little over an hour later there were three more flares about three miles away in the same direction.

At dawn a rubber raft with eleven Germans sailors on board landed at Galley Head. None of those on board could speak English, but one of the look-out post staff was able to talk to them in French. He learned they were from a U-boat which had sunk some 40 to 50 miles off the coast. He also learned that there were 37 others on two rafts at sea. The Courtmacsharry lifeboat put to sea and picked up the men about four miles from Glandore Harbour. None of the men were injured though two of them were somewhat exhausted and were hospitalised for observation. The others were taken to Collins Barracks that afternoon. They refused to talk about their mission or what had happened to them.

The crew consisted of five officers and 43 other ranks. The captain of the boat was *Oberleutnant* Klaus Becker, with *Oberleutnant* Karl Nagle as his number two; and there three *Leutnants*, Friedrich Bielecke, Gottfried Kuntze and Siegfried Dreschel. An officer from G2 questioned the crew, but they refused to say anything about what had happened to the U-boat. Kuntze, he noted, was more the artistic than military type, while Nagel was a dour individual, a strong party-man. Unlike the dispirited sailors rescued by the *Kerlogue*, these men's morale was high and they spoke "with the burning enthusiasm of school children" as they predicted that Germany would reverse the tide of battle against the Russians.

"We'll throw them back as we did before," one of the men said.

Kuntze, however, realised the war was all but lost. "Well, anyway," he said, "England has lost the war too." He was particularly worried about his home in Silesia, which had already been overrun by the advancing Soviet forces.

Nagel produced the official line without trimmings. The Irish intelligence officer asked if Germany would align with the west against the Soviets after the war. "Of course," Nagle replied. "Anything is possible in politics. It is such a high art; only the great brain can compass it. We cannot hope to comprehend it."

Both Kuntze and Nagel had some English, but they refused to use it. Werner Banisch, one of the NCOs, had good English, as he had been in England before the war, but Nagle shut him up immediately. The sailors were all transferred to the Curragh on 16 March 1945, still refusing to talk about their mission or what had actually happened to the U-260. The Irish naturally assumed the submarine had been abandoned after being damaged by the bombing on Sunday evening, but one of the men later told a different story.

After the attack the U-boat had surfaced under cover of darkness and everything seemed tranquil, so Becker ordered that half the crew at a time should take turns on deck for an hour of fresh air. After a couple of hours they were clearing the decks when an RAF Sunderland suddenly appeared out of the sky and caught the submarine in its searchlight. As the U-boat dived it was damaged by a number of explosives. Although leaking badly, it managed to stay submerged until the plane departed. Becker then ordered them to the surface and the crew abandoned ship, but not before opening the sea cocks to ensure the U-boat went to the bottom.

There was an interesting sequel to the sinking of the U-260. Some days later a couple of fishermen found a metal container floating in the sea near Glandore. It contained signal codes and ciphers, as well as other documents, among them reports from U-boat commanders detailing their experiences and the kind of action they took in certain circumstances. G2 was particularly interested in documents relating to Ireland.

"Ireland forbids the entry of warships into its territorial waters under penalty of internment," Grand Admiral Doenitz instructed in January 1942. "This prohibition must be strictly observed in order to maintain her neutrality." Further instructions were issued in August 1944. "Irish ships and the occasional Irish convoys should not be attacked inside the blockade area for political reasons, if recognised as such," he ordered. "There is no special obligation however to establish the neutrality of ships inside the blockade area." Although there had been numerous unfounded reports about U-boats supposedly being succoured in Irish harbours, there was no indication of this in the documents, and there was no advice as to how any such help might be sought. As usual this information was shared with Allied intelligence.

With the war now drawing to a conclusion, some of the internees began looking for work outside the parole area, pending their release. Hempel had already agreed in 1943 to an arrangement whereby the managers of local labour exchanges would have to certify that there were no local people available for a particular job before any of the internees could accept it. In the past, camp authorities had realised that some of the men had outside jobs during parole hours, but they had turned a blind eye to this practice until the internees began canvassing for employment throughout the country.

"There seems to be no doubt that they feel the war is lost," Collins-Powell wrote. "The internees feel that there are no prospects in Germany and the majority are anxious to stay in Ireland." Hence they were looking for employment. He wanted to restrict them to collective work, such as turf cutting or tree planting, or even preparing a site for a new gymnasium at the Curragh, but the men secretly mailed letters applying for employment at various centres around the country. Although the applications were not submitted through censorship, G2 intercepted some of the replies with job offers from places like Cork, Dundalk, and Tullamore. Collins-Powell complained to

Quedenfeld on 17 April about the breach of standing orders and instructed him to suspend all unauthorised employment forthwith.

There were normally 40 turf cutting vacancies, but the internees never took up many more than 30 of those. The announcement of vacancies for 72 internees in 1945 was not greeted with any enthusiasm; most of the men preferred to find work elsewhere and eleven of them already had other jobs. They and 41 others formally applied for permission to work in the Curragh area, but Collins-Powell opposed their applications.

"I do not recommend that the internees should receive employment as individuals as I am afraid that there would be repercussions from the local labour force," he wrote to Army Headquarters. "Up to the present I have not granted any permission and have asked Lieut. Comdr. Quedenfeld to submit a certification from each prospective employer indicating that local labour is not available."

The Department of External Affairs agreed with the army on this occasion. Boland warned his counterpart at the Department of Defence that an embarrassing situation might arise "if the German internees engaged in paid employment of a kind likely to irritate the local labour interest or cause resentment in the area". In August 1944, for instance, the manager of the local labour exchange explained there was no objection to the men working with farmers in harvesting, but the parliamentary secretary at the Department of Industry and Commerce "strongly disapproved of any suggestion to employ alien labour to the detriment of our people". Traynor sought de Valera's advice on the matter. In reply, the Taoiseach suggested that those who already had jobs should be allowed to continue to work pending a general settlement of the problem. The issue had not yet been settled when Hitler killed himself.

By then Buchenwald death-camp had been liberated and the true face of Nazism had been exposed. "A feeling of revulsion swept through the Curragh, not so much towards the German internees as for what they represented," one of the Irish soldiers recalled. "The internees professed as much horror as we did. Their morale slumped and they did not march or sing any more." The news of Hitler's death was received with mixed feelings among the German internees as the pro-and anti-Nazi factions confronted each other on the streets of Newbridge in a rare display of internal dissention.

In the circumstances de Valera's reaction in visiting Hempel to express condolence seemed all the more inappropriate. Although he made no favourable comments about Hitler and did not ask the Dáil to adjourn as a mark of respect, as he had done following the death of Roosevelt three weeks earlier, his gesture of condolence set off a fire-storm of criticism in the foreign press. De Valera made no public attempt to justify his actions, and he instructed the Department of External Affairs not to defend his gesture. "An explanation would be interpreted as an excuse, and an excuse as a consciousness of having acted wrongly," he wrote. "I acted correctly, and, I feel certain, wisely."

The Taoiseach's gesture was welcomed by most of the German internees at the Curragh. But why did de Valera go to such lengths to express sympathy for the death of a man he despised?

"Common gentlemanly feelings of sympathy with Dr Hempel in the hour of the country's collapse called for a gesture," de Valera explained privately. "I was damned if I was going to treat him any different from other representatives on whom I had called in similar circumstances, especially as Hitler was dead and there was no possibility of my reinforcing an already lost cause."

De Valera's annoyance at Gray was undoubtedly an important factor in the whole affair. In the final months of the war the American minister had been deliberately goading the Taoiseach. On 30 April 1945, the eve of the announcement of Hitler's death, Gray had presented the Taoiseach with a formal request for permission to seize the German legation in the hope of capturing German codes before the legation staff could destroy them. He contended that the codes could be used to save lives in the event of some U-boats trying to carry on the struggle, or in case there were armed pockets of German resistance. As this would have amounted to abandoning his wartime policy at the eleventh hour, de Valera refused.

Having recently paid what even Gray described as "a moving tribute" to Roosevelt, de Valera argued that it would have been an "unpardonable discourtesy to the German nation and to Dr Hempel himself" if official Irish condolences had not been proffered. As Taoiseach, de Valera was not about to insult Hempel, for whom he had a much higher regard than he had for Gray. "During the whole of the war," de Valera wrote, "Dr Hempel's conduct was irreproachable. He was always friendly and invariably correct – in marked contrast with Gray. I certainly was not going to add to his humiliation in the hour of defeat."

The war was just about over and Berlin had fallen when the Irish were surprised by the arrival of the latest model JU 88 on the airstrip at Gormanston army camp on 5 May 1945. It had a crew of three, who had been stationed at Grove near Aalborg, Denmark. With the formal liberation of Denmark that day, they were told they could fly to wherever they wished. *Oberfeldwebel* Herbert Gieseke decided on the two-and-a-quarter hour trip to Ireland. Irish authorities were in a quandary, not knowing whether to treat the men as internees or as deserters.

Gieseke, a 34-year-old Berliner with fluent English, was an intriguing character. An adventurer, it was hardly surprising that the other two – *Unteroffizier* Horst Schmidt, a 24-year-old from Hamburg, and *Obergefeiter* Bernhard Kruschyna, a 20-year-old from Kallowitz, Poland – decided to go with him, because he was a natural survivor. At the age of 21 Gieseke had gone to work in Spain and then Morocco before returning to Germany to take up civil flying in 1934. Next he went to South Africa gold-mining and married a girl from Johannesburg. He returned to Germany in 1939 and joined a Condor unit which had recently returned from fighting in the Spanish Civil War. He sent his wife back to South Africa and became a flying instructor for the *Luftwaffe* in Greece, from where he took part in the successful invasion of Crete in 1941. He served in the Middle East, Romania and in the Crimea. While on the Eastern Front he was once shot down with two companions over the Caucasus Mountains, and they spent the next six weeks travelling by night to cover the 200 kilometers necessary to get behind their own lines. He was temporarily discharged from the *Luftwaffe* because of diabetes, but got back as a night-fighter pilot in 1943. Since November 1944 he had been stationed in Denmark.

About 40 planes took off from Grove that morning, according to Gieseke. Some were going to Bohemia to fight the Russians, and others to neutral countries, especially Spain. He and his colleagues left at 3.30 a.m. after it was announced that all German forces would capitulate to the Danes at eight o'clock that morning. They flew the most direct route. While crossing over England one airfield turned on its landing lights, and they responded by turning on their lights, but continued until they reached Gormanstown.

Kruschyna had been reared in Poland as part of that country's German minority. Now that the Russians had occupied the area, he was particularly anxious not to return. After three weeks in Gormanston, the Irish were satisfied that the airmen were not deserters and would be accepted by the other internees. The three were transferred to Tintown. They had the distinction of being the last foreigners to be interned.

Three days after the Gormanston landing, Germany formally surrendered. That day there was a violent thunderstorm in the Curragh. As some soldiers and internees sheltered together, lightning hit the barbed wire around the magazine and it began to glow. "Some of the soldiers made the sign of the cross in anticipation of the magazine blowing up," Chris O'Callaghan recalled. "Nothing like this happened, but I do recall one of the Germans exclaiming: 'God is angry with the German people.'"

ANOTHER CURRAGH MUTINY

IN THE IRELAND of the 1940s it was probably inevitable that religion would somehow get mixed up in events. In July 1944 the Germans heard that Fr Doyle, the parish priest of Naas had made some disparaging remarks during a sermon in which he purportedly advised his congregation not to associate with the German internees because they had low moral standards. Indeed, there were widespread rumours that the naval ratings were infested with venereal diseases.

Following their internment all of the men had had medical check-ups and the instance of venereal disease was not uncommonly high. However, coming from the continent where the war had brought in its wake a decline in sexual morality, the men found the sexual climate in Ireland rather repressive. The ratings frequently resorted to prostitutes, and this inevitably led to instances of venereal disease; there had earlier been several instances of infection among both the British and German officers at K Lines. A special medical ward was set up to deal with venereal diseases; disdainfully known as the "Black Hut", it was reserved for the more serious cases. The German sailors themselves tended to regard the ailment as a symbol of distinction, as if they had been wounded in the service of their country.

Quedenfeld was deeply offended, however, by what Fr Doyle had supposedly said and ordered all Roman Catholic internees not to attend Sunday Mass. On hearing the reason for his action, the camp chaplain made enquiries and was quite satisfied that there was no substance to the rumours about Fr Doyle's sermon. The chaplain requested Fr Faeckler, a German Jesuit priest based at Milltown Park, Dublin, to speak to Quedenfeld and the Catholic internees about the matter, but Quedenfeld refused to meet him. What was more, he ordered the internees not to talk to him either. Although forewarned, Fr Faeckler decided to visit the Curragh anyway.

As he approached the camp he met three of the internees and saluted them in German, but they ignored him. He then met *Feldwebel* Heinz Kapp, who advised him not to go into the camp as he would not be received. The German priest still persisted and managed to meet Quedenfeld, but they only got into a heated argument.

Mollenhauer and Quedenfeld were both Lutheran, and their attitudes to the Roman Catholic Church were probably influenced by the fact that the three greatest trouble-makers in the camp, as far as they were concerned, all happened to be Roman Catholic: Josef Weber and two *Luftwaffe* NCOs, Josef Emmerich and Karl Macht. They caused Quedenfeld some of his biggest problems, and he blamed them for causing discontent among the lower ranks.

Realising that the affair could have damaging repercussions, Hempel made enquiries of his own and concluded that "the whole incident seemed to have its origin in idle and wholly false statements made to internees by some local girls". He asked Quedenfeld to reverse the order, which he did after the chaplain assured him that there was no substance to the story about the offensive sermon. That storm blew over, but there were other difficulties in the following months.

In early 1945 Macht ran foul of the law when he tried to hold a raffle without a licence. When the Gardaí intervened and explained that he was unlikely to get a licence unless the raffle were for a charitable purpose, he claimed that he had made arrangements with the prior of the Dominican Order in Newbridge. In fact the Dominicans would have nothing to do with Macht, and the prior refused even to speak to him. A notice inserted in the local newspaper, the *Leinster Leader*, announced that the Dominicans had absolutely no involvement in the raffle. As a result Commandant Guiney summoned Macht and – in Quedenfeld's presence – demanded that the raffle be abandoned immediately.

No disciplinary measures were taken in the matter, despite a strong call for action by Guiney, but Macht was back in trouble with the police within a month. During the early hours of 3 March 1945, someone tried to enter the open bedroom window of a house in Newbridge. The intruder actually tried to wake up the woman inside by throwing some objects at her before starting to climb through the window. As he was half-way into the room, she began screaming, and he fled. She was convinced he was one of the German internees.

The finger of suspicion immediately pointed at Macht, who was the only one out of the camp at the time. He had failed to return by the midnight curfew because, he said, he had bicycle trouble in Naas. He insisted that he had passed through Newbridge without stopping on his way back to the camp, but the police had little doubt he was the man they were looking for. He already had quite a reputation as a womaniser, and at one point had become engaged to a local school-teacher without bothering to tell her that he already had a wife back in Germany. In addition, he had had a number of affairs with local married women. On this occasion he may well have mistaken the house of one of those women, given that he did deliberately try to wake the woman before entering. The police were determined to pursue the matter. Macht was placed in a line-up at the camp, but the woman was unable, or unwilling, to pick him out. The police had to drop the matter.

Emmerich, the other main trouble-maker in the eyes of the authorities, was involved in a whole series of incidents. At a camp dance on 25 August 1944, for instance, he had to be physically restrained when he accosted one of the civilian women employed at the camp. He had been friendly with her and the fracas apparently developed because he did not want her to attend the function. He was so abusive that Commandant Mackey ordered his expulsion from the hall. Other charges against Emmerich were that he had stolen a bicycle belonging to one of the camp doctors, that he had misappropriated £70 worth of bar property while he was bar NCO, and that he had been habitually late on returning from parole during the past year. As a result Quedenfeld sentenced him to 14 days confinement in the camp on a restricted diet of tea and plain bread. He was given a mattress which, he complained, smelled of urine, and he was left with only his shirt trousers and two blankets in an unheated bathroom for the fortnight.

One of the Irish NCOs overheard Mollenhauer balling out Emmerich. "You are a swine," he said. "If I were in a position to have you out of here and in Germany I would treat you in a far worse manner."

There was a further incident in April 1945 after Emmerich asked for four days parole to stay with Fr Doyle in Naas to help with the activities of the choir over the Easter weekend. The request was rejected on the grounds that the extra parole was not needed. Emmerich then reported that Colonel Collins-Powell had asked him to have Quedenfeld speak with Fr Doyle. Before talking to the parish priest, however, Quedenfeld checked with the camp commandant, only to learn he had not made any such request. As a result Emmerich again found himself in hot water, and he was confined to camp on Easter Sunday for lying to Quedenfeld. This led to further complications with the parish priest, who was appalled that the German commander should prevent one of his men from attending Mass on Easter Sunday. To make matters worse, Emmerich stirred things up further a few weeks later when he told Fr Doyle that Quedenfeld had deliberately prevented all of the Roman Catholic internees from attending Mass on Sunday, 13 May, by requiring them to attend a parade in the camp that morning.

Fr Doyle complained to the Department of Defence about what he believed was the victimisation of Roman Catholic internees. He also called on Collins-Powell at his home on Saturday, 19 May, to protest that the victimisation had been going on with the knowledge of the Irish officers. When Collins-Powell asked for specific instances, Fr Doyle contended that "Quedenfeld was a menace and was active in his antagonism to the Catholic Church." He mentioned the latest charges by Emmerich who, he said, had also told him that a German officer had referred to "Catholic priests in a disrespectful manner" during Sunday's controversial parade. Moreover, he said Emmerich told him that the officers had mismanaged the camp by diverting money to their own use, and by wrongfully imprisoning Weber. The parish priest added that he had been professionally advised that, since the surrender of Germany, there were no longer any legal grounds for holding Weber in the Curragh military prison. The men were on the brink of mutiny because "the officers were no longer in a position to command", he contended.

Fr Doyle's charges had enormous implications. The Irish army was being accused of supporting Nazi officers who were supposedly persecuting Roman Catholic internees by preventing them from practicing their religion. The charges were taken very seriously by the Department of Defence, which ordered an immediate investigation.

There was, however, no basis whatever to the charge that Quedenfeld had called for the parade in order to prevent the internees attending Mass. It was actually Collins-Powell who had suggested the parade in the first place, because he wanted the German commander to warn the men that they were becoming lax in their observance of parole regulations. The Commandant even suggested Sunday morning as the best time to get all the internees together, seeing that so many of them were working on other days. The parade broke up shortly after 10.30, which gave the Roman Catholic internees plenty of time to get to Mass. Fr Doyle had based his whole case on what Emmerich had told him, but army authorities had no time for his evidence in view of his past record.

Yet Emmerich was undoubtedly close to the truth when he said that many of the men were on the verge of mutiny. At Fr Doyle's instigation, Emmerich drew up a petition demanding Weber's release. This was signed by 110 of the sailors, but, on being passed to the *Luftwaffe* NCOs, it was torn up, and this sparked a virtual mutiny on 20 May. Feelings were running so high in the camp that Quedenfeld asked Guiney to transfer all German officers from the compound because their lives were in danger. He said that a communist element had taken control and the NCOs no longer recognised the authority of the officers. He also contended that any effort to punish the ring-leaders would only aggravate the situation.

Quedenfeld was obviously panicking: the Irish authorities "were not satisfied that the position was as bad as represented". They asked him to resume control, or else all parole would be suspended. The German commander agreed, but he asked that three *Luftwaffe* and one naval NCO should first be removed from the camp. They included Emmerich and Macht. Collins-Powell, who was not satisfied the step was necessary, refused and warned Quedenfeld not to discriminate against those NCOs. If difficulties arose, he was to work in close collaboration with the camp authorities. Guiney was instructed to take precautions to ensure that the German officers were not attacked. A military police patrol was placed in the compound to keep an eye on the officers' huts.

The four NCOs named by Quedenfeld were brought before Collins-Powell who warned them to behave themselves. Macht and one of the others expressed loyalty to their officers, but said there were grounds for complaint regarding the distribution of finances, while Emmerich maintained there was religious victimisation. The fourth man, the naval NCO, said he did not understand what was happening. The men were told parole would be suspended indefinitely if the authority of their officers was usurped. And to emphasise the point, parole was cancelled for the day for all but those who were employed outside the camp.

The crisis quickly passed. Within a few days Quedenfeld wrote to Collins-Powell that the patrol around the officers' hut could be withdrawn. "Some of my best senior NCOs will protect us in case there would be any danger," he wrote. "Things do not look as serious today as they did on Sunday last and I found out that most of the men did not really know what was going to happen and found themselves defrauded. I am told by especially the senior NCOs that everything will be alright again if those four ring leaders would be removed." He again asked for the removal of Emmerich, Macht and the other two. "Those four, in my opinion and that of my senior NCOs," Quedenfeld continued, "are the only ones who are responsible for all the trouble. In case you are going to do that I think it would be necessary not to lock them up here but further away from the Curragh Camp and that there would be no possibility for any of my men to contact them."

It was now Emmerich who needed protection. Shortly before two o'clock next morning, eight German NCOs broke his window and tried to get into his room. He screamed for help and the alarm was sounded. The sergeant of the guard saw the men running and followed them to their hut, but some of them held the door until the others got to their rooms. On gaining entry the sergeant immediately accosted one of the attackers.

"It is all right, sergeant," the NCO said as the Irish guard raised his baton. "We did not do him any harm. We only wanted to cut his hair."

Emmerich was very frightened and asked to be withdrawn from the camp. He was removed for the night and the NCOs were warned about their conduct the following morning. Emmerich was then returned to the camp, while the Department of External Affairs took another look at the case against Weber.

What had happened to Weber, who was considered "a model prisoner" by his Irish guards, certainly did not reflect very well on the Irish army's sense of justice. In the opinion of William Warnock – who investigated the case upon his return from Berlin, where he had been chargé d'affaires at the Irish legation throughout most of the war – Weber was imprisoned simply because he "had threatened to desert to the British". For this he was jailed not only until Germany surrendered but for almost three weeks thereafter. He was only released and allowed to return to his colleagues following the threatened mutiny.

Repatriation

In June 1945 the British asked the Irish government to hand over all German internees and captured spies. De Valera flatly refused to surrender the latter, but he did agree to hand over the internees on condition Britain guaranteed that none of them would be executed, nor forced to return to the Soviet Zone of Germany.

Believing that Dublin was trying to split the wartime alliance by having Britain and America discriminate against their Soviet ally, the American minister was bitterly opposed to any such guarantees. He tried to persuade the State Department to put pressure on the British to reject de Valera's conditions but, since Roosevelt's death, Gray no longer enjoyed the same influence in Washington. His advice was rejected and the State Department instructed him to co-operate with Maffey, who by this time had already agreed to the Taoiseach's conditions.

Arrangements were made for the British to pick up the internees at Rosslare on 11 July 1945. Army authorities anticipated some trouble from the men once they learned they were to be repatriated, so a meeting of the top army brass was held in the office of the acting chief-of-staff on 4 July to discuss the repatriation arrangements. In all it was planned to repatriate 266 men, comprising 22 officers, 96 NCOs and 148 of other ranks. The meeting was particularly concerned about the possible reaction of the 21 men on parole in Dublin.

Those present at the meeting were reportedly afraid that some of the men "might seek through influential friends to have their repatriation deferred, or might attempt to go into hiding until repatriation of the main body had been completed, if they were aware that their repatriation was fixed for an early date". Consequently, it was decided to take "prompt and discreet action to secure the return of all the paroled internees". Someone suggested the police should round up those on parole, but the acting chief-of-staff disagreed, because he believed the Department of External Affairs would object.

Walshe explained next day that the British had agreed to provide a destroyer to pick up the internees, who would be taken to Fishguard, then transferred by train to Tilbury where they would embark for Germany, via Ostend. The British had already agreed that the men should be repatriated as civilians rather than POWs and that none of them would be compelled to go to the Soviet Zone against their will. However, a hitch had developed when the British back-tracked somewhat by stating they could no longer guarantee that those internees ordinarily resident in the Russian sector would not be obliged to return to their native areas. De Valera's response was adamant. If Britain did not stick to its original guarantee, the whole thing would be called off. Meanwhile the Irish authorities went ahead with their arrangements. The men were to be told of the assurance that none would have to return to the Soviet Zone, but Walshe tried to keep this very quiet, because he was afraid of "the international repercussion likely to follow any publication of details of the guarantee".

It was decided that the police would inform the internees on parole of their imminent repatriation, assure them of the guarantee concerning the Soviet Zone, and instruct them to return to the Curragh on 8 July. They were also to be told they would be deported as undesirable aliens if they attempted to evade repatriation. The others were to be confined to camp from the same date, and visits were to be suspended. All the arrangements fell through when the British rescinded their guarantee concerning the Soviet Zone, but after further negotiations the guarantee was reaffirmed and new arrangements were made with the British to pick up the men in Dublin on 13 August 1945. On 30 July, Guiney informed Quedenfeld of the impending repatriation and asked for a breakdown of the zones from which the men had come and the number wishing to return to those zones. Of the 266 men, only 138 wished to return to their homes; this included 43 whose homes were in the Soviet Zone.

For a country that had been and still was largely dependent on emigration to provide a livelihood for its citizens, one might have expected a more sympathetic view to be taken of the wishes of those who desired to remain in Ireland, especially those who had already found employment, but the men were not given the choice of remaining. Their only option was to return home or, in the case of those coming from the French or Soviet zones, to choose between their homes and either the British or American zones of occupation. Instead of being moved by the spirit in which the Irish no doubt liked to see their emigrants welcomed in other lands, the Dublin government was more concerned with preventing aliens from securing jobs that might otherwise be filled by native voters. It was a selfish attitude which reflected little credit on the government or the people it represented. But in fairness to de Valera, he did at least take a stand against forceful repatriation to the Soviet Zone, which was desired by the American minister.

Guiney assured Quedenfeld that the Irish government had secured guarantees that the men would be treated as honourable demobilised soldiers and that none would be interned. Quedenfeld asked for formal documents about their status from the Irish government and these were duly furnished. On 2 August Guiney requested the men on parole in Dublin to return to the Curragh within five days. All but three, Arthur Klanke, Ernst Lorra and Hans Biegel, returned by the appointed time. Klanke notified the camp he was ill and could not travel, while the other two simply disappeared.

Although the authorities hoped to keep the incident out of the press, the national newspapers got hold of the story. On 4 August *The Irish Times* reported that the internees were to be repatriated via England as the German civilians living in Ireland had been in 1939 following the outbreak of war. They would be transported through England in a sealed train before embarking for the continent from one of the North Sea ports. One of the internee sailors from Dussleldorf told the reporter he was anxious to get back to Germany as he had had no news of his family for a long time.

"All we know about what is happening is what we read in the

papers," he said. "What we see in them is not encouraging." He praised the treatment the internees had received at the Curragh but said that all of the men wished to go home.

Two days later, however, the same newspaper reported that 50 of the Germans had signed a petition asking to be allowed to remain in Ireland. The report quoted one of the internees, who said that he would rather remain in the country as he saw little hope for Germany, but added that they had been told by Quedenfeld that they had no option. Some of the internees were bitter about being forced to return, according to the *Irish Independent*. "We are no longer free," one of those from the Soviet Zone said. "We can be bought and sold and sent from one place to another. No place can we call home."

The Irish authorities had already decided on the wording of the statement to be issued to the men at the camp on 8 August. It read:

> You will be glad to learn that you are soon to be returned to your country. Arrangements have been made to have you conveyed by sea and rail to the British and American zones of occupation in Europe, according to your home addresses. In practice it is unlikely you will be moved into any other zone unless you so wish. You will probably be leaving within the next few days. In the meantime you should arrange for the disposal of such of your property that you cannot take with you. The only luggage you will be permitted to take will be personal belongings, clothing, currency, etc. The remainder of your belongings may be disposed of as follows: Property may be handed to representatives of the Red Cross with a view to its being sold and the proceeds placed to your credit. Property may be assigned to any friend or legal practitioner named by you for the purpose as directed by you. Currency in excess of the amounts which you are permitted to take may be placed on deposit in the banks, post office for recovery at a later day, or handed to the Red Cross representative. You would be well advised to provide for the safe keeping here of any papers, documents, or cameras. It is unlikely you will be able to retain these. The military will not accept responsibility for storage. You will not be permitted to

> leave the camp again before your final departure. It is not proposed to permit any large number of persons to visit the camp. You will travel in civilian attire.

Army Headquarters decided the men should not be given actual details of when they were to leave until the eve of their departure; they would not be told their actual route at any stage. Camp authorities were told what to say in the event that some of the men did not want to go back to Germany. "If there is any suggestion that individuals do not want to go home," headquarters ordered, "they will be advised that these arrangements have been specially made to convenience them and that they cannot reasonably expect to remain here. They would be well advised to avail of them now. Such a favourable opportunity may not come again."

When told of their impending repatriation several of the men asked for permission to return to Dublin to finalise some matters, and a further 48-hour parole was accorded to them. Alfred Heinzl and his fiancée, Eithne Rea of Dublin, had planned to get married in September, so they brought the date forward to 10 August. He then made representations to be allowed to stay in the country. He was brought to Dublin, where he met with de Valera, who authorised him to stay. Others were desperate to remain. Bruno Hullmann vanished from the camp through the barbed wire on 9 August and Karl Macht and Horst Huse failed to return from local parole next day, as did four of those who had been given the extra 48-hour parole to fix up their affairs in Dublin. They were Kurt Nitz, Rudolf Lauer, Eric Kruger and Georg Fleischmann.

Fleischmann was friendly with Dan Breen, a sitting member of the Irish parliament and one of the heroes of the Irish War of Independence. If necessary he was prepared to hide Fleischmann at his home, but first he interceded with de Valera, who authorised Fleischmann to remain in Ireland on condition he kept his presence secret from anyone in Austria. Two other Austrians, Bruno Arndt and Arthur Klanke, were also authorised to remain. The grounds for granting the Austrians political asylum was a fear that they might be charged with treason in Austria because they had considered themselves Germans.

So many Germans failed to return to the camp that Guiney decided to suspend parole on 11 August. Word quickly filtered out to the nearby towns, and friends of all description descended on the camp. Various traders, such as shoemakers, tailors and retailers, were allowed into the compound to purchase items the internees had made, but others were not admitted. There were some pathetic scenes as distraught girlfriends were refused entry and resorted to shouting through the barbed wire. "Some girls tried to get through the wire in a desperate effort to get to their lovers, even at the risk of being shot by sentries," one Irish soldier recalled. The army was called out to surround the perimeter fence.

"It was a comic, tragic scene as the Germans attempted to throw all of their possessions over the wire to their girlfriends, who struggled past soldiers to retrieve some momento," the soldier added. "Eventually sense prevailed and the visitors were permitted to enter the camp by authorised routes." Guiney did provide a courier service for the internees to send messages out, and two further marriages were hurriedly arranged under these circumstances at the camp. Rudolf Hengst of Chemnitz married Mona McElroy from Kildare on that Saturday and Josef Emmerich married Kitty Hopkins of Kildare next day.

Mrs C.G. Ceannt, the head of the Irish Red Cross, visited the camp with money for the men. This was divided among them, with the officers getting £5 and the other ranks £3 each. She expressed grave disappointment that those who wished to live in Ireland were not being permitted to stay. Guiney told her of the assurances secured by the Irish government and she seemed pleasantly surprised. He brought her into the camp, having first notified Quedenfeld to assemble his officers in their anteroom to meet "the very distinguished visitor with her generous gift".

"On our arrival in the anteroom I naturally expected to see all officers present," Guiney reported. "I was amazed on discovering only three were there who treated us with complete indifference. I asked for *Kapitaenleutnant* Quedenfeld and was told he was in his bedroom. I then requested one of the three to go and get him. Expecting him to arrive suitably attired, I was dismayed at seeing him appear in a dirty suit of overalls."

Guiney introduced Mrs Ceannt to Quedenfeld and the other officers present. She then addressed them sympathetically, and Quedenfeld thanked her.

"I thank you on behalf of my officers, NCOs and men," he said. And that was it.

"Aren't they very cold and undemonstrative?" Mrs Ceannt complained to Guiney on the way out.

"She seemed definitely disappointed and hurt at the manner in which she had been received and expressed the view that she thought it was well they were going away," Guiney noted. "So much had been done for them in this country and she did not see why we should embarrass our national position for the sake of them any longer."

On the eve of their departure Quedenfeld and Mollenhauer were brought to the Department of External Affair by Guiney. While he waited outside the two men met Freddie Boland, who assured them that they would be taken straight home by the British. Although *The Irish Times* reported the internees were not being "permitted to take home anything but their memories", they were allowed to take what personal belongings they could fit into their permitted amount of luggage. The ratings were allowed one clothing bag each, while the officers were permitted luggage weighing up to one hundredweight.

"We were also assured that we could take with us what we liked, personal belongings etc., and nothing would be confiscated," Mollenhauer recalled. The only thing specifically excluded was their bicycles. Each of the men was given a new pair of army boots, new clothing bag, new eating utensils, rations for three days, an army blanket, ground-sheet and three ounces of carbolic soap.

"The state of confusion within the compound prior to their departure was indescribable," according to Guiney. "There was a complete state of chaos – the officers lending no assistance in making final arrangements." The internees rifled the stores and left their quarters in an "appalling" mess.

"To start with the officers' quarters," Guiney wrote "the dining room is a most confused, disorderly and dirty condition, empty bottles, etc., presenting the aftermath of an orgy; anteroom and bedrooms seriously deranged, drawers pulled out of furniture, chairs tumbled on the floors, even bedding from the beds thrown on the floors and trampled on." The NCOs's quarters were in much the same state, with food strewn on the floors, while the "ratings' quarters presented a terrible spectacle, food strewn around the whole place (cooked and uncooked), obvious evidence that the food from the cookhouse had made its way to here; beds and furniture thrown about in a most disorderly fashion. In all my experience as an officer I never saw such a state of infernal disorder and neglect." The guards had seen all this going on, but Guiney had told them to keep a low profile to avoid any clashes.

It was shortly after midnight on 13 August when the convoy left the Curragh. The internees were in ten buses preceded and followed by four armoured cars and lorries with Irish soldiers. They had a rest stop at McKee Barracks, Dublin, before going on to Alexandra Quay, where they boarded the HMS *St Andrew*, which had soldiers of the West Kent Regiment aboard to guard the internees.

"We completely bemused the British soldiers when we were brought on board ship," Arthur Voigt recalled. "We marched on board dressed in civilian suits, carrying tennis racquets, fishing rods and all speaking good English."

"Who the hell are they?" Voigt heard one soldier ask another. "Soldiers or bloody tourists?"

The ship set sail that morning. The Germans were on their long journey home. It was the eve of the Japanese surrender and the formal end of the Second World War.

Aftermath

In Ireland the search continued for the internees who had absconded. Hullmann was recaptured in Dublin during the first week of September when recognised by a plainclothes detective while walking down Grafton Street. He refused to give details about the person who had sheltered him, but the police quickly learned anyway that he had been staying in the workroom of a girlfriend in Dawson Street.

Macht and Huse also went into hiding in Dublin with the mother of a friend living in Rathmines. Each of them had been offered permanent employment in Ireland, and they were hoping they would be permitted to stay if they could hide long enough for the heat to die down. Macht had been offered a job as a knitting-machine operator in Milltown Malbay, Co. Clare, and Huse as a toolmaker and turner in a Nenagh factory.

They stayed in Rathmines for about ten days, then moved into a house on Mount Street for a further five days before moving back to Rathmines. There they spent their days playing cards and hardly left the house. In all they only went out five or six times, and then at night, singly, and never for more than 15 or 20 minutes. But the police still learned of their presence and they were arrested in the house on 29 September 1945.

By then Lorra, Nitz and Kruger had been recaptured. The latter two were actually taken in the early hours of 25 September while in the Belclair, Co. Galway home of a member of the Dáil, Mark Killilea, the father of the current member of the European Parliament with the same name. They had jumped parole in Dublin and Killilea had driven them to the home of a friend in Ballinasloe, where they remained for ten days before moving in with the Killilea family.

In all cases it was decided not to prosecute anyone for harbouring the fugitives. Of course, in the case of Killilea, opposition deputies asked some embarrassing questions in the Dáil.

The six recaptured men were taken to Gorchwood border post and handed over to the British authorities on 8 October 1945. Lauer was captured on 8 December and handed over to the British the following day, while Biegel managed to stay at large until 7 April 1946. He had been harboured first in the Fairview area of Dublin by a dairy worker from Galway before moving to the Marino area, where he was sheltered by a doctor for several months. He was arrested shortly after leaving the house of a girlfriend on Pembroke Road in the early hours of the morning. The police had been watching her house as they knew she was friendly with him, but they acted discreetly, perhaps in order to minimise the risk of the matter becoming a political issue: the doctor who had harboured him was a close friend of Kathleen Clarke, who was not only the widow of Tom Clarke, the executed hero of the 1916 Easter Rebellion, but also a disillusioned member of Fianna Fáil from which she would shortly defect.

The other internees had returned to the continent. "After quite a nice voyage we were brought ashore at Ostend and from there proceeded to a prison camp near Brussels, where we were held eight weeks more," Gottfried Berndt wrote to a friend in Ireland. "The treatment there was good, but still it was a prison camp and in our view it was not necessary to keep us so long."

Notwithstanding Boland's assurances to Mollenhauer and Quedenfeld that they would neither be interned nor have anything confiscated, and that the wives of those who had been married in Ireland would follow on without delay, none of these promises were kept. The men were frisked at the camp by British soldiers, who often took anything of any value off them, though they did get some indirect Irish help. "A major of Irish descent stopped it when we complained," Mollenhauer explained. The major also issued them with "vouchers that nothing should be taken from us", but those who had been robbed already did not get their belongings back. As a result Mollenhauer was initially quite critical of Boland's promises.

"Well," he exclaimed in a letter to his fiancée in Dublin, "we have seen what they were worth."

In the same letter, which was written a fortnight after his release, he noted that Walter Habich and the other Austrians were still being held, and he asked his girlfriend to inform Boland. Some of the Austrians, like Max Galler and Ludwig Wochner, were awaiting transport to Austria, but Habich was in a different category, even though he was just a meteorologist. "He was a '*Wehrmachtsbeamter im Offiziersrang,*' literally an administrative officer of the armed forces with the rank of a commissioned officer, but with the civilian title '*Regierungsrat*'," Mollenhauer explained. "Anyone with 'rat' in his title fell under a silly regulation of automatic arrest." Habich was not released from the Brussels POW camp until the spring of 1946.

On later reflection Mollenhauer came to realise that all of them "might have been detained for a longer period", had they not "asked a visiting Red Cross commission to inform the Irish Legation in Brussels that we were still there". Moreover, when they were let go, those from the Soviet Zone were given the option of going to the British or American areas.

"We were set free in Münster and brought from there to the German liberation points of the English government districts, for me, Cologne," Gottfried Berndt wrote. "From Bonn onwards I started the journey into unknown. On seeing Germany again was for all of us a great disillusionment." When the *Luftwaffe* officer was first interned in Ireland, Germany was at the height of her power, in control of most of the continent. Now things were very different.

"I was staggered," Berndt wrote in December 1945. "One must put up with the fact that we lost the war, but I cannot get over the fact that the German people are lost too. It is all so terribly shameless. The German girls and women throw themselves on the necks of the occupation troops. German men are lickspittle, denounce their own fellow countrymen and think only of their own well being. I thought I should be able to work for the German idea, but one finds it no more.

"I was looking forward to Germany so," he continued, "and I have been so bitterly disappointed. If I could, I should gladly return to Ireland and get through life there and not in Germany – that is no longer Germany. Oh, to be a flyer again in Ireland!"

Although Berndt chose to settle in Bielstein in the British Zone, his home was in Grunlichtenberg near Waldheim, Saxony, deep in the Soviet Zone. Within a matter of days he decided to undertake the hazardous journey to see his family. The following is his own account, written on 2 December 1945:

> After I was here in Bielstein for eight days, I set out to look up my parents. I succeeded too. The joy of my parents was great, when I suddenly arrived at their place by night. Unfortunately I was able to be at home only two days as the journey thither lasted ten days longer than expected. For these two days I was three weeks on the road and slept almost exclusively in sheds, waiting rooms and goods wagons and had to live like a real tramp. One has to slip home and steal away like a criminal. I could not stay any longer in the Russian Zone on that account because officers are very much prized articles among the Russians. They seize them all ... From all I could learn it would have been even riskier to get into the French Zone as the French also in the hinterland are continually carrying out checks, whilst the Russians leave one completely at peace there. There it was only hard to get over the frontier and a few bullets whistled by me fairly close.

On the other hand, Mollenhauer found things "comparatively good" at his home in Cuxhaven, which had suffered very little war damage.

The three repatriated internees who had been married in Ireland had great difficulty getting their wives to Germany. Entry permits were refused as long as John B. Hynd remained minister in charge of the Control Office for Germany and Austria. It was not until he was replaced by de Valera's good friend, Frank Pakenham (now Lord Longford), in early 1947 that the wives were allowed to join their husbands.

The Germans seem to have retained fond memories of their stay in Ireland. Most, if not all the German airmen believed in the cause for which they were fighting at the time but, when the true nature of the Nazi regime became apparent after the war, few could have felt that their sacrifices had really been in a worthwhile cause. Many of the men interned in Ireland undoubtedly had their internment to thank for their lives, and consequently retained much happier memories of Ireland than their Allied counterparts.

George Fleischmann wrote a novel about the camp, entitled *Die Gefangenen der Grunen Insel* (Prisoners of the Green Isle). He married and settled in Ireland, as did Alfred Heinzl, and a couple of his colleagues returned to settle down in the country later. Arthur Voigt was one of those who initially decided to return to his home in Leipzig, in the Soviet Zone, but he fled East Germany in 1951 and came back to Ireland, where he settled and married a girl he had met while interned. Kurt Kyck, one of those who got married while at the Curragh, likewise returned to settle in Ireland, and Mollenhauer married Paula Mecklenberg once he could bring her to Germany.

Others have visited the country since. Konrad Neymeyr and the members of his crew, Erwin Sack, Willi Krupp, Hans Biegel and Ernst Kalkowski returned in 1980 at the invitation of the then Taoiseach, Charles J. Haughey, who had bought and built a house on the island on which they crashed many years earlier. He loaned them his house for a two-week holiday on the island.

Each year for more than four decades the former German and Austrian internees held a reunion in Germany, until the ravages of time began to eat so greatly into their numbers that such reunions became painful reminders of friends who had passed on.

Most of the former Allied internees seemed to lose touch with each other, and some remained extremely bitter about their internment. Only Maurice Browne came back to settle in Ireland. Not all of the Allied bitterness was directed against the Irish; Diaper, a member of Calder's crew, became quite vitriolic at the mention of Calder's name in 1983. Others, like Wolfe, did not know when contacted that some of their fellow internees had not survived the war.

All the Allied airmen returned to service before the end of hostilities, when the war was going much better for the Allies. As a result they tended to look on their period in the Curragh as lost time – time in which they were prevented from flying and playing their part in the struggle against Nazi tyranny. Many lost their lives in the war. Hobbs was killed very soon after his escape, Mayhew was killed the following year, and Webster was killed in the landing at Dieppe. Fleming's plane was shot down while on a reconnaissance flight over southern Germany in September 1944, and both Welpy and Shaw also "bought it", in the words of one of their colleagues. Hugh Verity survived the war, rising to the rank of Group Captain and winning the Distinguished Service Cross and Distinguished Flying Cross. He commanded the famous Lysander Flight of 161 Squadron which engaged in the hazardous moonlight "pick ups" and drops to the resistance in occupied Europe. He has covered this part of his career in his book, *We Landed by Moonlight*.

When the different Allied and Axis archives were opened after the war, all revealed dark and shameful secrets. In his book *The Last Secret*, for instance, Nicholas Bethell disclosed the horrific story of thousands of Cossacks who were savagely butchered after they were forcibly handed over to the Soviet Union by the British and Americans. The Irish archives certainly do not reflect well on the de Valera government which insisted on the repatriation of Germans who wished to remain in Ireland, but it was to his credit that de Valera resolutely refused to hand them over until he had received guarantees as to their safe conduct.

In more recent times it has become fashionable to question aspects of de Valera's policy during World War II, but criticism has usually come from people unaware of the real nature of his overall stance. Very little has been written about the internment of belligerent servicemen in Ireland, because their governments never made a public issue of the matter, yet Ireland's internment practice reflects well enough the policy of benevolent neutrality which de Valera adopted. Allied personnel were often secretly spirited over the border or released on a pretext, while German airmen and sailors were almost invariably confined for the duration of the war, even when strictly they might have been released in accordance with international law.

In Ireland de Valera's adroit wartime leadership was so popular that he served out his term and was elected Taoiseach on two further occasions before quitting active politics to become President of Ireland in 1959. After two seven-year terms he eventually retired from public life at the age of 91.

BIBLIOGRAPHY

Berger, Alexander, *Les Prisonniers de L'Ile Verte*, Paris, Press de la Cité, 1966

Bethell, Nicholas, *The Last Secret: Forcible Repatriation to Russia 1944-7*, London, André Deutsch, 1974

Bullock, Alan, *Hitler: A Study in Tyranny*, London, Pelican Books, 1962

Calder, Jack, "I Flew into Trouble," *MacLean's Magazine*, August 1942

Carroll, Joseph T, *Ireland in the War Years 1939-45*, Newton Abbot, David & Charles, 1975

Carter, Carolle J, *The Shamrock and the Swastika: German Espionage in Ireland in World War II*, Palo Alto, Pacific Books, 1977

Clive, John, *Broken Wings*, London, Granada, 1983

Duggan, John P, *Neutral Ireland and the Third Reich*, Dublin, Lilliput Press, 1989

Dunne, James, "The Cushiest Prison Camp of the War," *Sunday Mirror*, 21-28 November 1976

Dwyer, T. Ryle, *De Valera – The Man and the Myths*, Dublin, Poolbeg Press, 1992

Dwyer, T. Ryle, *Strained Relations: Ireland at Peace and the USA at War, 1941-45*, Dublin, Gill & Macmillan, 1988

Fisk, Robert, *In Time of War: Ulster and the Price of Neutrality, 1939-45*, Dingle, Brandon Books, 1983

Fleischmann, George, *see* Berger, Alexander

Forde, Frank, *The Long Watch: The History of the Irish Merchantile Marine in World War II*, Dublin, Gill & Macmillan, 1981

Foot, M.R.D. and Langley, J.M, *MI9*, London, Futura Publications, 1980

Longford, Lord and O'Neill, Thomas, *Eamon de Valera*, Dublin, Gill & Macmillan, 1970

McAree, J.V, "Interned Airmen Held in the Curragh," Toronto *Globe and Mail*, 21-8 November 1976
O'Callaghan, Chris, "The Germans in Ireland," *Irish Independent*, September 1979
Peterson, Basil, "The War Years," *Irish Times*, 24 January 1983
Quigley, Aidan, *Green is My Sky,* Dublin, Avoca Publications, 1984
Share, Bernard, *The Emergency: Neutral Ireland, 1939-45*, Dublin, Gill & Macmillan, 1978
Spraight, J.M, *War Rights on Land*, London, Macmillan, 1911
Stephen, Enno, *Spies in Ireland*, London, MacDonald, 1963
Sturm, Herbert. *Hakenkreuz und Kleeblatt: Irland, die Alliierten und das Dritte Reich 1933-1945*, Frankfurt, 1984
Turner, John Frayn, *V.C.s of the Royal Navy*, London, George Harrap, 1956
Warlimont, Walter, *Inside Hitler's Headquarters*, London, Weidenfield & Nicholson, 1964
Wheatley, Dennis, *The Deception Planners: My Secret War*, London, Hutchinson, 1980

INDEX

Other Books from Brandon

Gerry Adams

Selected Writings

The best of Adams's work, a substantial selection from a substantial body of writing. *Selected Writings* is essential reading for anyone seeking to understand the present state of Ireland.
Paperback £7.95

Falls Memories

"This nostalgic and very personal account of a working-class community deeply steeped in Republicanism is especially valuable because it has been written by someone who has strong and deep-rooted ties and involvement in both the class and the Republican struggles." *Irish News*
Paperback £6.99

The Politics of Irish Freedom

"Adams' 'personal statement' must rank as the most considerable one to date from a leading member of the republican movement clarifying and defending its aims and methods. It thus has a role to play as one corrective among others to the flow of misinformation that passes for journalistic analysis of affairs in the North of Ireland, both in Britain and the Republic." *New Statesman*
Paperback £4.95

Cage Eleven

"He is a natural storyteller, with a warm and agile wit ... The writing is natural and, one might say, writerly. There are deft shifts of focus, a relaxed sense of timing, a Myles na Gopaleen-like sense of character and an infinitesimal attention to emotional naunce." *Listener*
Paperback £4.95

Ulick O'Connor
Executions
"He has taken the single most dramatic event in our Civil War ... and turned it into a drama that is compelling, moving heartbreaking and most of all deeply human." *Sunday Independent*
Hardback £12.99

O'Donovan Rossa
Irish Rebels in English Prisons
"I defy anyone who reads this book to doubt the courage and fortitude of the human spirit." Paul Hill
Paperback £7.99

Eamonn McCann
Bloody Sunday in Derry: What Really Happened
"Moving and impressive ... it is cumulatively powerful ... The *tour de force* of this book is its deconstruction of Lord Widgery's Tribunal. As a mendacious and arrogant piece of judicial trumpery it can hardly be equalled." *Guardian*
Paperback £5.99

Micheal Farrell (ed)
Twenty Years On
"An important record of the activism of 1968 and the 20 years of turmoil and conflict that have followed." *Time Out*
Paperback £4.95

Steve MacDonogh (ed)
The Rushdie Letters:
Freedom to Speak, Freedom to Write
"*The Rushdie Letters*, which includes two letters from the condemned author, reaches beyond the world of literature, offering an emotional and inspiring reflection on the personal and global issues at stake in the 'Rushdie Affair'." *Boston Phoenix*
Paperback £7.95